Words without
Meaning

Contemporary Philosophical Monographs
Peter Ludlow, editor

Words without Meaning

Christopher Gauker

A Bradford Book
The MIT Press
Cambridge, Massachusetts
London, England

This book was set in Palatino by SNP Best-set Typesetter Ltd., Hong Kong and was printed and bound in the United States of America.

Library of Congress Cataloging-in-Publication Data

Gauker, Christopher.
  Words without meaning / Christopher Gauker.
    p.   cm.—(Contemporary philosophical monographs; 3)
  "A Bradford book."
  Includes bibliographical references and index.
  ISBN 0-262-07242-4 (hc. : alk. paper)—ISBN 0-262-57162-5 (pbk. : alk. paper)
  1. Semantics. 2. Language and languages—Philosophy. 3. Semantics (Philosophy). 4. Pragmatics. I. Title. II. Series.

P325 .G364   2003
401'.43—dc21   2002067839

To my father, Reid Stiers Gauker

Contents

Semantics

Beliefs

Preface

This book presents a critique of, and an alternative to, the received view of the nature of linguistic communication. According to the received view, the function of language is to enable speakers to reveal the propositional contents of their thoughts to hearers. So conceived, linguistic communication involves two kinds of meanings. First, there are the meanings that speakers express. These are the propositional contents of the thoughts that speakers intend to reveal to hearers. Second, there are the meanings that words possess. By virtue of these, a speaker's words express a complete proposition in the context in which they are uttered. Typically, a hearer will recognize the proposition that the speaker's words express in light of their meanings and the context and may infer that the meaning that the speaker expresses is that same proposition.

According to me, it is a mistake to try to explain linguistic communication in terms of meanings of these two kinds. No one has ever explained what having a propositional content in mind consists in, and such a conception of communication stands in the way of a correct account of a great variety of linguistic phenomena. Talk of meaning is one of the devices by which conversation is conducted, and we need to understand that kind of talk along with the rest, but the concept of meaning will play no role in a fundamental theory of how language works.

Others before me have balked at the concept of meaning as well (Wittgenstein 1953, Quine 1960, Davidson 1967, Kripke 1982, Schiffer 1987), but they have not succeeded in putting much of anything positive in its place. The primary value of the theory of meaning was that it seemed to offer us a set of linguistic norms. The theory of meaning tells us basically that we should strive to speak in such a way that what we mean is what another user of the language would think we meant judging by the meanings of our words and the context. If we give up on the theory of meaning, then we need an alternative approach to the norms of discourse; that is what I offer in this book.

The basic tools of my alternative are these: First, there are objective contexts. These are constituted by what is relevant to the goals of the interlocutors given the state of the world around them. They are objective in that interlocutors may be mistaken about the content of these contexts. Second, in precisely definable ways, some sentences will be assertible in such a context and others will not be. Of the assertible ones, some will go without saying and others not. The obligation of a speaker is to assert what is assertible if it does not go without saying. Using these tools, I will offer solutions to many outstanding problems in the philosophy of language.

I have discussed many of the topics of this book with Frank Döring and Marina Sbisà. I have discussed selected issues with Kees van Deemter, Kai von Fintel, Adam Morton, Zoltán Gendler Szabó, Tadeusz Zawidzki, Jonathan Berg, and Arthur Morton. Adam Morton, Michael Glanzberg, and Marina Sbisà read a draft of the entire manuscript, making many helpful suggestions. Countless others have pushed me along through e-mail correspondence and conversation at conferences. I thank them all for their help and their indulgence. Thanks too to Tom Stone, of MIT Press, and Peter Ludlow, the series editor, for recognizing the value of my work. The semantic theory of "believes" in chapter 12 was inspired by a paper by Walter Edelberg (1995). As always, my greatest debt is to my wife, Alice Youngsook Kim.

Chapters 4 through 10 and 12 are based largely on articles published elsewhere (1997a, 1997b, 1998, 2001b, forthcoming b, forthcoming c), but I have taken only a few brief passages out of those works verbatim.

The Issue

1   The Received View

According to the received view of linguistic communication, the central function of language is to enable a speaker to reveal his or her thoughts to a hearer. The speaker has a certain thought in mind and intends the hearer to recognize that he or she has that thought in mind. The speaker chooses his or her words in the expectation that on the basis of the words spoken and the circumstances of utterance, the hearer will be able to infer that the speaker has that thought.

In the case of a sentence in declarative mood, the thought that the speaker thus reveals to the hearer is typically a belief. More precisely, the speaker reveals to the hearer that he or she has a belief with a certain propositional content. In the case of a sentence in the imperative mood, the speaker reveals to the hearer that he or she has a desire with a certain content. In the case of a sentence in the interrogative mood, the speaker reveals the content of an act of wondering. For purposes of elaborating on this received view, it will be convenient to focus on the case of sentences in the declarative mood.

Of course, there has to be some basis on which the hearer is able to infer the speaker's belief from the speaker's choice of words and the circumstances, and the speaker has to choose his or her words in light of the hearer's basis for inferring the speaker's belief. According to the received view, this basis is the speaker's and hearer's shared understanding of the meanings of words. Typically, the hearer will recognize that, in light of the meaning of the speaker's words and the circumstances of utterance, the speaker's words express a certain proposition, and may infer that the belief the speaker intends to reveal to the hearer is a belief having that same proposition as its content, and the speaker intends the hearer to do just that.

For example, suppose I see that you are about to walk out behind my house and wish to warn you that there is poison ivy back there. In other words, I believe that there is poison ivy back there and intend to bring it about that you believe it too. I ask myself, "How can I get you to believe that there is poison ivy behind the house?" I reason that if you believe that I believe that there is poison ivy back there, then you might believe that too (since you might trust me). I reason, further, that if I say, "There is poison ivy behind the house," then you will recognize that I believe that there is poison ivy behind the house. Why? Because I know that you will recognize that my words express the proposition that there is poison ivy behind my house and that you will infer that the proposition my words express is the one I expect you to interpret me as believing.

We can discern two different concepts of meaning in this theory. First, there are meanings such as the speaker intends to reveal to the hearer through his or her act of speech. In the case where the speaker intends to reveal the content of a belief, this meaning is the propositional content of the belief that the speaker intends the hearer to recognize in the speaker on the basis of the speaker's choice of words and the circumstances of utterance. Second, there are the meanings of words and sentences, shared knowledge of which enables the hearer to recognize meanings of the first sort on the basis of the speaker's choice of words and the circumstances and enables the speaker to choose his or her words. My aim in this book is to criticize these uses of the concept of meaning and to show that it is possible to understand the nature of linguistic communication without these two concepts of meaning. My aim in this first chapter is to characterize in more detail the received view with which my own approach contrasts.

First, I need to say a little more about the nature of beliefs and propositions. A belief is supposed to be a relation to a proposition, or propositional content. To believe something is to stand in the belief-relation to a proposition. A proposition may be thought of as a category to which the world might or might not belong. A proposition is true or false depending on whether the world does or does not belong to the category. To believe a proposition is to accept a classification of the world as a whole as belonging to one type rather than another. For example, to believe the proposition that *some reptiles can swim* is to classify the world as one in which there are reptiles that can swim. Thus, a proposition is sometimes modelled as a set of possible worlds, or a function from possible worlds into truth values. It is supposed to be the set of possible worlds in which the proposition is true. For some purposes, for instance, for purposes of

distinguishing between distinct beliefs, it is useful to conceive of propositions as possessing more internal structure
than a mere set of worlds possesses. Thus, propositions may
be conceived, not as sets of worlds, but as structures built
up from individuals and properties, or they may be thought
to incorporate "modes of presentation" (a technical term).

A proposition is nothing like a mental image. If I say,
"Some reptiles can swim," and you understand me, then,
according to the theory, you will grasp the propositional
content of my thought. But you may or may not share with
me a mental image. If I form an image as I speak, I may
imagine a snake, and though you understand me perfectly
well, you may imagine an alligator. More likely, no mental
image of a reptile accompanies my act of speech at all.
Equally, a proposition is not a "bundle of experiences." This
idea that the contents of thoughts are exclusively images, or
bundles of experiences, may be one source of the sopho-
moric insight that no two people ever have exactly the same
thought. That's false, of course, because if you and I both
believe that some reptiles can swim, then we believe exactly
the same thing, namely, that some reptiles can swim—whatever differences there may be in the way we each believe it.
As Frege says, "one cannot well deny that humanity has a
common treasure of thoughts that it carries over from one
generation to the next" (1892/1994, p. 44).

At any given time there will be many propositions that
the speaker believes, and there may be several propositions
that the speaker expects the hearer to interpret the speaker
as believing as a result of the speaker's act of speech. Among
these there is supposed to be one that the speaker expects

the hearer to recognize as the content of the speaker's belief *on the basis* of the speaker's choice of words, that is, by a direct application of their shared understanding of the meanings of words. Let us call that proposition *the thought expressed*. In the case where the speaker is successful in leading the hearer to recognize the thought expressed on the basis of the speaker's choice of words, we may say that the thought was successfully *conveyed*. If the speaker is not successful in leading the hearer to recognize the thought expressed, then we may still say that that proposition is the thought that the speaker *intended* to convey. (So expressing a thought, or proposition, is the same thing as intending to convey that proposition.) In addition to expecting the hearer to recognize that the speaker believes the thought expressed, the speaker may intend the hearer himself or herself to believe the thought expressed, but this is not essential. The speaker may not expect the hearer to regard the speaker as authoritative, and the speaker's intention may be merely to reveal his or her own beliefs to the hearer without expecting that the hearer will come to share those beliefs.

Typically, proponents of the received view hold that if a person believes that p, then that person's brain contains a *mental representation* whose propositional content is the proposition that p. One person's belief that p is distinguished from another person's belief that p inasmuch as the mental representation that bears the content that p in the first person is numerically distinct from the mental representation that bears the proposition that p in the other. If there is no such mental representation, then the person does not explicitly believe that p, but he or she may nonetheless implicitly believe that p if his or her brain contains mental representations whose propositional contents imply that p. When a speaker attempts to express in words the content of an explicit belief that p, the mental representation bearing the propositional content that p is supposed to play a special role in the etiology of the speaker's act of speech. For instance, it might be supposed to serve as a template on which the words are somehow formed. I will refer to the mental representation that plays this role as that which *underlies* the speaker's act of speech.

As I have described the received view so far, it might seem that a proponent of the received view is committed to the existence of peculiar entities called *propositions*, but actually, that commitment is not essential. For many purposes one could think of all talk of propositions as shorthand for talk of an equivalence class of actual and possible sentences or, more generally, representations. Certain actual and possible representations may belong in a single class, which we think of as those that *bear the same propositional content*. Talk of bearing a propositional content, one might say, is just a way of referring to such an equivalence class of representations. A proponent of the received view can often formulate his or her theses in terms of equivalence classes of representations rather than propositions. For example, the speaker's aim in communication, one might say, is to enable the hearer to recognize that the speaker has a mental representation belonging to a certain equivalence class. It is not obvious that a proponent of the received view can always dispense with the concept of a proposition in this way, but I am not going to make an issue of the existence of propositions.

In addition to what I am calling the thought expressed, the speaker will of course believe various other propositions and may intend the hearer also to recognize some of those other beliefs in the speaker *as a result* of the speaker's act of speech, but not *on the basis* of the speaker's choice of words. For example, if I say "The first person to walk on the moon was born in Ohio," then the thought I express will be just the proposition that the first person to walk on the moon was born in Ohio, but in addition I may expect you to know that Neil Armstrong was the first person to walk on the moon and to regard this as common knowledge and consequently to infer that I believe that Neil Armstrong was born in Ohio. In a different sort of example (taken from Grice), a motorist has run out of gasoline and is approached by a passerby who informs him, "There is a gas station around the corner." In this case, the thought that the passerby expresses will be just the thought that there is a gas station around the corner. But the passerby may not only expect the motorist to recognize that the speaker believes that there is a gas station around the corner but may also expect the motorist to infer that the passerby believes that the gas station is open and has gas to sell. Yet a third sort of case is that in which a mother asks her son whether he has done his homework and he replies, "Some of it," implying thereby that he has not done all of it. If it is part of the speaker's intention in speaking that the hearer will recognize that the speaker believes such additional propositions as a result of his or her act of speech, then they may be classified as part of the *speaker's meaning*, but they must still be distinguished from the thought expressed.

Again, the thought expressed is the proposition that the speaker intends the hearer to interpret the speaker as believing on the basis of the speaker's choice of words, that is, through a direct application of their shared understanding of meanings. How exactly is the hearer supposed to interpret the speaker on the basis of the speaker's choice of words? A simple picture would be that in virtue of the meanings of the speaker's words, there is a certain proposition that the speaker's *sentence* expresses and that the hearer may simply assume that the thought expressed is that very same proposition. So if the speaker says, "Some reptiles can swim," then that sentence, by virtue of the meanings of the constituent words and their grammatical composition, expresses the proposition that some reptiles can swim, and the hearer may assume that the belief that the speaker wishes to reveal to the hearer on the basis of his or her choice of words is a belief with the propositional content that some reptiles can swim. Common knowledge of the propositions that sentences of their language express thus enables speakers to choose their words and enables hearers to recognize the thoughts that speakers express.

For many reasons this simple picture will not work, as probably all proponents of the received view would acknowledge. First of all, there are cases of transparent insincerity and nonliterality. The problem is not deliberate lies. If I lie, there may be a mismatch between the proposition my sentence expresses and what I believe, but it might still be the case that the proposition my sentence expresses is the proposition that I expect my hearer to regard as the content of my belief. The problem is transparent insincerity, such as irony and sarcasm, as when one says, "That's brilliant!" meaning just the opposite. Then there is nonliterality. If I say "This university is a prison," the proposition my sentence expresses is the proposition that this university is a prison, but it may be questioned whether that proposition is actually the content of the belief that I expect the hearer to recognize on the basis of my choice of words. (It depends on whether the content of a belief can itself be metaphorical.) But perhaps we can set such phenomena to one side on the grounds that they are not typical and what we have to understand first of all is the typical uses of language.

Something we cannot just set aside is the problem of context-relativity. Typically, the proposition that a sentence expresses depends not only on the meaning of the constituent words and their grammatical composition but also on the *context* in which the sentence is uttered. Here is a partial list of types of context-relativity:

• *Indexical reference:* "I am sick." The proposition expressed will depend on who is speaking, which will vary from one context to another.

• *Demonstrative reference:* "That one is nice." The proposition expressed will depend on which object is the referent of "That one."

• *Domain of discourse:* "Everyone is present." If the domain of discourse is students still enrolled in the course, then the proposition expressed will be the proposition that every student still enrolled in the course is present. If the domain of discourse is students who have been attending recently, then the proposition expressed will be the proposition that every student who has been attending recently is present.

• *Incompleteness:* "Mary is too tired." Is she too tired to go to work, too tired to get up, or too tired to live?

• *Lexical ambiguity:* "Right!" In response to the question "Should I turn left?," this can mean either "Yes, you should turn left," or "No, you should turn right."

• *Logical ambiguity:* "Every rhyme is not a poem." In response to your poetry homework, this might mean not every rhyme is a poem. Said by a radical poet, it could mean no rhyme is a poem.

• *Grammatical ambiguity:* A sign on the Interstate through Oklahoma reads, "Hitchhikers may be escaping convicts." What are the hitchhikers fleeing from, convicts or jail?

Proponents of the received view usually hold that in such cases the sentence by itself does not express a proposition. Rather, something somehow assigns to the sentence a *meaning*, which resolves the ambiguities, and then the context in which the sentence is (or might be) uttered together with this meaning (or, in Kaplan's [1989] terminology, *character*) determine the proposition expressed. Suppose that a teacher enters a classroom, looks around and declares, "Everyone is present." Taken out of context, this sentence does not express any particular proposition, because, taken out of context, there is no particular domain of discourse relative to which we may interpret "everyone" and no particular time and place that "present" might refer to. Nonetheless, the sentence, as a sentence of English, carries a certain potential for expressing propositions, and this potential is, in one sense, its meaning. The meaning of this sentence is such that in this particular context, an utterance of it might express the proposition that all of the students enrolled in the course are, at the time of utterance, located in the classroom where the utterance takes place; whereas there is no context in which it might express the proposition that there will be no lecture on that day, and there is no context in which it might express the proposition that the sky is made of glass. What speakers and hearers know in common about the sentences of their language is this kind of meaning, which together with a context of utterance determines a proposition.

So sentences may fail to express a proposition all by themselves, but may nonetheless express a proposition *in a context*. When a speaker utters a sentence in some context, we may describe the proposition that the sentence expresses in that context as *what is said*, or *what the speaker says*. However, proponents of the received view may disagree over how we should conceive of the context and how a context, together with the meaning of the sentence used, determines a proposition. There are at least two big questions here. One question is how much context-relativity we should recognize in our understanding of the very meanings of words and how much we should treat as a matter of bringing the context to bear in a way not governed by the semantic rules of language. In all of these cases, is this relativity built into the very meaning of the sentence so that to understand the meaning of the sentence is to recognize the presence of a variable that must be evaluated in light of the context? Or in some cases does this so-called context-relativity merely show that the words a speaker speaks may not tell us everything we want to know about the background from which that act of speech arises? (See Stanley and Szabó 2000, Stanley 2000, Bach 2000, 2001.)

The other big question, easily confused with the first, is, what determines the actual value of a contextual variable? At one extreme, someone might hold that there is just never any distinction between the proposition that the sentence expresses in context and the thought expressed, so that the pertinent context is really nothing other than the thought expressed. Somewhat less extreme, one might hold that the context relative to which we should interpret a sentence as expressing a proposition is always some aspect of the speaker's mental contents. For example, it might be said that the pertinent domain of discourse is just the set of things that the speaker has in mind in speaking. At the other extreme, someone might hold that the pertinent elements of the context lie entirely outside the mind of the speaker and that there are definite semantic rules that generate a proposition from the context and the meaning of the sentence. Indexicals such as "I" provide the paradigm, for we may suppose that there is simply a rule that says that the referent of "I" is always whoever is the speaker in the context. On this matter the received view faces a difficult dilemma, to which I will return in chapter 4.

Besides insincerity, nonliterality, and context-relativity, there is another complication that stands in the way of a simple account of the process by which the hearer recognizes the thought expressed, namely, the phenomenon of presupposition. Here are some examples:

• *Contrastive particles:* "Milosevic is a war criminal too." By virtue of the particle "too," this sentence in some sense presupposes that someone besides Milosevic is a war criminal. Or else it presupposes that Milosevic is something other than a war criminal.

• *Factives:* "Matt knows that his paper is late." In some sense this sentence presupposes that Matt's paper is late.

• *Possessives:* "Mrs. Champlain's free gift is still here." This sentence presupposes that Mrs. Champlain is associated in some way with a free gift.

• *Cleft constructions:* "It was not the maid who took the leftover bourbon." This sentence presupposes that someone took the leftover bourbon.

As with context-sensitivity, there is room for disagreement between proponents of the received view over the proper treatment of presupposition. One question is what it takes for a proposition to be presupposed. Proponents of the received view have typically followed Stalnaker in treating presupppositions as, roughly, background assumptions mutually acceptable to the interlocutors (Stalnaker 1973, 1974). The presuppositions of sentences, as opposed to speakers, are conditions that the background assumptions must meet if the use of the sentence is to be appropriate. For example, in any context in which an utterance of "Milosevic is a war criminal too" is entirely nondefective, there will be some $x \neq$ Milosevic such that a proposition to the effect that x is a war criminal is mutually believed by the interlocutors. Another question is what kind of defect we should find in a sentence if one of the propositions that the sentence presupposes is not really presupposed by the interlocutors.

Does the sentence in that case express no proposition? Is it false? Or is it merely misleading?

Thus, what the speaker and hearer bring to the discourse situation is supposed to be a knowledge of meanings, where the meaning of a sentence is supposed to be something which, at least when the presuppositions are fulfilled, combines with a context of utterance to generate a proposition. To interpret the speaker *on the basis* of the speaker's choice of words is to identify a proposition as a function of the meaning of the speaker's sentence, the context of utterance and the presuppositions. If the speaker has chosen his or her words well, and the hearer has correctly interpreted on the basis of the speaker's choice of words in this way, then the proposition so identified will be the thought that the speaker expresses, which, if the speaker is speaking sincerely and literally, the hearer may interpret the speaker as believing.

So what determines the meaning of a sentence? For a proponent of the received view, this question is not the general problem of intentionality. In philosophy, the general problem of intentionality is to explain what it takes for a concrete particular to qualify as a representation, and what it takes for a concrete representation to qualify as a representation of one thing rather than another. For a proponent of the received view, the general problem of intentionality is first of all a problem about the intentionality of thought: how it can be that something in the brain bears a propositional content, and bears the propositional content that, say, *some reptiles can swim*, rather than the content that, say, *all butterflies have been caterpillars*. But a solution to this problem is not itself part of the received view of linguistic communication. Within the framework of the received view of communication, one just takes for granted that beliefs have representational content and on that assumption explains what it is for a sentence to have a meaning. (In the next chapter I will argue that this is a problematic assumption.)

One idea within the camp of the received view traces the meanings of words and sentences back to the propositional contents of the thoughts expressed. Roughly, the meaning of a sentence is the thought that speakers typically express with it, or, in Grice's (1989) phrase, *have it in their repertoire* to mean by it. This idea is known as *intention-based semantics*. One problem with this idea is that it assumes that a sentence does, apart from context, express a proposition. Another problem is that it does not yield a theory of the meanings of individual words. Relatedly, it does not explain how novel sentences—sentences that have never been used before but which can be grammatically constructed from the given vocabulary of the language—might have meanings. Intention-based semantics in the strict sense would require us to explain the meaning of each word of a language in terms of speakers' intentions toward that particular word and then to explain how speakers' intentions with respect to each sentence are a product of their intentions toward each word (see Grice 1989, essay 6). As far as I can tell, no one believes in intention-based semantics in this strict sense anymore; so I will say no more about it.

A better idea, which has become fairly standard, is this: A language, considered as an abstract object, is a mapping of sentences to meanings. Inasmuch as the meaning of a sentence is a specifiable function of the meanings of its components, this mapping can be expressed in the form of a recursive definition. This definition comprises the *semantic rules* of the language. At the basis of this recursive definition will be an assignment of meanings to subsentential expressions. For example, the predicate "is nice" might be assigned the property of *being nice* and the expression "That one" might be assigned a certain function f from contexts into objects. Then the definition will imply that the meaning of "That one is nice" is a function F from contexts into propositions such that, given any context c, if $f(c) = x$, then $F(c)$ = a proposition to the effect that x is nice. A community can be said to *use* a language, conceived as such a context-relative mapping of sentences into meanings, if there prevails among them a practice, or convention, of interpreting one another in accordance with it. More precisely, a community uses a language, conceived as a mapping from sentences into meanings, if there prevails among them a convention according to which (a) a speaker utters a sentence of the language (in the declarative mood) only if he or she expresses the proposition that is the product of the meaning of the sentence, as determined by that mapping, in light of the context of utterance, and (b) when a speaker utters a given sentence (in the declarative mood), the hearer may interpret the speaker as expressing the proposition that is the product of the meaning of the sentence, as determined by that mapping, in light of the context of utterance. (The view I have described here is roughly that of Lewis 1975. What I have said here differs from what Lewis says in its use of the concept of expressing a proposition.)

One of the virtues of the received view is that it provides a framework in which we can articulate certain *norms of discourse*. Above all, we can characterize successful communication as an episode in which the hearer, on the basis of the meanings of the speaker's words, comes to recognize in the speaker the thought that the speaker expresses, that is, comes to recognize in the speaker a belief whose propositional content is the belief whose propositional content the speaker intended the hearer to recognize in the speaker on the basis of the speaker's choice of words. Consequently, we can characterize effective speech as acts of speech from which the speaker can reasonably expect success, that is, as acts of speech such that the speaker can reasonably expect the hearer to recognize the thought expressed on the basis of the speaker's choice of words. And we can say that one should strive to speak in such a way that the proposition one expresses is the proposition that another user of the language would think one was expressing judging by the meanings of one's words and the context.

In terms of the expression of propositions we can define the concepts of logical consistency and logical implication, which we can then use in formulating a maxim to the effect that one should not make assertions that are logically inconsistent and a maxim to the effect that one may draw whatever conclusions one's premises logically imply. Logical consistency and logical implication may be defined as first of all relations between propositions. For example, if we think of propositions as sets of possible worlds, then we can say that a set of propositions A is logically consistent if and only if the intersection of the propositions in A is non-empty, and we can say that a set of propositions A logically implies a proposition q if and only if the intersection of the propositions in A is set-theoretically included in q, the idea being that any world in which the premises are all true is a world in which the conclusion is true. Logical relations between sentences and acts of speech may then be defined in terms of logical relations between propositions. A set of sentences is logically consistent if and only if there is a context such that the propositions that the sentences in the set express in that context are consistent. Alternatively, we might say that a set of sentences is consistent *in a context* if and only if the propositions that the sentences in the set express in that context are consistent. An argument, consisting of sentences, a set of premises and a conclusion, is logically valid (the premises logically imply the conclusion; the inference from the premises to the conclusion is valid) if and only if for every context, the propositions that the premises express in that context logically imply the proposition that the conclusion expresses in that context. Alternatively, we might say that an argument is valid *in a context* if and only if the propositions that the premises express in that context imply the proposition that the conclusion expresses in that context. A person speaks consistently if and only if the sentences that he or she utters are consistent. A person argues validly if and only if his or her argument is valid.

Given that words are supposed to have more or less constant meanings, the received point of view provides a framework in which we can formulate discourse norms pertaining to particular lexical items. The received view of linguistic communication is not itself in the business of ascribing particular meanings to particular words, but nonetheless it provides a framework in which we can understand what we are doing in ascribing particular meanings to particular words. If we say that as a consequence of its meaning (or character) in English, a sentence of the form "That is a cat" expresses in context a proposition to the effect that a certain thing is a cat, then we may say that, barring some special excuse, one should not use that sentence among English speakers to try to convey a proposition to the effect that a certain thing is a dog, or a proposition to the effect that a certain thing is a small, furry pet. Or if we give an account of the meaning of "if . . . then . . ." according to which arguments of the form "not-p; therefore if p then q" are valid, then we may add that one may—one is permitted—draw conclusions in that way.

To say that the received view of linguistic communication allows for the articulation of norms of discourse in this way is not yet to say that the theory is itself a normative theory, as opposed to a descriptive account of how linguistic communication actually works. Whether a given form of words has a certain meaning is a natural fact, it may be said. The meanings of words are somehow entirely a matter of how words are used in fact, even if people sometimes express a proposition that is false or do not mean to express the proposition that their words express or fail to express a proposition by their use of words at all. So although we may make normative recommendations on the grounds that a certain sentence under certain conditions expresses a certain proposition, our doing so does not mean that the claim that such a proposition is expressed is itself a normative claim. Though theorists might defend their claims about the meanings of particular forms of words on the basis of assumptions about which sentences are true or about which forms of argument are valid, that does not mean that their debate is really a debate about which norms we should adopt; rather, their contentions about what is true or what is valid are in effect hypotheses about what the meaning of the form of words in question, as a matter of natural fact, really is.

The viability of this characterization of the received view of linguistic communication, according to which it presents the outlines of a descriptive science of language and is not in itself a framework for the formulation of norms of discourse, will depend on exactly how we are to understand what it is for words to have the meanings they have. If we think of this in the manner described above, as a conventional selection of a mapping of sentences into meanings, then, contrary to the point of view just sketched, we will find it hard to avoid the conclusion that the enterprise of defining that mapping is an intrinsically normative enterprise. That is because any attempt to characterize the linguistic conventions that prevail in a community will be at the same time a recommendation, a codification, a regularization of practices that are not already very regular.

We might try to avoid the normative conception of the received view by supposing that in describing the conventionally accepted mapping of words into meanings we would be practicing a kind of anthropology in which we merely observed which such mapping the members of a

community do strive to conform to. But we would necessarily be defeated in any such project because we would not
find enough uniformity in what people say to identify any
particular such mapping as the language that the members
of the community conventionally use. Everywhere we
would face an indeterminate choice between interpreting
the community as conforming to convention A, and consequently interpreting speaker X but not speaker Y as expressing his or her thought well, and interpreting the community
as conforming to convention B, and consequently interpreting Y but not X as expressing his or her thought well.

So instead, we might deny any pretensions to identifying
the language that they really do use and content ourselves
with merely describing the various conventions that the
various members of the community regard themselves as
following. The trouble here is that we have to take account
of the fact that the members of a linguistic community do
think of themselves as striving to speak the same language
as their fellows. When they lack a word to express some
concept, they ask what it is and do not simply make one up.
They are prepared to alter their usage when they detect that
in some respect their own usage is not in conformity to that
which prevails around them. They may even take college
classes to improve their understanding of words like "if . . .
then . . ." or "probable." So unless we are prepared to
declare that their practice in this regard, as well as our own
in our own linguistic community, is entirely based on an
illusion, we have to accept that we can meaningfully speak
of *the* linguistic conventions that prevail in a community.
Thus we find ourselves having to characterize these

conventions in a way that respects actual usage without aiming merely to describe it, that is, by presenting a conception of what those conventions ought to be.

If this is right, then, the received view of linguistic communication is not a descriptive science, like biology. It is a framework for the formulation of discourse norms, as an ethical theory is a framework within which we may identify rights and obligations. That does not mean that the concepts employed in it do not also have a place in the explanation of human behavior. In particular, one might explain that people choose their words as they do because they believe that those are the words that they ought to choose, given the discourse norms that prevail in their community, if they wish to succeed in conveying the contents of their thoughts to others. In general, we may cite norms in explanation of behavior in those cases where we may assume that at some level people are cognizant of these norms and strive to conform to them.

Whether he or she thinks of the theory of linguistic communication as normative or descriptive, in either case a proponent of the received view must make some basic assumptions about the nature of thought. Again, the primary function of linguistic communication is supposed to be that it enables people to grasp the propositional contents of people's thoughts, in particular, their beliefs and desires. To suppose that linguistic communication may be described in this way is to presume that this conveying of contents has some value. That value will be explained in terms of a general conception of thought, according to which thinking itself is largely a transition between mental representations bearing propositional contents, a process by which the thinker comes to stand in various relations to propositions, such as believing them to be true and desiring them to be true. Linguistic communication is important because other people's beliefs and desires may be important inputs to this process of thinking by which each person forms his or her own beliefs and desires and because knowing what other people believe and desire may enable a person to coordinate his or her behavior with that of others. In thus explaining the value of linguistic communication, a proponent of the received view is committed to the beginnings of a theory of thinking. Whether a proponent of the received view can live up to his or her commitments in this regard is the question that will occupy us in the next chapter.

2 Mental Representation

The basic argument against the received view is not that it is incoherent but just that in many ways it fails to provide a good explanation of language. Its particular shortcomings will be in evidence throughout this book. The topic of this chapter is a foundational problem that will not arise elsewhere. The question is: What can it mean to say that a belief, considered as a representation in the brain, has a certain propositional content? My aim in this chapter is to instill despair concerning the prospects for answering this question.

Recall that a proponent of the received view is committed to conceiving of thought as a transition between mental representations bearing propositional content. Even for a proponent of the received view, it is not necessary to think of thinking as exclusively a matter of thus manipulating propositional contents. Other, nonpropositional processes may mediate or intervene. But the manipulation of propositional contents will have to be conceived as an essential feature of the thinking of language-using creatures if the conveying of propositional contents by means of language is supposed to have some point. For the most part, people working on the nature of language have assumed that they could leave to others the business of explaining what it takes for a person to have a certain belief and, in particular, what it takes for a belief to have a certain propositional content. I'm here to say that a proponent of the received view of linguistic communication needs to face up to this problem.

A proponent of the received view may acknowledge that in many ways propositional thought is dependent on language. What we think depends on what people tell us, of course, but, moreover, what we *can* think may depend a lot on language. The things we think about are often linguistic objects, such as books. Many of the things we think about would not be countenanced outside the context of a linguistic community—such as Wednesdays, or tax codes. Some thoughts would be very hard to hold in mind without the aid of symbolic expressions—such as thoughts expressed by mathematical equations. Most importantly, we often acquire concepts only as a result of trying to grasp the thoughts that others intend to convey. Even learning the meanings of basic words like "bird" and "chair" might involve such a process.

Still, a proponent of the received view cannot maintain that the reason why a belief has a certain content is just because the believer attempts to convey the content of that belief by means of a certain sentence that expresses that content in context; otherwise, he or she could not maintain that speakers choose their words by deciding whether the proposition that a given sentence expresses in the context is the proposition they wish to express. The ways in which language affects thought must not be supposed to contradict the basic asymmetry that allows us to explain the use of words as the expression of thought. (Elsewhere, in my forthcoming a, I have drawn far reaching consequences from this basic constraint.) So the question is this: How, compatibly with the explanatory asymmetry between thought and language, might we explain what it takes for a belief to have one propositional content rather than another?

As I have explained in chapter 1, a belief is supposed to be a relation between a believer and a proposition, and the propositional content of a belief is supposed to be carried by a mental representation in the person's brain. We can also use the term "belief" to refer to the mental representation that carries the propositional content of an explicit belief. So a particular explicit belief, in a particular person's head at a particular time, is a particular mental representation, and, intrinsically, it might be said, a mental representation is a piece, or aspect, of the brain, having a certain neural, chemical, electro-magnetic structure. Inasmuch as the propositional content of a belief can be expressed in a sentence, the mental representation that bears this content presumably has a structure analogous to the structure of the sentence that expresses its content. Thus, believing a proposition (explicitly) entails having in one's brain somewhere a sentence-like mental representation having a distinctive physical structure bearing a certain propositional content. In these terms our question becomes: What are the conditions under which a given mental representation bears a given propositional content? Why is a certain squiggle in my brain a belief that *some reptiles can swim* rather than a belief that *all butterflies have been caterpillars*?

The contemporary literature contains many proposals for answering this question, but in my opinion all of them fail so miserably that we ought to seek a conception of mind and language that does not pose the question in the first place. I will not attempt to demonstrate a priori that all answers to this question must fail, because I do not know of any means of doing so. Nor will I be able to examine all of the ideas that are currently in play. Some of these ideas are quite remote from common sense (which is not in itself any strike against them), while others are theoretical articulations of hunches that come to mind rather readily. What I will do is attempt to instill a skeptical attitude toward the whole project by criticizing those theories that seem to be the starting point and fall-back position of almost all who are engaged in this enterprise. (Consequently, I will ignore the specific theories of Millikan 1993, Dretske 1988, Churchland 1989, and Gärdenfors 2000. I have criticized Millikan's theory in my 1995 review.)

One idea that occurs to people readily is that the content of mental representations is a matter of brain-world correlations. "Having a concept," writes Fiona Cowie, "is a matter of resonating to the property that the concept expresses" (1999, p. 132). A whole belief, then, is presumably a composition of such concepts expressing properties by virtue of such resonances. It is hard to find a clear statement of this theory in the writings of the authors who espouse it, but maybe the idea is this: Consider just the case of some person's belief B, considered as a brain state, whose propositional content is that some particular thing, *that thing*, has some property *being P*. According to this theory, a necessary condition on B's having the propositional content that *that is P* is that whenever the person is presented (via some sensory modality) with an object having the property *being P* (a P-thing), a belief having the same physical structure as B (relative to some given standard of sameness) arises in his or her brain (as an effect of this presentation). Perhaps we also have to add that we should expect the belief to arise only when the person's attention is turned on, his or her senses are working properly, and so on.

Even if this condition is necessary, we cannot maintain that it is also sufficient for brain state B's having the content that *that is P*. Suppose Q-things are always also P-things, as sparrows are always also birds. If it were true that a state like B arises in the brain whenever a P-thing is present (and the other conditions are satisfied), then likewise it would be true that a state like B arises in the brain whenever a Q-thing is present (and the other conditions are satisfied). The problem is that a state like B might be a belief to the effect that *that is P* without also being a belief to the effect that *that is Q*. We might remedy this by saying that a state like B is a belief to the effect that *that is P* if and only if (i) a state like B arises whenever a P-thing is present (and the other conditions are satisfied), and (ii) a state like B arises *only* when a P-thing is present. In other words, we might propose that a state like B is a belief to the effect that *that is P* if and only if the property *being P* is the most inclusive property of which we can say that a state like B occurs whenever a thing having that property is presented to the senses (and the other conditions are satisfied). For example, there might be a certain kind of brain state that occurs in a person whenever he or she is looking at a bird, although there is no broader class of objects such that we can say that that kind of brain state occurs in the person whenever he or she is looking at a member of that broader class. In that case we might say that brain states of that kind represent things *as birds* and that this particular brain state represents *that* as a bird (namely, the bird whose presence is causing the brain state). That brain state will not represent things *as sparrows*, even though it occurs whenever the person is looking at a sparrow, because there is also a broader class of things, namely birds, such that that brain state occurs whenever the person is looking at a thing in that broader class.

Certainly this sort of theory will not work for mental representations representing things that do not come and go or are not perceptible at all. For example, the belief that air contains oxygen cannot be very well accounted for along these lines, because it is not the case that the fact that the air contains oxygen comes and goes, so that we might look for correlations between the occurrence of that fact and events in our brains. But maybe this theory will work for some sorts of mental representations, such as the representation of the presence of a bird, and then maybe we could explain the content of other mental representations in terms of their relations to those. Unfortunately, it does not seem to work even for mental representations representing the presence of a bird. A thought to the effect that a bird is present may occur to us not only through observation of a bird but also through reasoning or the testimony of others. Further, the thoughts that result from observation depend not so much on how things are but on how they appear. We may think that something is a bird when it is only an imitation of a bird or is really a squirrel in the branches of a tree, so that the broadest category of things that regularly cause our representations of something as a bird will be not *birds* but *birds-or-imitation-birds-or-squirrels-in-the-branches-of-a-tree*.

In response to this last sort of difficulty, Fodor (1987) proposes that the types of situation that brain states depend on in this way are, in his terms, "asymmetrically dependent" on the types of situation that we should cite in identifying a belief state's propositional content. For example, the reason why some brain state whose content is the proposition that *that is a bird* occurs in a person, even though what that person is presented with is only an imitation bird, is that there are other occasions on which that kind of brain state occurs in the presence of an actual bird; whereas we cannot likewise maintain that that kind of brain state occurs in the presence of a bird only because there are other occasions on which that kind of brain state occurs in the presence of an imitation bird.

One problem with this answer is that in whatever way the misrepresentation of nonbirds as birds is dependent upon the representation of birds as birds, so too the representation of atypical, nonparadigmatic birds as birds is liable to be dependent on the representation of typical, paradigmatic birds as birds. Some paradigmatic kinds of birds might be sparrows and crows. Some nonparadigmatic kinds of birds would be penguins (which are almost like seals) and hummingbirds (which are almost like insects). Now consider the brain state that, according to Fodor's theory, is supposed to represent birds as such. I submit that if that brain state were not caused by penguins and hummingbirds, it might still be caused by sparrows and crows; whereas if that brain state were not caused by sparrows and crows, then it would not be caused by penguins and hummingbirds, for in that case we would never have formed the category *bird* in the first place. So just as Fodor's theory tells us, correctly, that representations of birdlike nonbirds as birds are still really representations of things as birds, so too the theory will tell us, mistakenly, that representations of atypical, nonparadigmatic birds as birds are really representations of atypical birds as typical, paradigmatic birds. (Fodor 1987 addresses this objection in footnote 9, pp. 164–165; but he does not apply his own theory properly. What he is supposed to do is consider *nearby* possible worlds in which typical birds do not cause the brain state, and then ask whether in that world penguins do; but instead he considers a world in which sparrows turn out to be reptiles.)

A much more promising idea is that we might explain the representational content of our mental states by an analogy to cartographical representation. This idea is much more widespread than its representation in the literature would suggest, but it does crop up in some of the literature too (e.g., Haugeland 1985, even Millikan 1993, but especially Cummins 1996). When push comes to shove and a philosopher is forced to defend his or her conviction that there must be some way to explicate the meaning of mental representations, this is what he or she usually falls back on. The basic idea is that our beliefs, considered as brain states, are analogous to the marks on an actual map. Assigning a propositional content to a particular belief is analogous to determining what aspects of the terrain are represented by some particular marks on a map.

One good thing about this idea is that it acknowledges that the propositional content of one representation will depend on the propositional content of other representations to which it is related, since it is only the arrangement of marks on the map as a whole that dictates one interpretation rather than another. Another good thing about this idea is that it gives us some sense of how it could be important to have brain states that qualify as beliefs with propositional content. Just as we can use an actual map to find our way around within the terrain, no matter the reason why we might want to go somewhere, so too we can use our beliefs to find our way around in the world, no matter the reason why we might want to do something in it.

One might suspect that there is a crucial disanalogy between maps and mental representations as well. In the case of an actual map, what makes it the case that the map represents the relationships between the towns and the roads and the mountains, one might say, is not just the fact that the mapping from marks on the map to objects in the terrain is an isomorphism from the structure of the map into the structure of the terrain; for we can find indefinitely many systems of uninteresting objects—ant hills, blades of grass, trajectories of birds, radio waves, arbitrary paths across the surface—to which the map is likewise isomorphic. Rather, the map represents certain roads, towns, mountains, and so on, just because we *think* of those lines and dots on the map as standing for those roads, towns, mountains, and so on. By contrast, in explaining what it takes for a system of brain states to qualify as having certain propositional contents rather than others, we obviously cannot fall back on how we *think* about those brain states. The meaningfulness of maps, one might say, rests on the prior capacity of those who use them to think contentfully; but the contentfulness of thoughts cannot likewise rest on a prior capacity to think contentfully.

However, to raise this doubt is not yet to offer any actual criticism of the cartographical theory. We can insist that there really is such a disanalogy only once we have independently shown that the cartographical theory is mistaken. So now I will try to explain why it actually fails. In order to define the cartographical theory of mental representation more precisely, and to criticize it more directly, I first need to explain what logicians mean by *interpreting* a language in such way that a *theory* formulated in that language is true. This will be a little complicated, but it will enable me to make a very important point that many philosophers (such as Cummins) seem to be ignoring. (For other, later purposes too, it will be useful to have gone through this here.)

First, for illustration's sake, I need to invent a simple language, which I will call *the simple language*. Let the *names* of this simple language be just two: *"a"* and *"b"*. Let the *variables* of the language be just *"x"* and *"y"*. Let the *predicates* of this language be just *"is blah"* and *"is a koob"*. Let the *logical vocabulary* consist of: *"not"*, *"or"*, and *"for all"*. The language will also contain parentheses: *"("*, *")"*. We may jointly specify as follows the conditions under which a string of

words from this language qualifies as a *formula* of the simple
language and the conditions under which a variable qualifies as *bound*:

Definition of formula and bound variable:

1. If P is a predicate and t is a name or a variable, then t followed by P is a formula (in particular, it is an *atomic*
   formula).

2. If F is a formula, then *"not"* followed by F is a formula too.

3. If F and G are formulas, then *"("* followed by F, followed
   by *"or"*, followed by G, followed by *")"* is a formula.

4. If F is a formula and v is a variable, then *"for all"* followed
   by v, followed by F is a formula and v is bound.

5. No string of words in the simple language is a formula
   unless it qualifies as one by the above rules, and no variable in a formula is bound unless it qualifies as bound by
   rule 4.

For example, by rule 1, *"x is blah"* and *"x is a koob"* are (atomic)
formulas; by rule 2, *"not x is blah"* is a formula; by rule 3,
"(not x is blah or x is a koob)" is a formula; and by rule 4, *"for
all x (not x is blah or x is a koob)"* is a formula and *"x"* is bound
in it. We can now define a *sentence* of the simple language as
any formula in which all variables are bound.

Let us say that a *universe U* is a set of objects, such as o_1,
o_2, and o_3. Define an *interpretation* of the simple language as
a function *Int* that assigns an object in the universe to each
name in the language and assigns a property to each predicate. (In logic, predicates are usually assigned sets, not

properties, but, as we will see, it will favor the received view to assign properties.) So, for example, on one interpretation, we may have $Int("a") = o_1$ and $Int("is\ blah") =$ the property of being blue. Further, we will need the concept of a *variable assignment*, which is a function f that assigns an object of the universe to each variable of the language. In addition, let us say that $f[v|o]$ is a variable assignment just like f except that instead of whatever f may have assigned to v, $f[v|o]$ assigns object o to v. So while we might have $f("y") = o_3$, we have $f["y"|o_2]("y") = o_2$, but if v is not $"y"$, then $f(v) = f["y"|o_2](v)$. Let us say that a *structure* is a triple $\langle U, Int, f \rangle$, consisting of a universe U, an interpretation Int, and a variable assignment f.

Now we can define the conditions under which a structure *satisfies* a formula of the simple language:

A structure $\langle U, Int, f \rangle$ *satisfies* a formula H if and only if either

(a) H consists of a name n followed by a predicate P and $Int(n)$ has the property $Int(P)$, or

(b) H consists of a variable v followed by a predicate P and $f(v)$ has the property $Int(P)$, or

(c) H consists of $"not"$ followed by a formula F and $\langle U, Int, f \rangle$ does not satisfy F, or

(d) H consists of $"("$ followed by a formula F, followed by $"or"$, followed by a formula G, followed by $")"$ and $\langle U, Int, f \rangle$ satisfies either F or G, or

(e) H consists of $"for\ all"$ followed by a variable v, followed by a formula F and for every object o in U, $\langle U, Int, f[v|o] \rangle$ satisfies F.

Then in terms of satisfaction we can define the conditions under which a sentence is *true* on *Int* in *U* thus: If *S* is a sentence, then *S* is true on *Int* in *U* if and only if for every variable assignment f (on the domain *U*), $\langle U, Int, f \rangle$ satisfies *S*.

For example, suppose $U = \{o_1, o_2, o_3\}$, where o_1 is a blue cube, o_2 is a red sphere, and o_3 is a red cube. Suppose also that:

$Int("a") = o_1$,

$Int("b") = o_2$,

$Int("is\ blah")$ = the property of being blue, and

$Int("is\ a\ koob")$ = the property of being a cube.

For example, the sentence *"a is a koob"* is true on *Int* in *U* if and only if for every variable assignment f, $\langle U, Int, f \rangle$ satisfies *"a is a koob"*. By clause (a) in the definition of satisfaction, this will be so, for arbitrary variable assignment f, if and only if o_1 is a cube, which is true. So *"a is a koob"* is true on *Int* in *U*. For another example, *"for all x (not x is blah or x is a koob)"* is true on *Int* in *U* if and only if for every variable assignment f, $\langle U, Int, f \rangle$ satisfies *"for all x (not x is blah or x is a koob)."* But by clause (e), for any given variable assignment f, $\langle U, Int, f \rangle$ satisfies *"for all x (not x is blah or x is a koob)"* if and only if for every object o in *U*, $\langle U, Int, f["x"|o] \rangle$ satisfies *"(not x is blah or x is a koob)"*, which, by clauses (d), (c), and (b), is so if and only if for every object o in *U*, either o is not blue or o is a cube. So *"for all x (not x is blah or x is a koob)"* is true on *Int* in *U* if and only if for every object o in *U*, either o is not blue or o is a cube, which is true. By contrast, *"for all x (not x is a koob or x is blah)"* is not true on *Int* in *U* because o_3 is a cube but is not blue.

Finally, let us say that an interpretation *Int* in a universe *U* is a *model* of a set of sentences in the simple language if and only if every sentence in the set is true on *Int* in *U*. The crucial fact for my criticism of the cartographical theory of mental representation will be that if a set of sentences has one model in a universe *U*, then it necessarily has more than one (provided that *U* contains more than one object). For example, recall that o_1 is in fact a cube, and every blue object in *U* is a cube. Then, by the example of the last paragraph, we have seen that the set of sentences {*"a is a koob"*, *"for all x (not x is blah or x is a koob)"*} has a model in *U*, namely, *Int*, as specified in the example. But without altering the nature of the objects in *U* (that is, without imagining a different reality), we can easily construct another, different model of that set of sentences. We can specify a second interpretation *Int** in which we simply switch the roles of o_1 and o_2, thus:

Int*("a") = o_2,

Int*("b") = o_1,

Int*("is blah") = the property of being either blue and not identical to o_1 or not blue but identical to o_2, and

Int*("is a koob") = the property of being either a cube and not identical to o_1 or not a cube but identical to o_2.

Although o_2 is not a cube, it is identical to o_2; so *"a is a koob"* is true on *Int** in *U*. Likewise, since every member of *U* that is either blue and not identical to o_1 or not blue but identical to o_2 (which is so for just o_2) is also either a cube and not identical to o_1 or not a cube but identical to o_2 (which is so for o_3 and o_2), "*for all x (not x is blah or x is a koob)*" is also true on *Int** in *U*. Further, "*for all x (not x is a koob or x is blah)*" is false on *Int**, just as it was false on *Int*, because while o_3 has the property assigned to "*is a koob*" (since it is a cube not identical to o_1), it does not have the property assigned to "*is blah*" (since it is neither both blue and not identical to o_1 nor both not blue and identical to o_2). It is evident (and provable by induction on the complexity of formulas) that every sentence of our simple language that is true on *Int* in *U* is true on *Int** in *U* and conversely.

The reason to present this conception of interpretation is that the cartographical theory can be defined in terms of it. As far as I am aware, no one who endorses the cartographical theory has attempted any very precise definition of it. However, if not cast simply as a vague analogy to maps, then I think it would have to include at least the following three claims: *First*, a person's explicit beliefs, considered as concrete particulars, can be treated as tokens of sentences in some kind of mental language. It is not important whether beliefs have a syntax very like that of the languages of logic. So long as they have some kind of structure such that the propositional content of one of them is a function of the interpretation of its components or aspects, then we will be able to speak of beliefs as containing mental names and mental predicates, and my question, which I am working up to, will be the same. *Second*, for some interpretation of that mental language comprising some universe of actual and possible objects and the properties they actually possess and the relations they actually stand in, that interpretation in that universe is a model of the person's true beliefs (and, we might add, a model of the negations of the false ones). *Third*, a belief has the propositional content that *p* if and only if on that same interpretation in that same universe, the belief is true if and only if it is true that *p*.

I am now in a position to explain my doubt about the cartographical theory of mental representation very neatly: Just as there is never just one model for a set of sentences, there will never be just one model for any set of mental representations. If a set of mental representations has one model, then (assuming the universe is as large as in any case it has to be), it will have many, many, wildly divergent models. If there is a model of your mental representations according to which one of your thoughts is about the chair you are sitting on, then there is another model of your mental representations according to which that same thought is about the biggest elephant in Africa. So the cartographical theory of mental representation does far too little to pin down the propositional content of a person's beliefs. This is so even if we suppose, unrealistically, that we are dealing with a person whose beliefs are exclusively true, who believes nothing false.

Before considering how one might respond to this problem, I ought to comment on one aspect of my characterization of the cartographical theory that might seem wrong to its proponents. In characterizing the cartographical theory as holding that the correct interpretation of a person is a model of the person's *true* beliefs, I seem to presuppose that we can pick out the true beliefs independently of their interpretation. The problem with this is that it might seem that there would be no way to identify the true beliefs apart from their interpretation, in which case, if the cartographical theory requires a prior identification of the true beliefs, then there will be no need for the cartographical theory of the interpretation of mental representation. But the only alternative is to strengthen the cartographical theory to the claim that the correct interpretation of a person's beliefs is a model of all of his or her beliefs, whether true or false in actuality, but then to weaken the definition of "model" so that an interpretation of a language qualifies as a model of a set of sentences in the language provided only that every sentence in that set is true on that interpretation *in some possible* (actual or fictitious) *world*. By increasing the number of beliefs that have to be modelled, we do somewhat restrict the class of models, but by not requiring that all beliefs be interpreted as actually true, we throw the class of admissible interpretations wide open again. So this version of the cartographical theory still does nothing to pin down the propositional content of a person's beliefs.

So the cartographical theory of mental representation faces a very basic question: What more can be added to the theory to sufficiently narrow down the range of permissible interpretations? This question goes well beyond the question whether there is a plurality of models. I am not the first person to have pointed out that there is always a plurality of models. Hilary Putnam, for one, has done so before me (1981, chapter 2). The problem with Putnam's exposition is that he blends his demonstration of this point with his discussion of further constraints in such a way that a reader might not clearly realize that the availability of alternative models is really quite trivial. In his exposition, the point is made to seem like a difficult metaphysical contention that might possibly be challenged by a more sophisticated metaphysics. What is really not trivial is what I am about to claim next, namely, that there is no good way to identify the correct interpretation from among the class of models.

We could narrow the class of permissible interpretations by requiring that any interpretation belong to a coherent class of interpretations that includes interpretations of the person's true beliefs at each time in his or her history, or includes interpretations of true beliefs that the person would have in each of a number of counterfactual histories. Perhaps we could also narrow the class of admissible interpretations by insisting that our interpretation of each person's beliefs must belong to a uniform interpretation of the beliefs of everyone else in that person's community. However none of these strategies will answer the basic point that wherever there is one model there are bound to be many, many others, so that the cartographical theory does little by itself to pin down the propositional content of a person's beliefs.

The only way to answer our question would be to supplement the cartographical theory with further constraints on interpretation beyond the requirement that the interpretation must constitute a model for certain beliefs. The correct interpretation of a person's beliefs, we might say, is that which is a model of certain beliefs *and* meets these further conditions. For example, one idea would be to stipulate that the interpretation of beliefs can assign to basic, noncompound mental predicates only properties that are in some sense privileged. In that way we might rule out the sort of gerrymandered property that I appealed to (in the definition of *Int**) in demonstrating that there is never just one model. (This is why I said it would be helpful to the received view to interpret predicates with properties rather than sets.) One version of this idea would be that the only properties to which we can appeal are properties that are directly perceptible, such as colors and shapes. But that is not right, since we can certainly think about such things as electrons, and propositions about electrons cannot be reduced to propositions about the directly perceptible properties of things. Another version of this idea would be that the properties to which we can appeal are those that in some sense "carve nature at the joints." But that cannot be right either since we can certainly think about properties and kinds that do not carve nature at the joints such as *dwellings*, *songs*, *dictators*, and *surprises*, and our thoughts about these cannot all be reduced to thoughts about properties that carve nature at the joints.

Another version of this idea would be that the only properties that we can appeal to are those that the human mind is especially suited to think about (Gärdenfors 2000). If "suited to think about" is taken narrowly, then such interpretations will misinterpret our thoughts of things that we are not particularly suited to think about. Thus, we might rule out the correct interpretation of our thoughts about electrons. If "suited to think about" is taken broadly, then again there are liable to be too many interpretations. For example, we might find a model in which *"is a koob"* is interpreted as expressing the property of being a cube, but we might also find a model in which it is interpreted as expressing the property of being either a cube and not identical to o_1 or not a cube but identical to o_2.

A different idea might be to return to the correlation theory and insist that at least for certain sorts of beliefs, such as those that do not result from a process of inference, the interpretation must interpret those beliefs as having the sort of propositional content characterizing situations of the kind with which beliefs of that kind are correlated. But first, we did not find that the correlation theory yields an adequate theory of the meaning of any kinds of belief at all, and, second, it is not evident that pinning down the meanings of just a small class of beliefs in this way would enable the cartographical theory to pin down the meanings of the rest. In any case, I am not aware that anyone has ever proposed a theory of this kind.

Finally, an idea I have encountered (in discussion with a prominent philosopher) is that the correct interpretation of a subject's beliefs must be not only a model of his or her true beliefs but in addition must *explain* the subject's success in negotiating his or her environment. So, for instance, we might want to say that we should select an interpretation that maps a given mental representation into Main Street if that mental representation is involved in the mental processes by which the thinker negotiates his or her way down Main Street. If in this way we interpret only some of the elements of the system of mental representation, then we will still have to face up to the plurality of models in the interpretation of the rest. If, however, the proposal is to interpret all elements of the system of mental representation in this way, then what is proposed is no longer a version of the cartographical theory of mental representation. In any case, this proposal does not seem very promising, since we cannot assume that every representation involved in negotiating Main Street denotes specifically Main Street and the theory as described does not tell us how to distinguish between those that do and those that do not.

If mental representations were not conceived as having the structure of sentences, but rather a structure more like the structure of topographical maps or road maps, then we would want to define the cartographical theory differently. We would want to define it as holding that the structure of mental representations was isomorphic to a structure of objects in the world. Say that an *n-ary relation* on U_Γ is a set of n-tuples of members of a domain of objects U_Γ. By a *structure* Γ, I will now mean a set of relations on U_Γ. (Structures in this sense are different sorts of things from the structures I introduced above in defining satisfaction of a formula.) Say that Π is a *projection* of one structure Γ into another structure Δ on domain U_Δ if and only if Π is a one-to-one function from the relations in Γ into the relations in Δ such that for every n-ary relation R in Γ, $\Pi(R)$ is some n-ary relation in Δ. A function h is an isomorphism from Γ into Δ relative to a projection Π if and only if h is a one-to-one function from U_Γ into U_Δ such that for all $x_1, x_2, \ldots, x_n$, $\langle x_1, x_2, \ldots, x_n \rangle$ is in R if and only if $\langle h(x_1), h(x_2), \ldots, h(x_n) \rangle$ is in $\Pi(R)$. It is easy to prove that for any structure Γ on domain U_Γ, if h is a one-to-one function from U_Γ into a domain U_Δ, then there is a structure Δ on U_Δ and a projection Π from Γ

into Δ such that h is an isomorphism from Γ into Δ relative to Π. So if all we say about mental representations is that they represent what they are mapped into by some isomorphism from the structure of representations into some structure in some domain of objects in reality, then we thereby do nothing at all to pin down the representational content of those representations.

As I say, I think the cartographical theory is the primary source of inspiration for those who hold out hope for a theory of mental representation. Since the cartographical theory appears to be hopeless, we should seek a theory of language and mind that, unlike the received view of linguistic communication, does not commit us to conceiving of thinking as essentially a matter of forming beliefs with propositional contents.

3   Elements of an Alternative

Typically, conversations have goals. One sort of basic goal that people might have in conversation is finding something: finding prey, finding water, finding a good place to sleep. Other goals have to do with the management of society: settling a territorial dispute, arranging a marriage, deciding how to punish a misbehaving child. I do not assume that all such goals serve survival. Our goals may include finding a beautiful vista, or learning how to play a flute.

In a world permeated with language, our goals may themselves be linguistic. Our goal may be to tell a funny story, to answer an outstanding scientific question, or just to get the message through. Such goals are possible only where language has, so to speak, taken on a life of its own. In this chapter, however, my focus will be exclusively on cases where our goals are not themselves linguistic in this way. In particular, I will not consider *informing* to be a goal of the pertinent sort. Where the practice of language has taken root as a means of achieving practical goals, the goal of keeping everybody informed about recent events can become a goal in itself. But if we find ourselves thinking of informing as a basic goal of language, whose nature we can understand without a prior, independent grip on the nature of language, then we are liable to fall back into the received view of linguistic communication.

Of course, not every conversation has a definite, practical goal. People can chat quite aimlessly about things that happened during the day or the activities of acquaintances. In some of these cases we might nonetheless characterize the interlocutors as feigning a goal. For instance, in chatting about the weather, we might talk as if the question were whether tomorrow would be a good day for a hike. In other cases, for instance, in recounting recent events for no other reason than to inform, we may have no independent practical goal, whether real or merely feigned. But this is an art that we humans can master only insofar as there are other, more practical goals that sometimes shape our discourse. Our sense of relevance on such occasions is shaped by those conversations in which we have some practical goal, and while our sense of relevance may sometimes reach out aimlessly, our interlocutors may reach in the same direction.

The goals of a conversation are, broadly speaking, interpersonal goals, shared by all those engaged in the conversation. They do not have to be self-regarding goals. An interlocutor need not have a personal stake in the achievement of the goal quite apart from his or her participation in the conversation. Rather, an interlocutor may adopt something as his or her goal for no other reason than that he or she recognizes it to be the goal of someone else and is willing to help out. We do not have to suppose that whenever a person adopts a goal, that is an expression of some deeper personal interest. A fortiori, we do not have to suppose that whenever someone is willing to help someone out, he or she does so because he or she has a self-regarding interest in the well-being of the person being helped.

The goals of a conversation may be set in various ways. The needs of the interlocutors may be evident without anyone's having to say anything. If a child is absent when everyone else is present, then finding that child will spontaneously become a goal. Some of these goals will be the product of periodic routines. If it is time to cook and we have no water, then getting water will become one of our goals. If it is time to bring in the cattle, then bringing in the cattle will become one of our goals. In other cases a goal may be set by the commands, or requests, or proposals issued by someone with adequate authority. If the chief commands the building of a new house, and no one challenges him, then the villagers acquire the goal of building the chief a new house. If the leader of the builders tells the builders to cut timber, then the builders acquire the goal of cutting timber.

Thus one sort of speech act serves to establish goals. Call these speech acts *commands*. Not every command will actually establish a goal. A speaker with adequate authority and otherwise well placed to establish goals may indicate to the others that that is what he or she is doing by choosing a particular form of sentence, a sentence in the imperative or propositive mood. Thus a distinctive form of sentence, the imperative or propositive, may acquire as its function the setting of goals. But others, not well placed to set goals cannot always be prevented from attempting to create a goal by speaking in the imperative or propositive mood. Thus, a speech act may qualify as a command by virtue of its mood without achieving that which it is the function of such speech acts to achieve, namely, the establishing of a goal.

Usually, there is more than one way to try to achieve a goal, and some of these ways will be better than others. Oftentimes, what is better is a matter of what is most likely to succeed. For example, if the goal is to hunt buffalo, then it may be better to hunt them near the lake, rather than in the valley, because their actual location may be near the lake. Other times, what is better is a matter of the utility or disutility of side effects. For example, if the goal is to obtain water for cooking, then it will be better to use the clean pail rather than the dirty pail because it would be bad to let the water get dirty. Sometimes what is better may be simply a matter of the tastes of the person who sets the goal. For example, the chief may specify that his new house is to be built on the hill.

The primary function of assertions, I contend, is to shape the manner in which interlocutors attempt to achieve their goals. For example, "Herds are near the lake" directs the hunters to hunt near the lake. "That pail is dirty" directs the cooks away from the dirty pail. "The house will be on the hill" directs the builders to build the house on the hill. As a speech act may qualify as an imperative by virtue of its mood, and yet fail to fulfill its function of establishing a goal, so too a speech act may qualify as a declarative by virtue of its mood, a distinctive verbal form, and yet fail to perform its function of directing interlocutors in their attempt to achieve their goals.

One of my basic assumptions will be that an action in pursuit of a goal may or may not *accord* with a set of declarative sentences. For example, consider the following set of sentences:

{Water is in the well. The well is next to Namu's house. Water is not in the barrel. *This* pail is not clean. *That* pail is clean.}

If the goal in force is obtaining clean water for cooking, then an action in accordance with this set of sentences would include fetching water from the well next to Namu's house using *that* pail, not *this* one. Actions not in accordance with it will include taking the clean pail to the barrel, taking the dirty pail to the well next to Namu's house, and sweeping the floor.

For another example, suppose Namu and Balam have it as their goal to meet the next day so that they can exchange goods. The following set of sentences bears on their situation:

{Namu is busy in the morning. Balam is busy in the evening. The meeting place is the village center.}

Actions in accordance with this set of sentences will include meeting in the village center in the afternoon. Actions not in accordance with it will include meeting in the morning, meeting in the evening, and meeting elsewhere than in the village center.

The simplest kind of sentence consists of one or more demonstrative pronoun and a predicate, for example, "This is a pail" and "This is clean", or "That is ripe" and "That tastes good", or "This is larger than that". Call such sentences *atomic*. Only slightly less simple are negations of such sentences, such as "This is not clean". Atomic sentences and negations of atomic sentences are what I call *literals*. If a literal is an atomic sentence, then its *opposite* is its negation; if a literal is the negation of an atomic sentence, its *opposite* is the atomic sentence negated. Literals are basic in my scheme inasmuch as my formulation of the norms of discourse will rest on them. (Throughout this book, I will assume that we are dealing with languages in which officially the "not" goes in front of the sentence that it negates; but for ease in comprehension I will often insert the "not" in the predicate, as in English.)

When I write of *demonstrative pronouns* in identifying this most basic form of sentence, what I mean is not just words of a certain form, such as "this" and "that". Rather, a demonstrative pronoun is a kind of index that serves to link atomic sentences in a manner that I will explain further in chapter 7. I will suppose that for purposes of formulating the norms of discourse, we can think of a language as containing as many different demonstrative pronouns as we happen to need (although never more than countably many). Two occurrences of a given word, such as "this", may be recognizable as distinct demonstrative pronouns by virtue of something about them other than their sound. For example, one occurrence may be accompanied by an act of demonstration toward one thing while the other is accompanied by an act of demonstration toward another thing. But accompanying acts of demonstration are not the only means of distinguishing between distinct ones. I call these objects *demonstrative* pronouns merely as a reminder that something other than phonetic and graphemic properties plays a role in their individuation. Rather than try to build some representation of their distinguishing features into the representation of these pronouns, I will often simply put lower case Roman (and sometimes Greek) letters in their place and will assume that we have as many of these as we need. If we were working within the received point of view, we might say that it is context that determines what a demonstrative pronoun refers to, but here we will have no use for any such notion of context. Rather, as I will explain presently, contexts will be defined in terms of demonstrative pronouns.

A central concept throughout this book will be that of a *context*. I use this term not in any ordinary sense but as a defined term. In terms of contexts we will define the concept of *assertibility*, and in terms of assertibility we will define some basic norms of discourse. In this chapter I will define only what I call a *primitive context*. In terms of this, I will define the *assertibility conditions* for sentences in a simple language. In later chapters I will introduce languages that incorporate further devices, such as quantifiers, conditionals, truth predicates, and the predicate "believes". For each of these devices I will have to introduce further complications into the definition of context. Whenever I take a major step in the formulation of assertibility conditions for additional kinds of sentences, I will introduce a corresponding innovation into the definition of contexts, and whenever I introduce a new kind of context, one has a right to expect both a formal and a substantive account of it (although sometimes my substantive account will fall short of what might be desired).

The formal theory of primitive contexts is very simple: *Formally*, a primitive context is just any consistent set of literals, that is, any set of literals in the language such that for every atomic sentence p, not both p and the negation of p belong. (In chapter 9, I will introduce a slight amendment to this definition of primitive contexts to accommodate the identity sign.) At a later stage, in developing the theory of assertibility for a more sophisticated language, we might recognize relations of inconsistency between literals other than that between an atomic sentence and its negation (such as that between "x is a fish" and "x has lungs"), but such relations are not countenanced in the definition of primitive contexts.

The *substantive* account of any kind of context will tell us what it takes for an object of the kind defined by the formal account to be *the* context of that kind pertinent to a given conversation. In the case of primitive contexts, we can formulate the substantive theory in terms of the concept of accordance as follows:

The *primitive context for a conversation* (in language L) is the set of literals (in language L) such that:

(i)   all courses of action in accordance with it relative to the goal of the conversation are good ways of achieving the goal, and

(ii) no proper subset of that set has that property.

In other words, a primitive context is the smallest set of literals such that every action in accordance with it relative to the goal of the conversation is a good way of achieving the goal. We may assume that the primitive context for a conversation, so defined, satisfies the formal definition of a primitive context in that it cannot contain both a sentence and the negation of that same sentence. For now I will make the simplifying assumption that for every conversation there is a unique set of literals that satisfies these conditions. That is not right in fact, and later (in chapter 8), I will accommodate our conception of contexts to that fact.

For example, if we translate the set of sentences in my first example above into a set of literals, we get something like this:

{a is a well. b is a house. b belongs to Namu. a is next to b. a contains water. c is a barrel. c does not contain water. d is a pail. d is clean. e is a pail. e is not clean.}

Such a set of literals may qualify as the primitive context for a conversation in which the goal is to obtain clean water, because any action in accordance with it is a good way of achieving the goal, and if we consider any subset of this set then there are actions in accordance with that subset that are not good ways of achieving the goal. For example, if we remove "c does not contain water", then the act of taking the clean pail to the barrel will accord, and that is not a good way of achieving the goal. If we remove "d is clean", then an action in accordance with the set relative to the goal will be to first clean e and then to use e to get the water, but that is not a good way of achieving the goal since it is inefficient; it is inefficient because one could more easily just use the clean pail.

One might be tempted at this point to say that the literals in the primitive context for a conversation *describe* the features of the situation that are relevant to the goal. This is innocent enough if it is taken merely as a way of acknowledging that the content of the primitive context for a conversation does depend on what the world is like around the interlocutors—for the best way to achieve their goal depends on this. Indeed, when I want a brief way (or just a vague way) of characterizing what is distinctive about my conception of context, I will say that, on my theory, the context comprises those *facts* that are most *relevant* in view of the goals of the conversation and the situation in which the conversation takes place. But this characterization should not lead one to look for a relation of *describing* between sentences and the world such that we can say that it is the relevant states of the world plus the relation of describing that determines which sentences belong to the primitive context. If, as I urged in the last chapter, we should despair of all attempts to explain what it takes for a mental representation to bear a propositional content, then even more readily we should despair of finding such a representation relation between the sentences of a natural language and facts in the world.

As for the literals of a language that do *not* occur in the primitive context for a conversation, there is an important distinction between two kinds. Some such literals could be harmlessly added to the set inasmuch as exactly the same courses of action would accord with the augmented set. For example, if in the above example, we added "*e* is red" or "*f* is a cat" and no others, then the ways of getting water in accordance with the resulting set would be exactly the same. I will take for granted that if any literal could be harmlessly added in this sense, then likewise its opposite could be. But other literals could not be so harmlessly added. In particular, if we removed any literal from the primitive context for a conversation and substituted its opposite, then the resulting set would be positively contrary to the goal of the conversation inasmuch as some actions in accordance with it would be positively bad ways of attempting to achieve the goal. For example, if in the above example we removed "*e* is not clean" and substituted "*e* is clean", then some courses of action in accordance with the set relative to the goal would involve using the dirty pail *e* to fetch the water.

If a literal belongs to the primitive context for a conversation, then we can see that it would be in one way helpful for an interlocutor to actually assert that literal, for insofar as the other interlocutors understand the language and accept that assertion, the actions they might undertake in pursuit of the goal are somewhat restricted in the direction of good ways of achieving the goal. So we can say that a literal is *assertible* in a primitive context and, accordingly, in the conversation to which that primitive context pertains, if and only if it belongs to that primitive context. Further, if a literal belongs to the primitive context for a conversation, then, as we have just seen, it would be positively misleading to assert the opposite of that sentence. So we can say that a literal is *deniable* in a primitive context, and in the conversation to which that primitive context pertains, if and only if its opposite belongs to the primitive context. If a literal could be harmlessly added to the primitive context and also its opposite could be harmlessly added, then that literal is neither assertible nor deniable in the primitive context.

The concepts of assertibility and deniability in a context can be extended to a language slightly richer than the language of atomic sentences and their negations as follows. Let us suppose that the language contains in addition a symbol for disjunction, "or", a symbol for general negation, "not", and parentheses as punctuation. That is, if **p** is a sentence of the language, whether atomic or not, then another sentence of the language is **not p**, which is the *negation* of **p**. If **p** and **q** are sentences of the language, then another sentence of the language is **(p or q)**, which is the *disjunction* of **p** and **q**. For example, the language contains the sentence, "Not (*a* is clean or not *a* is a pail)", which is a negation of a disjunction. (I am using boldface to represent *forms* of expression and I am putting quotation marks around particular instances of those forms.)

I will formulate the assertibility and deniability conditions for sentences of this language with a series of sufficient conditions and a closure clause. (In view of later developments, this is preferable to stating necessary and sufficient conditions for the assertibility/deniability of each type of sentence.) A consequence of what I just said about literals is that an atomic sentence **p** is assertible in a primitive context Γ if **p** is actually a member of Γ; and an atomic sentence **p** is deniable in a primitive context Γ if its negation **not p** is a member of Γ. To these conditions we can now add that a negation **not p** is assertible in a primitive context Γ if **p** is deniable in Γ; a negation **not p** is deniable in a primitive context Γ if **p** is assertible in Γ. A disjunction **(p or q)** is assertible in a primitive context Γ if either **p** is assertible in Γ or **q** is assertible in Γ; a disjunction **(p or q)** is deniable in a primitive context Γ if both **p** and **q** are deniable in Γ. Finally, we add the closure clause: A sentence is assertible or deniable only if it is assertible or deniable in one of these ways. To assert a disjunction is not quite to *specify* the content of the primitive context for the conversation, but asserting a disjunction does narrow down the range of primitive contexts that might be the primitive context pertinent to the conversation.

Not every sentence that is assertible in the context for a conversation need actually be asserted in order to ensure that interlocutors undertake a good way of achieving the goal of the conversation. Some assertible sentences may *go without saying* in the sense that, whether they are uttered or not, interlocutors will act as though they recognized that that sentence was assertible in the context pertinent to their conversation. For instance, it might be quite clear to everyone involved that the only convenient place to obtain water is in the well next to Namu's house. So although by my definition "The well is next to Namu's house" might be assertible in the conversation, there may be no need to actually assert it. Of course, it may happen that some things go without saying only after other things have been asserted.

Members of a linguistic community will recognize that there are certain costs associated with asserting something deniable or merely unassertible. If one asserts something deniable and one's assertion is accepted in the conversation, then the achievement of the goal of the conversation may be thwarted. If one asserts something merely unassertible but not deniable, no one who understands the goal will be led by that to act contrary to the achievement of the goal. But in so doing one presents oneself as tending to assert the unassertible, and to that extent one undermines one's worthiness to be listened to. Further, some interlocutors might get the idea that the goal of the conversation must be something other than what it is, for they may assume that the context pertinent to the conversation is such that the sentence uttered is assertible in it.

An interlocutor's goal in uttering declarative sentences is primarily to achieve the goals of the conversation. As a means to achieving these, an interlocutor aims to assert all of those sentences that both are assertible in the context for his or her conversation and do not go without saying. But at the same time, an interlocutor will strive to avoid asserting the unassertible because this, as we have noted, carries certain costs. Since an interlocutor will conform to these policies only insofar as he or she *takes* the context to be as it really is, each interlocutor will strive to take it as it really is. The speaker's speaking in accordance with these policies may be useful to the hearer inasmuch as the speaker's utterances, insofar as they really are assertible in the context that pertains to their conversation, identify for the hearer the content of the context and thereby help him or her to act in accordance with it. Insofar as the context so identified differs from what the hearer takes it to be, the hearer may adjust. Speaking may be useful to the speaker insofar as the consequent adjustment on the part of the hearer may be useful.

The evaluation of success in communication cannot be separated from the evaluation of success in achieving the goals of the conversation. If the goals are achieved, but would not have been achieved apart from what was said, then normally we will be able to say that the communication was successful. Even then there may be odd cases in which the right result is achieved by means of the communication, but not in the right way. A coincidence of misunderstandings may fortuitously produce the right result. If the goals of the conversation are not achieved, we might like to place the blame on unforseeable events and not blame the linguistic communication and still deem the linguistic communication successful. But there is no sharp criterion for success in such a case. At most we can try to make a judgment to the effect that the linguistic communication did as much as we could have expected toward the achievement of the goal.

We are now in a position to formulate some norms of discourse alternative to those of the received view. First of all, interlocutors ought to achieve the goals of the conversation. (We might say, instead, that interlocutors ought to *try* to achieve the goals of the conversation, but there is no reason to weaken the norm in this way; they ought to try because they ought to succeed.) The selection of goals might in turn be guided by other norms, and in light of these we might deem some goals to be wrong, but these other norms need not be especially norms of discourse. Further, interlocutors ought to assert whatever is assertible in the context for their conversation, provided it does not go without saying, and they ought to avoid asserting what is unassertible, especially what is deniable. Each interlocutor's assertions, we may suppose, are guided by his or her *take* on the context, and so we may also say that an interlocutor is obligated to make sure that his or her take on the context matches the context actually pertinent to the conversation.

As a community begins to reflect on its practices of assertion, it may superimpose over the basic norms additional, facilitating norms formulated in terms of the concepts of logic. On top of the requirement that one assert whatever is assertible provided it does not go without saying they may add a facilitating guideline to the effect that one ought not to make inconsistent assertions. Beyond that, they might try to identify circumstances in which one ought to be able to supply *reasons* for one's assertions. The pertinent relation of *having a reason* cannot be explicated simply as that of having a logically valid argument (since logically valid arguments are never ampliative), but logically valid arguments can be viewed as an extremum in the space of good arguments.

Accordingly, we must try to say in a theoretically acceptable way what logical consistency and logical implication really are. A set of sentences is logically *consistent* if there is a context in which they are all assertible. An argument is logically *valid* (that is, the premises logically imply the conclusion; the inference from the premises to the conclusion is valid) if and only if for every context in which the premises are assertible the conclusion is assertible too. For example, an inference from **(a is F or b is G)** and **not a is F** to **b is G** is valid in this sense. To see this, suppose both **(a is F or b is G)** and **not a is F** are assertible in an arbitrarily chosen primitive context Γ. Then since **(a is F or b is G)** is assertible in Γ, either **a is F** is assertible in Γ or **b is G** is assertible in Γ. But since **not a is F** is assertible in Γ, **a is F** is deniable in Γ. But **a is F** cannot be both assertible and deniable in Γ. So it must be **b is G** that is assertible in Γ. Since Γ was arbitrary, we see that for every primitive context in which both **(a is F or b is G)** and **not a is F** are assertible, **b is G** is assertible, which is what we had to show. In the chapters on quantification, conditionals and truth, I will be concerned to demonstrate the virtues of this approach to logic.

The logic that is generated on this approach is not in every respect classical. For example, in classical logic, every sentence of the form **(p or not p)** is supposed to follow from any premises whatsoever. On the present approach, on the contrary, no sentence of that form will follow from every arbitrary set of premises. A sentence **p** may fail to be either assertible or deniable in a primitive context Γ. In that case, neither **p** nor **not p** will be assertible in Γ, and so **(p or not p)** will not be assertible in Γ either. This is a reasonable result because there will be situations in which neither **p** nor **not p** is relevant to the goals of the conversation. If in a real conversation, we say something of the form **(p or not p)**, this may be taken as a challenge to figure out which, or as indicating that both options have consequences that we need to consider.

In one major respect the resources of the present approach for the formulation of norms really do fall short of those provided by the received point of view. From the present point of view, the class of logical words, whose use is constrained by norms of assertibility in a context, will be rather broad in comparison with the traditional categories and will include such terms as "true" and "believes". However, for all the terms in the complement of this class, such as "red", "cat", "gene", "freedom", and "love", the present framework offers little immediate guidance. We are free to identify paradigm cases of application, dimensions of variation within and beyond the paradigms, and leave it at that. Where we find analytic connections (such as the one between "bachelor" and "male"), we will be able to lay down special rules, as much as anyone else. But we will not imagine that we are saying something that might guide actual usage if we say something like this: The sentence "This is a cat" may be used to express a proposition to the effect that something is a cat. What really might be useful, unlike such a semantic guideline, is an explanation of what cats are. (For a salutary discussion of the semantic open-endedness of lexical items, see Pelczar 2000.)

Finally, it is necessary to say something about the operations of the mind. As we have seen in chapter 1, the received view is committed to the theory that the processes of thought may be explained as transitions between states having propositional content. The alternative conception of linguistic communication sketched here does not directly deny that conception of thought, but it does leave us free to deny it, which, as we have seen in chapter 2, is something we have reason to do. Further, it would be strange to reject the received view while retaining this theory of thinking, since it does seem that if thinking is a matter of having mental representations bearing propositional content, then thinkers would find some means of making those propositional contents known to others, and in that case we would inevitably suppose that language was just such a thing.

In addition, in my own positive account I have taken certain things for granted which, if not just taken for granted but explained, would open up the subject of cognition. In particular, I have taken for granted that there is such a thing as having a *goal*. I have taken for granted a distinction between actions that *accord* with a context and those that do not accord. I have supposed that one interlocutor may *accept* the assertions of another. And I have supposed that each interlocutor's assertions are guided by his or her *take* on the context. From the point of view of the norms of discourse, these things are basic, that is, not to be further analyzed. But that is not to say that they cannot be explained at all. What needs to be explained, in particular, is how the distinction between accordance and the lack of it can be reliably grasped and how it can be instilled in an agent through others' acts of speech. An investigation into these matters would lead us into the psychological side of the nature of language.

If we were to allow ourselves the theory of propositionally contentful mental representations, then explicating these things might seem easy. For instance, the goal of a conversation, we might say, is the object of a shared intention. But if we allowed ourselves to posit such propositionally contentful mental representations in the explanation of such things, then inevitably we would be drawn back into the received view of linguistic communication. Since, as we have seen, and as I will argue further in subsequent

chapters, we have reason to avoid that, we must suppose
that there will be some psychological framework by means
of which we can answer these questions without appeal to
propositional content.

In a framework in which one denies the received view of
linguistic communication, it is probably misleading to countenance the existence of propositional content at all. Propositional content, one might suppose, is essentially that which
is conveyed in linguistic communication as this is conceived
from the received point of view (which is not all by itself to
say that only linguistic creatures are capable of thoughts
with propositional content). So from the point of view of my
alternative, it might be best just to abandon the use of the
term "propositional content" altogether. In our new framework, we might continue to use the term "propositional
thought" as a term for a kind of thinking that just consists
in talking in a natural language, such as English, German,
or Korean. Not all such talking need be overt—we can use-
fully talk to ourselves—and we might acknowledge that fact
by describing talking to oneself, or talking in general, as
propositional thought. But in that case we should not go so
far as to say that thinking *tout court* is talking in natural languages. Most thinking must be on the order of that which
underlies our acts of speech in natural language, and on
pain of infinite regress, that cannot itself be talking in
natural language. Rather, we should acknowledge that a
lot of thinking is not propositional thought. (For more on
the limitations of talking to oneself, see Bickle forthcoming.)

So the question remains, what alternative conception of
thinking is open to us? The behaviorist program of explain-

ing all sorts of intelligent behavior as the product of various kinds of conditioning is certainly no longer on the table. One possibility, though, is that we will have to abandon the concept of representation altogether and explain mental processing wholly in neurological terms. On the other hand, there might still be room to posit some kinds of representations after all. For instance, there is imagistic representation, and it is not obvious that the relation of representation between an image and the thing imagined can arise in the mind only against a background of propositionally contentful thought (however we conceive of this). If I take apart a faucet to replace a washer, I might be able to remember how the parts go together by forming a mental image of the pieces and their arrangement. While I might, incidentally, think of some part as a ring or think of some other part as a handle, it is not evident that my ability to use the image to solve the problem depends on these conceptualizations.

Moreover, the brain may contain something like indicators that selectively respond to events of a certain type. (Hubel and Wiesel's edge-detectors are the paradigm, but now there are many other examples as well.) In the previous chapter, I disputed the claim that we could interpret mental representations as bearing propositional contents by construing mental representations as such indicators, but it might still be the case that the mind employs such indicators in some kind of nonpropositional thought. Such indicators might even form a kind of inner map of the environment. It's just that these indicators will still not bear propositional contents. An indicator does not "say" that some particular object belongs to some general kind.

Elsewhere (1994, chapters 8–10) I have developed in greater detail the idea that thinking may be largely non-propositional; I will not repeat that material here. My attitude in this book will be that, yes, my project rests on a major assumption that I will not develop here; but I have two excuses: First, I have already argued, in chapter 2, that it is doubtful whether there is any viable account of the contentfulness of thoughts such as we would need if we wished to explain language as the product of representations bearing propositional content. So it is not as though the psychology of language that I am rejecting in the absence of an alternative is already known to be well-founded. Second, the question of how we should formulate the fundamental norms of discourse is a sufficiently big question to merit a little book of its own such as this one, and if the framework I wish to propose here can prove its worth in dealing with that question, then that will provide a motive to undertake elsewhere the difficult task of developing a conception of cognition that does not rest on the hypothesis of nonlinguistic propositional thought. Even some psychologists have observed independently that the concepts of representation that appear in contemporary cognitive psychology do not bear much resemblance to the philosopher's conception of propositionally contentful thoughts (e.g., Pickering and Chater 1995). So I expect that many psychologists, to whatever extent they may feel themselves bound by the dogmas of philosophy in the first place, will find my assumption liberating.

Pragmatics

4   Domain of Discourse

Proponents of the received view will acknowledge that the proposition a sentence expresses depends on the context of utterance. At the very least, we will need to consider the context in interpreting indexicals, demonstrative noun phrases, and quantifier phrases. If someone points to a book and says, "I read that book, but I didn't like it," then the proposition expressed will be a proposition to the effect that a certain person—the one speaking—read a certain book— the one he is pointing at—and did not like it. Or if the clerk in a shoe store says, "All shoes are 20% off," that does not mean that all shoes in the world are twenty percent off, but only that all of the shoes for sale in that particular shop can be purchased at a twenty percent discount. What determines the proposition expressed in such cases will be something about the context in which the sentence is uttered.

A question for the received view is whether it can give an adequate account of the determinants of the reference of demonstrative phrases and of the content of the domains of discourse for quantified phrases relative to which we should interpret utterances as expressing propositions. For some expressions whose reference varies from context to context, there might be definite semantic rules that determine the referent in virtue of specific features of the context. For example, there might be a rule to the effect that the referent of "I" is whoever qualifies as the speaker in the context. However, there is no such simple rule for demonstrative noun phrases such as "that" and "that book" (and there are exceptions even to the rule for "I").

One point of view would be that to the extent that there are no semantic rules governing such things, the sole determinant is what the speaker has in mind. What a demonstrative noun phrase refers to, we might say, is just whatever object the speaker intends to refer to by it, provided that that object conforms to whatever description occurs in the phrase. So the referent of "that book" will have to be a book, but nothing determines which book it is but what the speaker has in mind. What makes it the case that the domain relative to which we interpret the quantified phrase "all shoes" is the things for sale in this particular shop, and not the things for sale in this particular town, we might say, is just that that is the class of things the speaker has in mind.

The relevance of what the speaker has in mind, on this theory, is not that what a speaker's words express is just whatever the speaker intends. We can still draw a distinction between the proposition that a *speaker* expresses and the proposition that a *sentence* expresses in a context, because there may be occasions on which a speaker expresses (intends to convey) a proposition that his or her words simply cannot express. If a speaker says "That cat has been digging in my flower beds again," then the proposition his or her sentence expresses cannot be a proposition about a ferret, not even if it is a ferret he or she has in mind. What the theory says is that when we have to look to the context to determine those aspects of the proposition that the speaker's words express that are not determined by the semantic rules of the language, the relevant features of the context are just what the speaker has in mind.

This is the answer usually taken for granted by proponents of the received view (e.g., Stalnaker 1972, p. 384; King 1999; Recanati 2001), and from that point of view it does seem reasonable. Again, the objective of communication is supposed to be that the speaker reveals the propositional content of his or her thought to the hearer. Interpretation of the speaker's words on the basis of semantic rules may not get as far as the selection of a complete proposition, just because no semantic rules pick out a referent for some demonstrative phrase or a domain of discourse for some quantified phrase. In that case we can appeal to that which we as interpreters are ultimately most interested in anyway, namely, what the speaker has in mind. If we determine referents or domains in any other way, then our interpretation will only be a detour on the way to our objective, namely, what the speaker has in mind.

On the other hand, this idea that the referents of demonstrative phrases and the domains for quantified phrases are always determined by what the speaker has in mind is certainly not mandatory for proponents of the received view. Indeed, it runs contrary to one of the basic elements of the received view, namely, the idea that the normal way to determine what proposition the speaker is expressing is to determine independently what proposition his or her words express in context and then to assume that the former is the same as the latter. Normally, we have little access to the content of people's thoughts apart from what they say. According to the received view, the primary function of language is to enable hearers to determine the propositional contents of people's beliefs by interpreting their words. If we have to determine what people have in mind in order to determine what proposition their words express, then to that extent words cannot serve their essential function. We do not understand words by reading minds; rather we read minds by understanding words. So even though the objective of interpretation is to discover the thoughts the speaker intends to convey, the rules of the language, it may be said, must assign a proposition to the speaker's sentence in light of the external context, quite apart from what the speaker has in mind, as a way of enabling us to do just that.

Still, it is hard to see what—if not what the speaker has in mind—might determine the referent of a demonstrative phrase or the content of a domain of discourse. (This is the dilemma that I referred to in chapter 1.) One might think that the referent of "That F" is always the most *salient* thing that is F and that the domain relative to which we should interpret "Every F" is always the set of minimally *salient* things. But this theory is clearly not right. Imagine a man who owns many cats—there are always some in every room of the house. But only one of these cats has a habit of ripping up pillows. While the naughty cat is out of the house, the man notices a ripped up pillow and declares, "That cat did

it again!" The referent of "that cat" in this utterance is the
naughty cat, even if other cats are more salient in the ordinary sense.

Or suppose a college professor, at the beginning of a class,
looks around and declares, "Everyone is present." This
could mean at least two things. It could mean that everyone
who is still officially enrolled in the course is present, or it
could mean only that everyone who has been attending
recently is present. The way to decide is not to see which set
of people is salient. In one sense, the "salient" people are
just those who are present, but we cannot take the domain
to be just those people, because we want to allow that what
the professor says may be mistaken; whereas it is trivially
true that the people who are present are present. In another
sense, the salient people might be just those whom one can
expect to be there. But this does not decide the matter
because there are different sorts of expectation. In one way
we expect everyone still enrolled to be there; in another way
we expect at most those who have been attending recently
to be there.

So let us go back to the idea that the determinant of
demonstrative reference and domain of discourse is what
the speaker has in mind. Insofar as this leaves us with the
question how a hearer could know what the speaker has in
mind, perhaps we just have to resign ourselves to dealing
with that. Maybe a shared understanding of the meanings
of words takes the hearer up to a certain point toward grasping the proposition the speaker aims to convey, and then
other considerations, concerning the speaker's interests and
background knowledge, enable the hearer to fill in the gaps.

Still, we must ask: Does this theory give a plausible account of communication in particular cases, and can we, without begging any questions, explain what it is for a speaker to have a certain referent or domain of discourse in mind?

Suppose that Suzy is sitting on the floor in her bedroom playing with glass marbles. All of the marbles in Suzy's room belong to Suzy, and some of them are red. Suddenly Tommy comes into Suzy's room and declares in a loud voice, "All of the red ones are mine!" As a matter of fact, when Tommy says this he is thinking of the marbles in his own room. The proposition he is expressing is the proposition that all of the red marbles in his room are his. Tommy is very proud of his possessions and on this occasion is exulting in his possession of red marbles. But there is no way Suzy could know that. She would naturally expect that he was talking about the marbles there on the floor in plain view of both of them. So of course she retorts, "No they're not!"

In this case, should we say that the domain of discourse pertinent to Tommy's utterance is the class of marbles in his own room, which are the marbles he has in mind, or should we say that it is the class of marbles in Suzy's room, which lie in plain sight on the floor in front of them? There is no question about what Tommy has in mind: by hypothesis it is that the red marbles in his room are his. The question is what he *says*, that is, what proposition his sentence expresses in the context. If the domain is the marbles in his own room, then we should interpret his utterance as expressing the proposition that all of the red marbles in his own room are his, which is true. In that case, that is the proposition that Suzy is claiming to be false; so what she says is false. Call this interpretation the *straight defense of Tommy*. If the domain is the class of marbles on the floor in front of them, then the proposition his sentence expresses is the proposition that all of the red marbles on the floor in front of them are his, which is false, and what Suzy says in denying it is true. Call this interpretation *the straight defense of Suzy*.

The straight defense of Suzy does not have to take the form of claiming that the pertinent referents and domains are always to be identified with what the *hearer* has in mind in interpreting the speaker's utterance. The idea might be rather that there is something about the environment that determines the content of the domain, which, as I have explained above, is in one way entirely consonant with the received view. In this particular case, that idea yields a defense of Suzy, since in this example Suzy has the right idea about the domain, so conceived, and Tommy does not. Still, in the framework of the received view, the straight defense of Suzy would be very problematic. The trouble with it is that it takes us back to the problem of having to say what determines the content of the domain if not what the speaker has in mind.

If we want to say that in general the domain of discourse is what the speaker has in mind, then we have to adopt the straight defense of Tommy, and we have to conclude that Suzy's retort is strictly speaking false. She denies the proposition that Tommy's sentence expresses in context, but that proposition is true, and so what she says is false. This does not have to mean of course that she has no excuse. We can agree that what she says is false while maintaining that her assertion was justified. Naturally, one would have assumed that the marbles Tommy was talking about were the marbles there on the floor in front of them. Since they were plainly there on the floor in front of them, those are the marbles Suzy could reasonably have expected Tommy to have in mind. It's just that in this case the justified interpretation of Tommy's utterance is in fact incorrect.

One problem with the straight defense of Tommy might seem to be that it presumes too much freedom on the part of a speaker to mean whatever he or she wants. Surely the speaker has an obligation to make sure that his or her words are interpretable by others as meaning what he or she means by them. The claims that we can hold a person to, expect a person to defend, or blame a person for in case they are wrong, are those that one could reasonably interpret the person as expressing. In the case at hand, that means we should side with Suzy. Tommy should have seen that Suzy would take the domain of discourse to be the things in her room, and so we can hold him responsible for expressing the proposition that all of the red marbles there on the floor in front of them are his. Our way of holding Tommy responsible is to interpret him as literally having said that all of the marbles on the floor in front of them are his, even though we know that that is not what he meant. So Suzy is not only justified in interpreting him that way; her interpretation of him is correct, and the proposition she expresses in responding "No they're not!" is true.

In any case, one might wonder why we really have to resolve the issue, since the disagreement between Tommy and Suzy seems "purely verbal." At first Tommy and Suzy might argue back and forth as if there were some genuine issue of fact. After Suzy says, "No they're not!," Tommy, still thinking of the marbles in his own room, may insist, "Yes they are, Mom gave them to me." Suzy may reply, "Dad got me those marbles and Mom doesn't even know I have them." After carrying on in this way for a while, it may occur to them that the problem between them lies not in the facts but in their language. Pointing to the marbles on the floor, Tommy might say, "I'm not talking about *those* marbles; I'm talking about the marbles in *my* room," or Suzy might ask, "Which marbles are you talking about?" What this makes plain is that the disagreement between Tommy and Suzy is merely verbal and not factual. It is resolved not by uncovering facts about the marbles but by examining one another's words.

In view of the purely verbal nature of their dispute, a proponent of the received view might conclude that in the case of Tommy and Suzy there really is no unique domain of discourse. In the case of Tommy's utterance, one might say, we have to remain neutral between Tommy's point of view and Suzy's. To put this in a more general framework, one might say that in general interpretation is subject-relative. For each utterance and each subject who contemplates that utterance, there is a domain relative to which we should interpret the utterance, and nothing makes it the case that one subject's domain or interpretation takes priority over another's as the correct domain or interpretation. The point is not merely that each interlocutor will in fact interpret the utterance employing what he or she takes to be the pertinent domain, but that there is nothing to say about which interpretation is correct beyond saying which interpretation is correct relative to each interlocutor's choice of domain. We may speak of *the* domain relative to which we should interpret an utterance, and *the* proposition expressed by the sentence in the context, only insofar as the domains of the several subjects in whom we happen to be interested coincide. In the case of Tommy and Suzy, there is no such coincidence of the domains of discourse relative to which they interpret Tommy's utterance; we simply have to specify whether we are talking about Tommy's domain or Suzy's domain. (For a version of this idea, see van Deemter 1998.)

The problem with this proposal is that it leaves us with nothing for the pertinent states of mind to be about. Perhaps we can identify the speaker's domain as whatever domain we must appeal to in order to interpret the speaker's utterance as an expression of the thought that he or she does intend to express. But on the present proposal we have to identify a domain of discourse for the hearer also, relative to which the hearer is supposed to interpret the speaker's utterance. The hearer will not think it permissible just to interpret the speaker's utterance relative to whatever class of things he or she, the hearer, happens to have in mind at the time. Even the hearer will think that he or she must interpret the speaker's utterance relative to the domain that is appropriate for that purpose and will interpret according to the domain that he or she chooses expressly because he or she considers it to be the correct choice. If we could suppose that the correct choice was indeed the domain the speaker had in mind or that which the external context determines in some way, then we could suppose that the hearer's domain was whatever the hearer represented the speaker as having in mind or whatever the hearer took to be determined by the external context. But on the present proposal there is no such correct choice and so there is nothing for the hearer to aim at in his or her interpretation of the domain of discourse, contrary to what hearers themselves suppose. Moreover, the speaker presumably attempts to choose his or her words in such a way that the hearer, employing his or her own representation of the domain, will understand the speaker. So if there is nothing for the hearer's domain to be a representation of, then by the same token there is no basis for the speaker's choice of words either.

Still, there might be ways of remaining neutral without denying that there is anything that the hearer's representation of the domain aims to capture. We could claim that a hearer's objective in choosing a domain relative to which he or she will interpret an utterance will be to represent the domain the speaker has in mind in speaking, but it should be reasonable for the speaker to expect the hearer to recognize that the speaker has that domain in mind (which is not to say the hearer actually succeeds in doing what the speaker may reasonably expect of him or her). If that condition fails, then there is no unique domain of discourse relative to which we may interpret the speaker's utterance, and the sentence expresses no unique proposition at all in such a context. In Tommy's case, there is indeed a mismatch between what he has in mind and what Suzy would reasonably suppose; so in this case there is no proposition that his sentence expresses in their context.

The problem with this second way of trying to remain neutral is that it leaves us unable to understand the dialogue that ensues between Tommy and Suzy. The argument between them may be productive. Ultimately, they may reach agreement. Accordingly, we should not find their discourse to be simply uninterpretable, not even if we acknowledge that they mean things *by* what they say. So if interpreting a discourse means identifying the propositions expressed in context by the sentences composing it, then we should find that Tommy's and Suzy's sentences express propositions in the context they are in. Even if, apart from Suzy's reaction, there were reason to conclude that Tommy's utterance is simply uninterpretable, we should not have to say that Suzy's retort is uninterpretable too. But to interpret Suzy, when she says, "No, they're not!" we have to interpret her as denying the proposition that Tommy's words express in context. (She might just as well have referred to it directly, saying, "That's false!") If there is no such proposition for her to deny, then her words fail to express a proposition in turn. But there is no such confusion on her part, no mismatch between what she has in mind and what a hearer might reasonably attribute to her on which we can blame this failure to express a proposition. For this reason we ought to reject the neutral solution.

Let us return then to the straight defense of Tommy, according to which the domain of discourse relative to which we should interpret an utterance is whatever domain the speaker has in mind. If we take this line, then we have to resign ourselves to the conclusion that whether the hearer could reasonably be expected to recognize the domain of

discourse has no bearing on what it really is. Suzy's accu-
sation may be justified, but that is nothing against the
conclusion that her interpretation was incorrect and what
Tommy said really was just that all of the red marbles in his
room are his. But there is another reason to question the
straight defense of Tommy, namely, that it ultimately begs
the question: It begs the question of the determinants of the
domain of discourse, because the same question arises at the
level of mental representation.

To see this, let us switch to a different example. Imagine
a goatherd in the Peruvian Andes whose community has
long been isolated from the rest of the world. The goatherd
possesses normal intelligence and plays a normal part in his
society. But he is not very curious or imaginative and it has
never occurred to him to wonder whether there might be
people beyond the farthest mountains that he can see. One
evening all of the people of the village are gathered together
for a traditional celebration and there appears in the sky a
remarkably bright falling star. Everyone looks up into the
sky and sees it. Over the next few days, the falling star and
its possible meaning are a favorite topic of discussion. As
a result, our goatherd forms a belief that he attempts to
convey in words that translate thus: "Everyone saw the
falling star." Call this the goatherd's *first utterance*.

Sometime later, our goatherd is out in the hills accompanied by a philosophical friend. Bored with tending goats, the
philosopher asks the goatherd, "Do you think there might
be people like us on the other side of those distant moun-
tain tops?" For the first time our goatherd contemplates the
question and forms the opinion that, yes, very probably

there are other people over there, people whom he has never seen and can barely imagine. To convey this thought, he chooses words that translate thus: "Not everyone in the universe lives in the village." Call this the goatherd's *second utterance*.

Surely the right thing to say about the goatherd's thoughts in these cases is that with his first utterance the goatherd expresses the thought that *everyone living in the village saw the falling star* and that with his second utterance the goatherd expresses the thought that *not everyone in the universe lives in the village*. So the mental representation underlying the goatherd's first utterance is about everyone living in the village, while the mental representation underlying the goatherd's second utterance is about everyone in the universe. What accounts for this difference in the domains that the underlying mental representations are about?

One answer would be that the mental representation underlying the first utterance actually contains a mental predicate meaning *living in the village*, which attaches to the mental expression meaning *everyone*, whereas the mental representation underlying the second utterance contains no such mental predicate attaching to the mental expression meaning *everyone*. But it is not very plausible that the mental representation underlying the goatherd's first utterance is qualified in this way, because he has never before contemplated the question whether anyone exists beyond the people who live in his village. Similarly, it is not plausible that he explicitly thinks, in a separate thought, *everyone who exists lives in my village*, or that he thinks, *the people who exist are my brother, my neighbor, my neighbor's children. . . .*

So literal translations of the mental representations underlying the goatherd's two utterances would have to be something like "Everyone saw the falling star," and "Not everyone lives in the village." But if we interpret these mental representations relative to one and the same domain of discourse, then one or the other interpretation is bound to be mistaken. If we take the domain to be people in the village, then the first bears the propositional content, *everyone who lives in the village saw the falling star*, which is fine as an interpretation of the mental representation underlying the goatherd's first utterance, but then the mental representation underlying the goatherd's second utterance bears the content, *not everyone who lives in the village lives in the village*, which is surely not what the goatherd was thinking.

If, on the other hand, we take the domain of discourse to be all people in the universe, then the mental representation underlying the goatherd's second utterance bears the propositional content, *not everyone in the universe lives in the village*, which is fine, but the mental representation underlying the goatherd's first utterance bears the content, *everyone in the universe saw the falling star*, which is not fine, since it is not reasonable to interpret the goatherd as believing something so patently false. One must not reply that this is not an unreasonable thought *for him*, since *for him* everyone in the universe *is* just everyone in his village, for when I use the words "everyone in the universe saw the falling star" to express an interpretation of the goatherd's thought, the proposition expressed is the proposition expressed by those words when I use them, and it is unreasonable to interpret the goatherd as having a thought with such a propositional content.

Apparently, then, the correct interpretation of the goatherd's underlying mental representations varies with context. When he makes his first utterance, the underlying mental representation has to be interpreted relative to a domain comprising only people in the goatherd's village, for those are the only people who saw the falling star, and at this point he has never considered whether there might be other people in the universe. However, when he makes his second utterance, the underlying mental representation has to be interpreted relative to a domain comprising everyone in the universe. At this point the goatherd's philosophical friend has explicitly raised the possibility of there being other people in the universe, and only if we interpret the goatherd's mental representation relative to such a broader domain does it amount to a reasonable thought.

What this shows is that even if we maintain that the domain of discourse relative to which we interpret an utterance is always just the domain of discourse that the speaker has in mind in speaking, still the external context in which the utterance takes place may not be screened off as irrelevant; for the correct interpretation of the underlying mental representation still depends on that. A similar thesis could be defended regarding the interpretation of demonstratives. We might want to say that the referent of a spoken demonstrative is always whichever object of the appropriate type the speaker has in mind. But we should expect to find that mental representations contain demonstrative expressions too and that their interpretation is a matter of the character of the environment in which the thinker is embedded (as argued by Perry 1993).

This conclusion can be accommodated within the received view up to a point. It would not be reasonable to suppose that hearers must always track the features of external context relative to which a speaker's underlying thought is to be interpreted. The goatherd's interlocutors may be no better able to represent explicitly the domains pertinent to the goatherd's thought than the goatherd himself can. But in order to accommodate the possibility of communication, as typically conceived, we do not have to suppose that they do so. As features of the external context may determine the proposition borne by the mental representation that underlies the speaker's choice of words, so too features of the external context may determine the proposition borne by the mental representation resulting in the hearer. To ensure that the hearer receives the intended proposition, the speaker need only choose his or her words in such a way that the mental representation that results in the hearer is one that in the given context bears the intended proposition. Since the external context for the speaker will normally be the same as the external context for the hearer, the speaker's choice of words need not normally be guided by those features of the proposition to be conveyed that are determined only by the external context, and those features need not be reflected among the underlying mental representations in the speaker. Coincidence of external context will not always ensure understanding in this way, even when words are rightly chosen, but misunderstandings do occur, and a theory of communication need not entail that there is always a way to avoid them.

Nonetheless, there is a problem for the straight defense of Tommy, which emerges when we ask: Why does the relevance of the external context to the proposition expressed by a sentence in context always have to go *through* the relevance of the external context to the proposition borne by an underlying mental representation? More precisely, why does the relevance of external context to those features of the proposition expressed by a sentence in context that are not generated by semantic rules always have to reduce to the relevance of the external context to the proposition borne by the underlying mental representation? Why cannot the external context have a direct bearing on the proposition expressed by an utterance, quite apart from the proposition borne by an underlying mental representation, even when there is no semantic rule that generates a proposition on the basis of the external context? If the external context were directly relevant in this way, then we might have to conclude that the proposition Tommy's sentence expresses in context was the false proposition that all of the red marbles there on the floor in front of him are his.

In a complete theory, a proponent of the received view would have to explain exactly how the interpretation of mental representations is sensitive to the external context. Perhaps such a theory would explain how mental representation and external context combine to determine a propositional content in view of the cognitive role that such a mental representation would play in an agent embedded in such a context. Or perhaps it would explain how mental representation and external context determine a proposition in light of the way an agent possessing such a mental representation in such a context ought to be regarded by other members of the community. But overt utterances too have a cognitive role. Overt utterances too are regarded in certain ways by other members of the community. So we might expect it to turn out that spoken sentence together with external context equally determine a proposition quite independently of the content of the intention with which the speaker speaks.

By virtue of sharing an environment a hearer may qualify as grasping the proposition that the speaker intended to convey although the hearer does not explicitly represent that proposition, for the mental representation that results in the hearer may bear that same proposition in virtue of the external context. Having conceded this much, one must grant that even the hearer's mere recognition of the meaning of the speaker's words may qualify as his or her grasping the proposition that the speaker intended to convey without the hearer's having to interpret them any further in light of the context. A fortiori, the hearer's interpretation of the utterance will often qualify as his or her grasping the proposition that the speaker's sentence expressed in context without the hearer's having to consider whether the presumed domain of discourse is that which the speaker had in mind. But according to the straight defense of Tommy, Suzy's interpretation of Tommy's utterance does not have this privilege. It does not qualify as a grasp of the proposition his sentence expresses in context. Why not? If a hearer's interpretation of a speaker's utterance may qualify as a grasp of the proposition that the speaker's sentence expresses in context even when the hearer does not explicitly represent the contents of the speaker's mind as such, then it seems *ad hoc* to insist that whenever there is a mismatch between the hearer's interpretation and the proposition the speaker intends to convey, the hearer's interpretation is incorrect.

The upshot is that the idea that the domain of discourse is the set of things that the speaker has in mind does not provide any stable resting point for the received conception of communication. We find that even the interpretation of the speaker's underlying mental representations will be sensitive to the context, which leads us to wonder why a hearer must interpret a speaker's words by interpreting them in light of what the speaker has in mind rather than by interpreting them directly in light of the external circumstances. We find that in order to account for the possibility of interpretation at all, the state of mind in the hearer that in the context qualifies as the correct interpretation amounts to hardly more than recognizing the meaning of the speaker's words. But in that case an interpretation that rests on an interpretation of the speaker's state of mind carries no special privilege.

Can we do any better if we adopt the alternative conception of communication adumbrated in the previous chapter? From this point of view, the question is very different, since there is no expectation that we will be able to interpret the sentences that a person utters as expressing propositions. Still, we have to draw a distinction between those contexts in which a sentence is assertible and those in which it is not, and we can expect that for purposes of evaluating sentences containing demonstratives and quantifiers, the content of the context will somehow come into play. In particular, we can suppose that the context will in some way identify the referents of demonstratives and will in some way specify the necessary domains of discourse. So we can ask whether it is the speaker's state of mind or something else that determines the content of these aspects of the context.

In the previous chapter, I explained how the content of what I called the primitive context depends on the goals of the conversation and the situation in which the conversation takes place. That account does not provide a suitable theory of context for languages containing demonstrative phrases of the form "That *F*" or for languages containing quantifiers; I will take up these matters in chapter 7. For now I will simply say that the central theme of my more elaborate accounts of context will continue to be that the content of the context is a matter of what is objectively relevant to the goals of the conversation in light of the situation in which the conversation takes place. The speaker's state of mind will of course not determine the content of the context so conceived, for the speaker may be mistaken about what is objectively relevant. In particular, the domain of discourse, which will be conceived as a set of demonstrative pronouns, not a set of objects, will be a matter of what is objectively relevant to the conversation in view of the situation in which the conversation takes place. In particular, it will include every demonstrative pronoun that occurs in any literal in the primitive context. Accordingly, its content is not determined by what the interlocutors have in mind.

When Tommy barges into Suzy's room and blurts out "All of the red ones are mine!" he may be unaware of his surroundings and may be talking only to himself. In that case, we may construe his utterance as not part of any real conversation but merely as part of a fantasized conversation. Relative to the imaginary context pertinent to his fantasized conversation, his sentence might even be assertible. The only actual context may be the empty context; the sentence he utters is neither assertible nor deniable relative to that. If we suppose that Tommy addresses himself to Suzy, albeit in a slightly detached frame of mind, then we can make out the rudiments of a conversation and a goal. It is the first move in a conversation with Suzy, and the goal of the conversation is to stake out a claim, to settle the question of who owns what with respect to marbles, and Tommy is seriously mistaken about the context. The domain in this case (speaking of it, for the time being, as a set of objects, not a set of demonstrative pronouns) will consist of all of the things that might be at issue between Tommy and Suzy in a question of ownership. It might include all of the marbles in both Tommy's room and Suzy's room, or it might, depending on their history, include all of the things in the house that presumably belong to one or the other of them. Relative to such a domain, the sentence Tommy utters is certainly unassertible.

Such an account of the domain of discourse rests on the assumption that, as an essential part of their function, words can have an influence on behavior quite apart from their being interpreted as expressing propositions in context. The context pertinent to a conversation is built up from atomic sentences and negations of atomic sentences as a function of whether the sorts of behavior that would be a good way

of achieving the goal of the conversation would accord
with such a structure. Positing relations such as accordance
between actions and linguistic structures is not strictly
incompatible with the interpretation of those linguistic
structures as expressing propositions, but it does render
such interpretation otiose. Such an account of the context,
including the domain of discourse, cannot rescue the
received view of communication; it undermines it.

5   Presupposition

Aside from demonstrative reference and domain of discourse, another complication for the received view of linguistic communication is the phenomenon of presupposition. The appropriateness of using a sentence in a given setting may depend on whether certain other propositions are *presupposed*. For example, if someone says, "The mail has not arrived yet," this will be appropriate only if it is presupposed that the mail will arrive within a certain period. In an office in Manhattan, the presupposition might be that the mail will arrive before noon of the day on which the sentence is spoken. In the mountains of Borneo, the presupposition might be that the mail will arrive sometime before the end of the week.

According to what is called the *semantic theory of presupposition*, a sentence *s* may be said to presuppose a sentence *r* if and only if *r* must be true in order for *s* to be either true or false (Keenan 1973, Martin 1975). For example, we might say that "Matt knows that his paper is late" presupposes "Matt's paper is late", because unless "Matt's paper is late" is true, "Matt knows that his paper is late" is neither true nor false. In a framework in which sentences are supposed to express propositions in a context, and propositions are conceived of as always true or false, the semantic theory of presupposition might be formulated thus: a sentence *s* presupposes a *proposition p* in a context if and only if: if *p* is false then *s* expresses no proposition in that context.

One reason to doubt the semantic theory of presupposition is that in many cases the presuppositions of a sentence seem to vary from one situation to another. For example, if someone says, "Milosevic is a war criminal too," what is presupposed is not simply "Someone else is a war criminal" or "Milosevic is something else." Rather, there has to be some person *x*, other than Milosevic, such that what is presupposed is that *x* is a war criminal, or there has to be some property *F* other than being a war criminal such that what is presupposed is that Milosevic is *F*, and which person is presupposed to be a war criminal, or which property Milosevic is presupposed to have, may vary. (This was pointed out early on in Karttunen 1974. See also Stalnaker 1973, p. 454.) Another problem is that the semantic theory of presupposition provides no good solution to the so-called presupposition projection problem, which is to explain how the presuppositions of a compound sentence depend on the presuppositions of its components. For example, the sentence "If Matt's paper is late, then Matt doesn't know that it's late" does not presuppose that Matt's paper is late, while the sentence "If Matt hasn't turned in his paper, then Matt doesn't know that it's late" does presuppose that Matt's paper is late. Why is there this difference?

For these reasons, the received view of sentence presupposition (part of it) has come to be this: For each use of a sentence, there is an associated set of propositions. In order for the use of a sentence s to be in every respect nondefective, the associated set of propositions C must satisfy certain conditions. If those conditions are met, then we say that C satisfies-the-presuppositions-of s, or that the presuppositions of s are satisfied in C. For some sentences s, the condition will be that C must contain the proposition that p, and in that case we may say that s presupposes the proposition that p. In other cases, there may not be any particular proposition that s always presupposes, but for any given use of s, there may be certain propositions in the associated set of propositions C by virtue of which C satisfies the presuppositions of s on that occasion, so that, speaking loosely, we might say that on that occasion s presupposes those. This associated set of propositions is sometimes called the *context set* (that's Stalnaker's term for it), but I will call it the *propositional context*. Like the domain of discourse and the referents of demonstratives, the propositional context constitutes an element of *the context*.

For example, the condition that a use of "Milosevic is a war criminal too" must meet is that either there be some person $x \neq$ Milosevic such that the propositional context contains the proposition that x is a war criminal, or there be some property $F \neq$ *being a war criminal* such that the propositional context contains the proposition that Milosevic has F. So if on some occasion the propositional context contains the proposition that Radovan Karadzic is a war criminal, then it may be by virtue of that fact that the propositional context satisfies the presuppositions of "Milosevic is a war criminal too." In that case, we might say, speaking loosely, that on this occasion "Milosevic is a war criminal too" presupposes that Radovan Karadzic is a war criminal.

Further, this approach offers some prospect of solving the presupposition projection problem. For example, we might say that the presuppositions of "If"ˆpˆ"then"ˆq are satisfied in propositional context C if and only if the presuppositions of p are satisfied in C and the presuppositions of q are satisfied in $C \cup$ {the proposition that p expresses} (i.e., the set theoretic union of C with the set containing the proposition that p expresses). Thus, in order for the presuppositions of "If Matt's paper is late, then Matt doesn't know that it's late" to be satisfied in C, it is not necessary that C contain the proposition that Matt's paper is late, because $C \cup$ {the proposition that Matt's paper is late} contains that proposition. (This approach to the presupposition projection problem was first developed in Karttunen 1974).

(A note on notation: We may think of the symbol "ˆ" as denoting a function that forms a single expression from the expressions that fall on either side of it. So when I write, "'We regret that'ˆp", "p" holds the place of the quotation name of a sentence. However, the same variables that I use to hold the place of names of expressions will on other occasions be used to hold the place of the expressions that those names name. For example, when I write "the proposition that p", "p" holds the place of a sentence. Sometimes, moreover, I will use the expression "the proposition that

p" as shorthand for "the proposition that the *sentence* p expresses".)

The kind of defect associated with presupposition failure may vary with different locutions. In the case of a sentence such as "The red book on the table is boring", we might say that if C does not contain a proposition to the effect that there is exactly one red book on the table, then the use of the sentence expresses no proposition. In the case of "Matt knows that his paper is late", if the proposition that Matt's paper is late does not belong to the propositional context, we might still allow that the use of the sentence expresses a proposition, but we might say that the manner of expressing that proposition was misleading. Leaving such distinctions aside, let us just say that the use of a sentence is *appropriate* only if the presuppositions of that sentence are satisfied in the pertinent propositional context.

Still, the question remains: What determines the content of the propositional context? What makes it the case that the propositional context pertinent to a given utterance or conversation is one set of propositions rather than another? The usual answer to this is that the propositional context pertinent to a speaker's utterance consists of those propositions that the speaker takes to be *common ground* with his or her interlocutors. What a person takes to be common ground is supposed to consist, roughly, of those propositions that he or she believes he or she shares with his or her interlocutors. To say that two people *share* the belief that p is to say at least that they both believe that p, but typically sharing is supposed to involve more than that, such as mutual recognition that the two of them both believe that p (see Clark 1992, pp.

69–71). In cases of pretense or hypothetical reasoning, what is common ground may not be shared *beliefs* but may still be described as shared *assumptions*.

The idea underlying this identification of the propositional context with the propositions that the speaker takes to be common ground is that what belongs to the propositional context is what we may say the *speaker presupposes* and that what a speaker presupposes is what the speaker takes to be common ground. On this view, if one presupposes that p, then one has no need to assert that p; rather one has reason to assert something only if it is not already common ground. This idea that a speaker's presuppositions may be identified with the propositions that the speaker takes to be common ground seems to have its origins in the early work of Stalnaker (e.g., 1972, 1973) and is known as the *pragmatic theory of presupposition*. The main use of the pragmatic theory of presupposition (indeed the only use as far as I am aware) is its use in characterizing the content of the propositional context, which is a notion we can then use in defining certain conditions on the appropriateness of using certain sentences.

A first question that can be asked about this conception of the propositional context is whether we really should say (following Stalnaker) that it consists of those propositions that the speaker *takes* to be shared, or whether we should say that it consists of those propositions that really are shared (as in Thomason 1990). There will be a difference when the speaker is mistaken about what is shared. A reason to take the latter stance is that, as I explained in chapter 1, what we are interested in are the norms of discourse and it is the set of propositions really shared that we ought to appeal to in formulating those norms. We want to say that if a condition on a sentence's being appropriate is that the proposition p belong to C, then the speaker has an obligation not to use that sentence to make an assertion unless the proposition that p belongs to C. Well, in the cases that interest us, we can say that a speaker has an obligation not to use the sentence unless the assumption that p really is shared; and so we might identify C with the set of assumptions really shared. For example, a speaker has an obligation not to say "Matt knows that his paper is late" unless it really is a shared assumption that Matt's paper is late. A speaker also has an obligation not to utter "Matt knows that his paper is late" unless he or she *takes* it that his or her interlocutors share the assumption that Matt's paper is late; but that is just not the strongest thing we can say about the speaker's obligations.

In any case, on either version, a problem for this conception of the propositional context is that propositional contexts turn out to be simply too broad. Suppose that two people are talking about the persons responsible for atrocities in the Bosnian civil war. At one point somebody says, "Karadzic is a psychiatrist too." The mere fact that the interlocutors share the assumption that Sigmund Freud was a psychiatrist does not assure the appropriateness of the use of "too" in this sentence, because Sigmund Freud is irrelevant in this context. Similarly, if someone says, "Milosevic is a war criminal too," it is not the fact that they share the assumption that Hermann Göring was a war criminal that secures the appropriateness of the use of this sentence;

although the fact that they share the assumption that Ratko Mladic is a war criminal might do that. So if the condition we place on the appropriateness of the use of sentences of the form $x\char`^$"is"$\char`^F\char`^$"too" is that there be some $y$ that does not denote the same thing as $x$ such that the proposition that $y\char`^$"is"$\char`^F$ expresses belongs to the propositional context (or that there be some other predicate $G$ such that the proposition that $x\char`^$"is"$\char`^G$ expresses belongs), then if the propositional context is the set of shared, or supposedly shared assumptions, then the condition will be too weak. At the very least we have to modify the theory to say that the propositional context consists of *relevant* shared assumptions.

A problem that cuts even deeper into the pragmatic theory of presupposition is the problem of *informative presuppositions*. For example, someone might say,

(*) We regret that children cannot accompany their
    parents to the commencement exercises,

intending to inform the parents who have come to see their children graduate from college that there is no room in the auditorium for the other children whom they have brought along. (The example is from Karttunen 1974.) We would like to say that (*) presupposes that the children cannot accompany their parents, which on the present theory means that the proposition that children cannot accompany their parents belongs to the propositional context. But precisely because (*) is used to inform the hearers of the truth of that proposition, we cannot say that the proposition is a shared assumption when (*) is uttered or even that the speaker takes it to be a shared assumption. (Stalnaker has been criticized on such grounds also by Simons 2001.)

The problem is that the following three propositions cannot be jointly maintained:

1. The propositional context = the set of (relevant) shared assumptions.

2. "We regret that"^p is appropriate only if the proposition that p belongs to the propositional context.

3. "We regret that"^p can be appropriate even when used to inform the hearers that the proposition that p is true.

At most two of these propositions can be true, since one cannot inform someone of something that he or she already assumes. Abandoning (1) is not an option, since it defines the theory in question. It is no help to identify the propositional context with the assumptions that the speaker *takes* to be shared, rather than with those that *are* shared, because "We regret that"^p can also be appropriate when the proposition that p expresses does not belong to the set of assumptions that the speaker takes to be shared.

We do not want to deny (2) either. The only reason to posit propositional contexts in the first place is that we want to define appropriateness conditions in terms of them and in that way explain what it is for a sentence to presuppose something. We might deny the particular claim about "We regret that"^p, but that is not much help because no matter what sort of sentence presupposition we consider, we will find cases of informative presupposition. For instance, it has often been remarked (e.g., Stalnaker 1974, Soames 1982) that possessive noun phrases can be used to inform the hearer of that which is presupposed. For example, if I speak of "my sister," what I say presupposes that I have a sister, but at the same time I may inform my hearer of this fact for the first time. To take a different kind of example, if I say "The mail has not arrived yet," I may inform my hearer of the fact that the mail is due to arrive soon.

Perhaps, then, we should deny (3). Someone might think that it really is inappropriate to utter "We regret that"$\hat{}p$ when the proposition that p is not a shared assumption, contrary to what (3) says, and if it seems not to be, then that is just because we sometimes do, and are even permitted to do, what is inappropriate. One violates a rule of language if one says "I love it!" speaking ironically, meaning one hates it, but sometimes a rule of language may be deliberately flouted in order to achieve some special effect. One may on occasion—one is permitted—say things that are literally false or ungrammatical or in other ways "inappropriate," for one can do these things in a way that has no tendency to mislead. In just this sense it might be permissible, though inappropriate, to utter "We regret that"$\hat{}p$ when the proposition that p is not a shared assumption; for even if inappropriate, doing so may have no tendency to mislead.

The problem with this answer is that it leaves us with the question: What is the sense of "appropriate" on which (2) is true and (3) is not? We cannot say that "appropriate" in (2) means *permissible* in the sense in which "We regret that"$\hat{}p$ is permissible even when used informatively, for then (3) will be true in the same sense and we will still have the contradiction. "Appropriate" in (2) cannot mean merely *true*, and it cannot mean merely *either true or false*, and it cannot mean merely *expresses a proposition*, because if we read it in any of those ways in both (2) and (3), we will find that (3) is true and incompatible with (1) and (2). We want to say that uttering "We regret that"ˆp when the proposition that p does not belong to the propositional context may be inappropriate in that it violates a rule of language, but it is hard to see what could possibly be wrong with it if doing so has no tendency to mislead.

Still, it is tempting to look for equivocation in the use of "appropriate," and to try to show that (2) and (3) are both true in their own way but do not contradict (1). Let us nail down the sense that "appropriate" has in (2), when (2) is understood as true, as its *primary sense*. (3) may be true too but only if "appropriate" in (3) has a broader sense. To say something appropriate in this broader sense is *either* to say something appropriate in the primary sense *or* to speak *as if* one were saying something appropriate in the primary sense. As (2) claims, saying "We regret that"ˆp will be appropriate in the primary sense only if the proposition that p is a shared assumption; but, as (3) claims, saying "We regret that"ˆp informatively may also be appropriate in the broader sense, for one may say "We regret that"ˆp informatively in speaking *as if* "We regret that"ˆp were appropriate in the primary sense, for in that case the proposition that p need not actually be a shared assumption.

The problem is it is not true that one may say "We regret that"ˆp informatively while acting as if the proposition that p were a shared assumption; so (3) is not true on this interpretation. When one acts as if something is the case, one acts as one might be expected to act if that thing were really the case (though not perhaps just as one would in fact act). If I act as if I did not notice your embarrassing remark, I continue talking just as one might have expected me to do if in fact I had not noticed. So if one were pretending or acting as if everyone already knew that children cannot accompany their parents to the commencement exercises, one would not announce that one regrets that that is the case. One might make such an announcement if one's regret per se were what needed to be communicated, but in the usual sort of case the regret per se would not be an issue. The point would be to inform the parents that the children cannot come, and one might put it that way in order to acknowledge that this news may be disappointing to some.

One might try to meet this reply by substituting a more sophisticated account of what it is to speak *as if* something were appropriate in the primary sense. To speak *as if* the proposition that p belonged to the propositional context, one might say, is to say something using a sentence that would *normally* be used only if the proposition that p belonged to the propositional context. (This appears to be Stalnaker's answer to the problem of informative presuppositions in his 1973 and his 1974, note 3.) One doubt about this strategy is whether this condition is satisfied in the case of "We regret that"^{p}, for this locution may normally be used to inform people that p. But the main problem with this answer is that it still does not yield a reasonable reading of (3). We do not identify a kind of appropriateness by saying that the use of a sentence is appropriate in the broader sense if either its use is appropriate in the primary sense or normally it is used only when its use is appropriate in the primary sense; for if the latter condition is fulfilled then every use of that sentence will be appropriate in this broader sense, so that no distinction is drawn between appropriate and inappropriate.

The problem of informative presuppositions is usually glossed over with the phrase "presupposition accommodation." In an influential article from 1979, David Lewis pointed out that, while certain presuppositions may be in force, if someone speaks as if other presuppositions were in force, then those other presuppositions might simply be "accommodated." For example, in telling a story, speaker A may adopt a point of view in Cincinnati and say, "Mr. Smith came to Cincinnati on Tuesday" (whereas if he had adopted a point of view outside of Cincinnati, he would have said, "Mr. Smith *went* to Cincinnati on Tuesday"). Picking up where A left off, B may continue, "Mr. Smith came to Columbus on Wednesday," thereby altering the point of view from Cincinnati to Columbus. B's utterance need not be considered inappropriate in any way, for the change in point of view can simply be "accommodated." Cases of informative presupposition have often been characterized as cases of such presupposition accommodation.

The concept of accommodation might be put to use in escaping our inconsistent triad by allowing us to weaken condition (2). Instead of saying that "We regret that"ˆp is appropriate only if the proposition that p belongs to the context set, we might say only that "We regret that"ˆp is appropriate only if the proposition that p can be *accommodated* into the context set. But if we are to appeal to such a condition in explaining the nature of presupposition, then it has to be a condition that could somehow fail to be satisfied. To explain how it might fail to be satisfied, we might (following Soames 1982) distinguish between cases in which a speaker's audience is *prepared to accept* the proposition that p and cases in which the audience is not prepared to do so and say that the proposition the p can be accommodated into the context set only in case the audience is prepared to accept that p. However, that will not work in the present instance, because we will want to say that "We regret that children cannot accompany their parents to the commencement exercises" may be appropriate even if the audience is not prepared to accept that children cannot accompany their parents to the commencement exercises. One can well imagine a parental revolt in which the parents insist that the children must be admitted and bring them into the auditorium whether the authorities permit it or not. No doubt there is some truth in the idea that presuppositions can be accommodated, but I do not see how it can be combined with the pragmatic theory of presupposition. (Indeed in his 1979 paper, Lewis did not employ any special theory of presupposition at all.)

We may conclude that the propositional context cannot be identified with the common ground or with what the speaker takes to be common ground. Once we have acknowledged this, we can recognize that presupposition poses a problem of coordination between speaker and hearer. In general, a coordination problem is a situation in which two or more people have to cooperate in some way but in which what each person should do depends on what the others are going to do. (I take the term and the concept from Lewis 1969.) For instance, if two people have become separated in a shopping mall and want to find one another, each must look for the other at the place where the other will look for him or her. Foolishly, someone might try to solve the problem by asking, "Where will he go?" and answering, "He will go where he thinks I will go," and then asking, "Where will he think I will go?" and answering, "He will think I will go where he thinks I think he will go," and so on. The only way to solve the problem is to stop thinking reflexively in this way and consider what the other might be disposed to do quite apart from such reflexive thinking, such as go out to the car in the parking lot. In fact, I doubt it is ever helpful to take even the first step into the infinite abyss of reflexive thinking.

A similar problem can arise in simply talking. A speaker, in choosing his or her words, will want to presuppose only what the hearer might be able to recognize him or her to be presupposing, and the hearer will want to attribute to the speaker only those presuppositions that the speaker really is making. Call this the *presupposition coordination problem*. For example, suppose A and B notice C getting into a rather beat-up automobile. A gestures toward C and says to B, "Her car was stolen." What is A presupposing in speaking of "her car"? One possibility is that A is presupposing that the car that C is getting into is the car that was stolen. The stolen car was returned in bad condition. Another possibility is that A is presupposing that the car that C is getting into is not her original car. C's original car was stolen, and that is why she is now driving this wreck. Assuming that the possibilities are just these two, how is B, the hearer, to decide which?

Here, as before, the abyss of reflexive thinking holds no solution. It is no help for the hearer to ask, "What is he presupposing?," and answer, "He is presupposing what he thinks I will think he is presupposing," and then to ask, "What will he think I will think he is presupposing?" and answer, "He will think I will think he is presupposing what he thinks I will think he thinks I will think he is presupposing," and so on. It is best not even to start down this path. The solution to the presupposition coordination problem is for the hearer to suppose that the speaker presupposes that which . . . what? We cannot answer that the hearer should suppose that the speaker is presupposing that which they believe in common, because we have already seen that the attitude of presupposing is not the attitude of taking something to be common ground. Nor can we answer that the hearer should suppose that the speaker presupposes what is most salient, because there may be several candidate answers, none more salient than the others. The assumption that C is getting into her original car is neither more nor less salient than the assumption that C is getting into a different one.

The upshot is that we need some kind of alternative to the pragmatic theory of presupposition and the identification of the propositional context with the speaker's presuppositions. An alternative that gets around all of the problems we have been contemplating is to identify the propositional context with the kind of context that I defined in chapter 3. Again, contexts in my sense are structures of sentences in a simple language. They are objective in the sense that the interlocutors in the conversation to which a context pertains may be unaware of its content. The context pertinent to a conversation may be characterized as describing the facts that are relevant to the conversation in light of its goals. (Again, the kind of structure in question will depend on the resources of the language in question, and, as I have explained, the characterization in terms of "facts," "relevance," and "description" is not fundamental.)

From this point of view, we may explicate the relation of satisfying-the-presuppositions-of as a relation between the objective context and a sentence. Satisfying-the-presuppositions-of is a favor that a context bestows on a sentence when the context satisfies certain conditions under which alone the sentence will be either assertible or deniable in the context. For example, we may find that a sentence of the form $x^\frown$"is"$^\frown F^\frown$"too" is either assertible or deniable in a context only if there is some other singular term y such that $y^\frown$"$\neq$"$^\frown x$ and $y^\frown$"is"$^\frown F$ are both assertible in the context (or there is some other predicate G such that $x^\frown$"is"$^\frown G$ is assertible in the context). In that case, we may say that a context satisfies-the-presuppositions-of $x^\frown$"is"$^\frown F^\frown$"too" provided that it satisfies that same condition. Obviously this accommodates very directly the observation that in order for the presuppositions of "Milosevic is a war criminal too" to be satisfied, there must be someone else who is *relevant to the conversation* such that it belongs to the context that that other person is a war criminal; for on the present theory what belongs to the context is never more than what is relevant to the conversation.

From this point of view, we can deal with the presupposition projection problem in much the same way as before. In explicating the semantics of logical operators, such as the conditional operator, we can explain that whether the context satisfies the presuppositions of the sentence as a whole depends on whether the presuppositions of the later part of the sentence are satisfied in the context in light of the earlier parts of the sentence. For example, we can say that the presuppositions of a conditional sentence of the form "If"ˆpˆ"then"ˆq are satisfied in a context Γ if and only if the presuppositions of p are satisfied in Γ and for every context Δ, if everything assertible in Γ is assertible in Δ and p is assertible in Δ, then the presuppositions of q are satisfied in Δ. (This is by no means a theory of the assertibility conditions for conditionals; it is only a supplement to that. I will present a theory of conditionals in chapter 8.)

Against this theory one might object that it is sometimes possible both to assert something and, in the same breath, to deny its presuppositions, as in:

(**) Matt doesn't know that his paper is late, because it isn't.

By the present account of sentence presupposition, we should say that "Matt knows that his paper is late" presupposes "Matt's paper is late" in the sense that "Matt knows that his paper is late" is neither assertible nor deniable in a context Γ unless "Matt's paper is late" is assertible in Γ. But the context-logical theory of negation tells us that "Matt doesn't know that his paper is late" is assertible in Γ if and only if "Matt knows that his paper is late" is deniable in Γ. But (**) denies that Matt's paper is late. So on the present theory, (**) is a contradiction, assertible in no context. The solution is to acknowledge that negation can play another role in language besides expressing the deniability of the sentence negated. It can also express the unassertibility of what is negated. That, I suggest, is how we understand it when we treat (**) as consistent. Understanding this sentence does require a certain double-take, and that is because it is not until we reach the second clause that we realize that we have to understand the negation in the first clause in this second way. (The idea that we need two kinds of negation to handle cases like this has been around for a long time. See, for example, Wilson 1975, pp. 32–35, 151.)

The present proposal yields a straightforward account of the possibility of informative presuppositions: A context satisfies-the-presuppositions-of a sentence of the form "We regret that"$^\frown p$ only if p is assertible in the context. In other words, "We regret that"$^\frown p$ is neither assertible nor deniable in a context Γ unless p is itself assertible in Γ. Thus an assertion of "We regret that"$^\frown p$ will serve to inform us that p is assertible in the context pertinent to our conversation if we were not already aware of that fact. For example, the context may be one in which in fact children will not be permitted to accompany their parents, although the parents may not be initially aware of that. In that case, an assertion of "We regret that children will not be able to accompany their parents to the commencement exercises" may serve to inform them. In general, if the assertibility and deniability conditions of a sentence are such that that sentence is neither assertible nor deniable in a context unless the context satisfies certain conditions, then the use of that sentence to make an assertion can serve to inform a hearer that the context pertinent to the conversation does satisfy those conditions.

Having characterized the propositional context as an objective context in my sense, we may characterize an interlocutor's "presuppositions," in one broad sense of the word, as whatever we may attribute to that interlocutor as part of his or her *take* on the context pertinent to the conversation in which he or she is engaged. Not every sentence assertible in the context pertinent to a conversation is actually a member of the context, as I have defined it, but all assertible sentences can be thought of as "describing" or "circumscribing" the content of the context, in the sense of placing constraints on its actual content. So everything that an interlocutor regards as assertible belongs to his or her take on the objective context. Using the term in this way, we should not try to divide a speaker's beliefs, or assumptions, into those that are presupposed and those that are, or might need to be, asserted. Rather, everything that a speaker takes to be assertible in the context is, in this broad sense, presupposed, including all that the speaker chooses to assert.

We might also use the term "presupposition" in a narrower sense. As I explained in chapter 3, some assertible sentences may *go without saying* in the sense that, whether they are uttered or not, interlocutors will act as though they recognized that that sentence was assertible in the context pertinent to their conversation. So someone may take it that something goes without saying, whether or not it does, and for that reason not bother to assert it. We might like to reserve the term "presupposition" for those things that the speaker takes to go without saying. Using the term in this way, we might distinguish after all between what a speaker presupposes and what he or she regards as needing to be asserted. So, we might explain that "she didn't *say* so because she *presupposed* it."

In these terms, the solution to the presupposition coordination problem is that a hearer may identify the speaker's presupposition by presuming it to be something assertible in the context. Suppose that what is in fact assertible in the story of C and her car is that the car C is getting into is not her original car, but a cheap car she bought to replace it. In that case, B may assume that A is presupposing *that*. If B, from what he sees and remembers, cannot make any presumptions about whether the car C is getting into is her old car or a different one, then he may be in no position to judge what A might be presupposing and will have to ask. But if he does have some reason to think that this is not C's former car, then he may fairly well assume that that is what A is presupposing.

Of course, this strategy for deciding what a speaker is presupposing is fallible. What a speaker is presupposing may not in fact be what is assertible, for the speaker may be mistaken about the content of the context. Suppose that in fact A has forgotten what kind of car C used to drive and has concluded that this is C's same old car returned in bad condition after having been stolen. In that case, what is assertible, namely, that C is driving a different car, will not be what A is presupposing. If B has some reason to think that A is mistaken in this way, then perhaps B should not assume that A is presupposing that C is getting into a replacement car.

But if B has no special reason to think this, then he will be justified, albeit mistaken, in assuming that A is presupposing that C is getting into a replacement car.

It does not follow that one may presume that one's interlocutors presuppose everything that is in fact assertible. If that were so, then one would never have a reason to assert anything, since everything assertible would go without saying. The picture is, rather, this: A speaker may sometimes say something whose assertibility depends on the context's satisfying certain conditions. But there may be many different contexts that would satisfy those conditions. In that case, the question arises what feature the speaker takes the present context to have such that the present context satisfies those conditions. The hearer may answer that question by assuming that the speaker's take on the context satisfies those conditions in the way that the actual context does. To adopt this strategy in solving the presupposition coordination problem is not to assume that the speaker's take on the context is in all respects identical to the actual context.

As for presupposition accommodation, that can happen in several ways. One possibility is that one interlocutor, upon discovering what another interlocutor is presupposing, recognizes that he or she was mistaken about the content of the pertinent context and corrects his or her take on it. Another possibility is that two interlocutors have different conceptions of what they are trying to do. If one interlocutor takes the goal to be one thing and the other takes it to be something else, then each may really be talking in a different objective context. Upon realizing this, one or the other party may yield to the goals of the other and in this way enter the other's objective context. Finally, as we will see in chapter 7, a context may involve the setting of certain parameters to certain values and there may be a certain amount of "free choice" as to how to do this. In that case, one interlocutor may acquiesce in another's decision to change the values of those parameters. That is what is happening when, in the example above, one speaker adopts a point of view in Cincinnati and the other shifts the point of view to somewhere else.

6 Implicature

Two of the most deeply entrenched dogmas in contemporary philosophy are Grice's theory of *meaning something by something* and Grice's theory of *conversational implicature* (Grice 1989). The first is a theory of what is distinctive in actions that amount to *meaning something*, and the second is Grice's explanation of the ways in which a person can mean something over and above what he or she literally says. This chapter is primarily a critique of Grice's theory of conversational implicature, although I will have a word to say about his theory of meaning something by something as well.

Perhaps many proponents of the received view of linguistic communication view themselves as "not Griceans," because they associate with Grice his intention-based conception of semantics, which they reject. Grice's theory of meaning something by something, which I will explain in a moment, allows that the normal case of meaning something by something exploits the conventional meaning, or in Grice's terminology, the "timeless meaning" of a form of words. According to Grice's theory of timeless meaning, the timeless meaning of an expression is the sort of thing that speakers of the language "have it in their repertoire" to mean *by* it (1989, Essay 6). As I mentioned in chapter 1, this conception of the conventional meanings of words seems to have been rejected by almost everyone. But many if not most proponents of the received view may still be described as Griceans because they accept the basic ideas behind his theory of meaning something by something and his theory of conversational implicature.

As we have seen in chapter 1, from the point of view of the received view, one supposes that, among all the propositional contents to which a speaker is in one way or another related at the moment of utterance, there will be one that we can describe as the thought that he or she expresses by his or her utterance. Grice's theory of meaning something by something is in effect an analysis of this relation of expressing a thought, and so it contributes an important element to the received view of linguistic communication. As for the notion of conversational implicature, that is perhaps not a necessary part of the received view of linguistic communication, but Grice's theory of it nonetheless plays a critical supporting role in the promulgation of the received view. That is because Grice's account of the interpretive process by which hearers are supposed to recognize conversational implicature seems to many proponents of the received view to be closely related to the interpretive processes on which linguistic communication in general rests.

According to Grice, meaning something by some act is a matter of intending to produce some result in an audience on the basis of the audience's recognition of one's intention to do so. For example if a speaker, or "utterer," *U*, utters what Grice calls an "indicative-type" utterance *s* to an audience *A*, then *U* means by this that *p* if and only if *U* intends (i) that *A* will believe that *p*, (ii) that *A* will recognize that *U* intends (i), and (iii) that (i) will be achieved on the basis of achieving (ii) (1989, Essay 14, first published in 1957). Subsequently, Grice introduced a variety of further complications and, in particular, replaced condition (i) with the condition that *A* recognize that *U* himself or herself believes that *p* (1989, Essay 5, first published in 1969).

Although Grice's conception of meaning something by something is widely accepted as a basically correct account of the relation of expressing a thought, no one, as far as I can see, neither Grice nor anyone else, has ever given any good reason to believe it. Grice's own persuasive strategy (I have been told that it is not an "argument") is to compare cases in which, intuitively, someone means something by something with cases in which, intuitively, someone does not mean anything, and then to conclude that some property lacking in the latter cases is present in the former. For example, Grice asks us to imagine that someone leaves *B*'s handkerchief at the scene of a crime, intending the detective to conclude that *B* did it. This, we are supposed to agree, is not a case of meaning something by something. The agent does not *mean* by his act that *B* committed the crime. In this case, Grice observes, the agent does not intend the detective to recognize the agent's intention. So we are supposed to conclude that in a case of really meaning something, it is necessary that the agent intend the audience to recognize the agent's intention to bring about a certain effect in the audience. However, considered as an argument, this is an obvious fallacy. From the fact that a case of not meaning something by something lacks some property, we cannot conclude that every case of meaning something by something possesses that property. If we want to know what alligators are, we cannot simply observe that alligators are not rabbits, that rabbits lack wings and then conclude that therefore alligators must have wings. This same fallacy can be observed at many stages in Grice's development of the complex conditions of his later analysis. Since I have never seen any argument for a Gricean analysis that does not commit this kind of fallacy, I think there is really no reason to believe that anything like Grice's analysis is correct.

Grice's theory of conversational implicature (in Grice 1989, Essay 2, first published in 1975) is more creditable than his theory of meaning something by something because it seems to provide explanations. A conversational implicature is supposed to be a proposition that a speaker conveys to the hearer indirectly, without literally expressing it. One of Grice's examples is the case of the motorist (mentioned already in chapter 1) who has run out of gasoline and is approached by a passerby who informs him, "There is a gas station around the corner." What is conversationally implicated is supposed to be that the gas station is open and has gas to sell. Grice's explanation of this is that the speaker expects the hearer to assume that the speaker is speaking cooperatively, and on that basis to assume that that is what the speaker must have had in mind in speaking (Grice 1989, p. 32).

As Grice defines it, a conversational implicature is a special kind of "implicature" and contrasts with "what is said." Various theorists define the expression "what is said" in various ways to suit their own purposes (although I doubt that any of these technical uses is supported by ordinary usage). For present purposes *what is said* has to be, roughly, the proposition that the speaker intends the hearer to attribute to the speaker on the basis of the timeless meaning of the speaker's words. As for implicatures, Grice does not define the general case, but presumably implicatures in general are supposed to be things *meant* in the sense defined in Grice's theory of meaning something by something; or perhaps implicatures comprise all things meant with the exception of what is explicitly said.

Further, in order for a person to be regarded as *conversationally* implicating something, he or she must be presumed to be conforming to the "Cooperative Principle," which says: "Make your conversational contribution such as is required, at the stage at which it occurs, by the accepted purpose or direction of the talk exchange in which you are engaged" (1989, p. 26). This principle, as Grice explained it, carries a variety of submaxims, such as that one's contribution should be just as informative as required, that one should avoid saying anything for which one lacks adequate evidence, that one should avoid ambiguity, and so on.

In terms of the concepts of implicature and the Cooperative Principle, *conversational* implicature is defined as follows: A speaker *conversationally implicates* the proposition that q by saying that p if and only if he or she implicates that

q and (1) he or she may be presumed to be conforming to the Cooperative Principle, and (2) in order to understand the speaker as conforming to the Cooperative Principle, it is necessary to suppose that he or she thinks that q, and (3) he or she thinks that the hearer will recognize that it is his or her thinking that q that explains his or her conformity to the Cooperative Principle (1989, pp. 30–31). This theory of what conversational implicature *is* yields a theory of how hearers *recognize* that a speaker is conversationally implicating that q, namely, that they reason from what the speaker literally says and the presumption that the speaker is speaking cooperatively to the conclusion that the speaker must have had it in mind that q. (What I have formulated as condition (3) is actually a weaker consequence of Grice's own words, according to which the speaker must expect the hearer to think that the speaker thinks that it is within the competence of the hearer to work out that the supposition mentioned in (2) is required.)

As Grice defined the concept, a speaker's conversational implicatures are in some respects independent of the speaker's expectations and intentions. In particular, the satisfaction of condition (2) is not simply a matter of what the speaker expects or intends. Though a speaker expects the hearer to think that the speaker thinks that q and intends thereby to conversationally implicate that q, the speaker may fail to conversationally implicate that q if in fact the specific supposition that q is not a part of the explanation of the speaker's conformity to the Cooperative Principle. In some cases, there may be many ways of interpreting the speaker as conforming to the Cooperative Principle, and in that case the speaker will simply fail to conversationally implicate that q even if he or she intends to do so. For later purposes it will be useful to note that in principle one could define a concept of conversational implicature that was even more "externalistic" than Grice's own, by substituting for (3) a condition to the effect that the hearer must in fact recognize that it is the speaker's thinking that q that explains the speaker's conformity to the Cooperative Principle. That is, one might define conversational implicature in such a way that there is conversational implicature only where there is actual uptake on the part of the hearer.

Insofar as Grice's theory has met with any criticism, the focus has been mainly on the Cooperative Principle. Some authors have claimed that it is pointless to try to construct a taxonomy of submaxims, as Grice did, and that the whole import of the Cooperative Principle can be reduced to a principle to the effect that what one says should be *relevant* (Sperber and Wilson 1995). Others have questioned whether in every case of conversational implicature the hearer can presume that the speaker is speaking cooperatively (Davis 1998). There has also been some dispute over exactly which phenomena belong under the heading of conversational implicature and which belong in some other category (Bach 1994, Levinson 2000).

In contrast, what I want to question is the very idea that in the sorts of cases at issue the goals of the conversation can be achieved only through the hearer's contemplation of what the speaker has in mind in speaking. It is essential to conversational implicature, as Grice conceived of it, that the speaker expects the hearer to contemplate what speaker had

in mind in speaking, that is, what the speaker must have
had in mind given that the speaker spoke cooperatively.
This is evident both in Grice's definition of conversational
implicature and in his account of the thought process that
the hearer is supposed to go through in working out the
presence of a conversational implicature (1989, pp. 30–31;
see also 1989, p. 370). I deny that that is necessary at all.
Typically, the hearer can infer the extra content from what
the speaker literally says and the external circumstances in
which the conversation takes place, without thus considering what the speaker might have had in mind. Hearers
can contemplate what speakers have in mind if they choose
to do so, and they will often do so when communication
is in some way defective, but what they find in that case
will not be that the speaker intended the hearer to recognize
that the speaker had a certain thought but that the speaker
expected the hearer to make an inference from what the
speaker literally said and the external circumstances of
utterance.

Consider again the case of the motorist and the passerby.
A, the motorist, says, "I am out of gasoline," and *B*, the
passerby, replies, "There's a gas station around the corner."
The ultimate goal of this conversation, we may suppose, is
to enable *A* to drive his car again. *B*'s more immediate goal
is to bring it about that *A* goes around the corner and gets
gasoline at the gas station there. To explain the success of
communication in this case, we have to explain how *A* is
able to conclude from what *B* explicitly says that he can get
gas at the gas station around the corner. According to Grice,
A recognizes that this must be what *B* is supposing if *B* is

conforming to the Cooperative Principle. But instead, we may explain that *A* reasons from the truth of what *B* says and the character of the external situation to the conclusion that if there is a gas station around the corner then probably it is open and has gas to sell. If *A* cares to contemplate what *B* has in mind, he may recognize that *B* thinks that the gas station is open and has gas to sell, but *A* need not suppose that *B* intended *A* to contemplate what *B* must have had in mind in speaking; rather, *A* may suppose only that *B* intended him to make an inference from what he, *B*, literally said, and the observable circumstances in which they find themselves. And that may indeed be all that *B* did intend.

Suppose for example that *A* and *B* are near a busy intersection in a heavily populated part of town in the middle of the day. In a place like this, one rarely finds the abandoned remains of a former gas station, with boarded up windows and the empty frame of a Texaco sign. Any gas station at a location like this is likely to be a thriving concern. Most people would know this. So in order for *A* to conclude that the gas station will be open and have gas, *A* need only understand and accept what *B* says, namely, that there is a gas station around the corner. If the circumstances were different, then *A* might not draw any such inference, even if it were what *B* intended him to conclude. For example, suppose the exchange takes place on a remote country road in the middle of the night. Nonetheless, there really is a gas station around the corner, it is open and has gas to sell. In this case, *A* will not conclude that the gas station is open and has gas to sell. Even if he asks himself why *B* might say this, how it could possibly be relevant to his predicament, *A* will not draw this conclusion—at least not without further questioning. If *A* asks himself why *B* spoke as he did, he might conclude that *B* was simply thinking out loud as he contemplated the issue. Or *A* might consider that *B* expected him to infer that he could get gas at the gas station; but even if so, the expectation he considers attributing to *B* need not be the kind that Grice takes to be characteristic of conversational implicature; rather he may expect only that *A* will draw an inference from what he, *B*, literally said and the external situation (an expectation which, as it happens, is not reasonable).

This is not to say that *A* would not walk around the corner to the gas station. He might, after all, ask *B* whether the gas station is open and receive an affirmative answer. But suppose *B* is driving by and does not stop but simply shouts out the window, "There is a gas station around the corner!" Even then, *A* might, in desperation, walk around the corner to see whether, against all odds, someone is there to give him gas; but the reason for his doing this will not be his presuming, on the basis of what *B* said to him, that the gas station is open. His reason will be that if there is even a small chance that someone is there, it is worth his effort to check it out. His reason would be just the same if in the moonlight he could faintly make out a darkened gas station sign off in the distance.

I am not denying that interlocutors may assume of each other that they are speaking cooperatively. They may assume so unless something special happens that ought to raise a doubt. There is a difference between assuming that the speaker is speaking cooperatively and not assuming that the speaker is speaking uncooperatively, but I do not wish to deny even that hearers may normally assume that speakers are speaking cooperatively. But to suppose that the hearer will normally assume that the speaker speaks cooperatively is not in itself to assume that the hearer contemplates the speaker's state of mind, for to speak cooperatively is to say something relevant to the situation, and the hearer may assume that the speaker's words are relevant without making any assumptions about the speaker's state of mind, beyond, perhaps, that he or she intends to say something relevant.

One of the attractions of Grice's theory of conversational implicature is that it offers a simple formula by which to explain many different cases. His examples are very different from one another in fact, and we have to think each one through in detail. For a second example, consider Grice's Professor *A*, who writes a letter of recommendation for his pupil, who is a candidate for a philosophy job. His letter reads as follows: "Dear Sir, Mr. *X*'s command of English is excellent, and his attendance at tutorials has been regular. Yours, etc." (1989, p. 33). In this example, Professor *A* is supposed to conversationally implicate that Mr. *X* is no good at philosophy. I think that for the example to be plausible the letter has to do a better of job of explaining the candidate's good points; otherwise, the reader might infer that the writer is simply a nincompoop whose opinion does not reflect on Mr. *X* at all; so let us imagine we are dealing with such a letter.

We cannot assume that Prof. *A* intends the reader to *believe* that Mr. *X* is no good at philosophy. A judicious reader could not be so influenced by a single letter of this sort, and Prof.

A will know this. At the same time, it would not be right to say that Prof. *A*'s objective in writing the letter is only to cause the readers of the letter to believe that Prof. *A believes* that Mr. *X* is no good at philosophy. This bit of information about Prof. *A* would have no value in itself, but is valuable only inasmuch as it is some evidence, to be weighed alongside other evidence, that Mr. *X* is in fact no good at philosophy. Thus if Prof. *A* does intend his readers to take some attitude toward the proposition that Mr. *X* is no good at philosophy, and does not merely unwittingly leave them to infer it, then the attitude he intends them to take must be one of regarding that proposition as one that the letter somehow supports.

In fact, this is not a case of conversational implicature in Grice's sense, because there is no reason why, in order to reach this conclusion, readers of the letter need to consider whether Prof. *A*'s belief that Mr. *X* is no good at philosophy explains Prof. *A*'s conformity to the Cooperative Principle; nor indeed need readers consider whether Prof. *A* does believe that Mr. *X* is no good at philosophy or contemplate Prof. *A*'s state of mind at all; accordingly, there is no reason for Prof. *A* to expect that readers will do this. Readers may simply reason as follows: "This is a letter of recommendation for a candidate for a philosophy job. The letter does not say anything about whether the candidate is good at philosophy. Therefore, there is some reason to doubt whether this candidate is good at philosophy."

If the reader reflects on his or her inference from the fact that the letter does not say that the candidate is good at philosophy to the conclusion that there is some reason to doubt whether he is, then the reader may reason as follows: "The purpose of a letter of recommendation is to describe the candidate's qualifications for the job. Being good at philosophy is obviously a relevant qualification for a philosophy job. So the fact that the letter does not say that the candidate is good at philosophy is some reason to think that he is not." Thus, the information pertinent to the reader's goals, namely, whether Mr. X is good at philosophy, is acquired by an inference from the situation and what the speaker actually says. The pertinent feature of the situation is simply that the document is a letter of recommendation.

In reply it might be said that the reasoning I have attributed to the reader requires the support of some further assumptions about the writer. If the reader is to assume that this letter will do what letters of recommendation are supposed to do, then the reader must assume that the letter writer is conforming to the Cooperative Principle. If the reader assumes that the letter does what it ought to do in addressing Mr. X's qualifications for a philosophy job, the reader must assume that in not saying that Mr. X is good at philosophy, Prof. A was in fact being cooperative, because Prof. A believes that Mr. X is no good at philosophy. Thus the reader must, at least implicitly, recognize that it is Prof. A's thinking that Mr. X is no good at philosophy that explains his conformity to the Cooperative Principle.

My reply to this reply is that, while the reader's reasoning about Prof. A's state of mind might in this way strengthen the conclusion that Prof. A thinks that Mr. X is no good at philosophy if the reader had independent evidence that Prof. A wished to be cooperative and consequently attempted to list all of Mr. *X*'s qualifying characteristics, typically the reader of the letter would have no other basis for supposing that Prof. *A* wished to be cooperative, and thus had described all of Mr. *X*'s qualifying characteristics, than the fact that the description of Mr. *X* occurred in the context of a letter of recommendation for a philosophy job. But if the facts about the contents of the letter and the conclusion that Prof. *A* is speaking cooperatively support the conclusion that Mr. *X* is no good at philosophy, and the sole basis for the conclusion that Prof. *A* is speaking cooperatively is that he has written this letter of recommendation, then the conclusion that Mr. *X* is no good at philosophy is equally well supported by the fact that the letter is a letter of recommendation with this content quite apart from the intermediate conclusion that Prof. *A* is speaking cooperatively. The reader's contemplation of what Prof. *A* might have had in mind given cooperativeness can typically add nothing to the force of the reader's conclusion. Borrowing a term from probability theory, we can say that the premise that the description occurs in a letter of recommendation *screens off* the premise that the writer is being cooperative.

In cases of what has been called "generalized conversational implicature," the pertinent features of the external circumstance may be more general (Grice 1989, pp. 37ff; Levinson 2000). In some of these cases, the hearer may simply make an inference from what tends to be the case when someone uses a certain form of words. If a speaker is reliable, then the context will tend to be such that his or her sentence is assertible in it, and the hearer may rely on that;

but in addition the brute matter of fact may be that when such sentences are uttered, or when they are uttered under circumstances such as those that obtain, certain other conditions tend to be satisfied as well, and the hearer may rely on that as well. Or the hearer may know that in response to a question, the speaker always, usually, or under circumstances such as those present, gives the logically strongest answer that is still assertible. Thus if the speaker says something logically weaker than he or she might have said, then on that basis, the hearer may infer that that logically stronger sentence is not assertible. In none of these cases does the hearer's inference require the hearer to contemplate what the speaker had in mind in speaking.

For example, suppose an employee for a manufacturer has been collecting information on how well the company's new product is selling at retail outlets around the country and is asked by a supervisor whether all of the data are in. The employee replies, "Some of the data are in." From this the supervisor may well conclude that not all of the data are in. In this case, the supervisor's reason for concluding that not all of the data are in may be just the fact that in general when people use a sentence of the form "Some F are G," it is often the case that not all F are G. This is of course not an assumption about what the speaker had in mind in speaking. Or the supervisor might know of this particular employee that when asked about the progress of projects he generally gives the strongest but still assertible answer he can give. This is still not an assumption about what the speaker must have had in mind in speaking but merely an assumption about the kind of answers this speaker tends to give in circumstances such as those present. The employee may indeed have intended the supervisor to infer that not all of the data are in, but he may not have envisioned any plan by which this intention would be realized, or if he did, then he may have intended the supervisor to draw the inference simply on the basis of what speakers in general tend to say or what he in particular tends to say, and if for any reason the supervisor considers what the employee might have had in mind, the intention she attributes to the employee may be just that one.

Under other circumstances, the hearer should not infer from the speaker's assertion, "Some of the data are in," that not all of the data are in. The exceptions are as much a matter of the external circumstances as is the general rule. For example, if the speaker is not the person collecting the data but is only some middle manager not actively engaged in the collection of the data, he may not be up-to-date on the status of the project. So the reason why he does not say "All of the data are in" may be not that he knows that not all of the data are in but just that he does not know more than that some of the data are in. In this case, the hearer may not infer that not all of the data are in, because she recognizes that the speaker is not up-to-date. The assumption that the speaker is not up-to-date is not so much an assumption about the speaker's state of mind as it is an assumption about the speaker's role in the community and what he might have been told; but even construed as an assumption about the speaker's state of mind, it is not an assumption about what the speaker had in mind in speaking.

Perhaps the Gricean theory of conversational implicature can be better motivated by considering a case in which the hearer recognizes what the speaker intends the hearer to believe but does not in fact believe it. For example, suppose that Jane tells Mireille that her advertising agent has been seen with Mireille's business competitor. Jane is insinuating that Mireille's advertising agent is working for Mireille's competitor. More precisely, Jane intends to plant in Mireille's mind the thought that possibly the agent and the competitor are working together. Mireille, however, knows that that is nonsense. Mireille knows that her agent and her competitor are simply friends who occasionally meet to socialize. So Jane does not succeed in getting Mireille to share her suspicions, but she does at least get Mireille to recognize that she, Jane, has those suspicions.

How does Jane's act of speech achieve this? Perhaps Mireille asks herself, in effect, "Why is Jane saying this to me?" The answer she gives herself may be something like "Because she thinks that what she is telling me, namely, that my agent and my competitor have been seen together, will be interesting to me, and the reason she thinks that is that she thinks it is evidence that my agent is doing advertising work for my competitor." This is not an explicit application of the principle that conversation will be co-operative in Grice's sense, but the presumption that Jane intends to say something of interest to Mireille may be construed as a corollary. So we may conclude that Mireille does in fact recognize that it is Jane's thinking that Mireille's advertising agent is working for Mireille's competitor that explains how Jane's speech is in conformity with the Cooperative Principle.

Above, I drew a distinction between Grice's own conception of conversational implicature and a more externalistic conception. I think that the story of Jane and Mireille gives us a plausible example of conversational implicature in the externalistic sense, but not an example of conversational implicature according to Grice's own conception. It is an example of conversational implicature in the externalistic sense if, as I have allowed, Mireille recognizes Jane's suspicions on the basis of the presumption that Jane is conforming to the Cooperative Principle. However, the story of Jane and Mireille does not give us a case of conversational implicature in Grice's sense because it is not the case that *Jane expects* that Mireille will recognize her thought on the basis of the presumption that Jane is being cooperative. Rather, Jane expects Mireille to think that her agent may be working for her competitor on the basis of an inference from what she, Jane, is telling her and everything else that Mireille knows about her agent and her competitor.

In any case, this example gives us no reason to think that there is conversational implicature in cases where the speaker succeeds in causing the hearer to share his or her belief. If in light of everything else Mireille knows, Jane's assertion does cause Mireille to worry that possibly her agent is doing work for her competitor, then Jane's assertion may have that effect on Mireille without Mireille's having to consider first whether Jane suspects that the agent is doing work for the competitor. Mireille may consider whether Jane suspects this if she pauses to consider why

Jane has told her this. But instead she may forget all about
Jane and rush off to confront her advertising agent. In that
case, there would be no conversational implicature in any
sense. As the story is told, Jane should not expect Mireille
to consider what she, Jane, had in mind; so we do not have
a case of conversational implicature in Grice's sense. And
since Mireille does not in fact consider what Jane had in
mind, we do not have a conversational implicature in the
externalistic sense either.

Part of the attraction of the theory of conversational implicature may be a conception of the distinction between those
conclusions on the part of the hearer for which the speaker
bears a special responsibility and those for which the
speaker bears no special responsibility. A hearer may draw
all kinds of conclusions from a speaker's act of speech, of
course. From the tone of voice, the hearer may infer that the
speaker is nervous. From the time of utterance, the hearer
may infer that the speaker is late for her bus. From what
a person says, we may draw all kinds of conclusions about
his or her motivation and underlying beliefs. But among
the conclusions that can be drawn from a speaker's act of
speech, there will be some for which we think the speaker
bears a special responsibility. That special responsibility
toward a proposition may include the responsibility for
giving reasons to believe the proposition, and it may entail
that the speaker may be deemed blameworthy if the proposition proves false. In ordinary language this distinction
may be represented in various ways, but in philosophy one
might try to represent it as a distinction between what is
meant and what is not, and the theory of conversational

implicature might serve us in identifying what we can say, in the pertinent sense, the speaker meant.

Grice's theory of conversational implicature might seem useful in explicating the pertinent relation of meaning. Roughly, a speaker *means* a proposition—in the way that gives the speaker a special responsibility toward that proposition—just in case the proposition is one that the speaker either literally expressed or conversationally implicated, for these, it might be said, are the propositions that the speaker intends the hearer to recognize as contents of the speaker's thought on the basis of the speaker's choice of words. Thus, in the gasoline example, if *A* goes around the corner and finds that the gas station is abandoned, *A* might have cause for complaint against *B* on the grounds that what he conversationally implicated was not true.

There is no simple relation between responsibility and intention. It is not true that we hold people responsible only for those effects that they intend; we also hold people responsible for things they do not intend but merely foresee and even sometimes for things they do not foresee but should have foreseen. Still, what a person intends may form the core, or minimum of what a person can be held responsible for, and so the theory of conversational implicature might play a role in identifying that core of the responsibilities that a speaker acquires through speaking.

But even supposing that conversational implicature in Grice's sense were a common occurrence, we could not maintain that the only conclusions a speaker might intend his or her hearer to draw on the basis of his or her act of speech would be those that the speaker intended the hearer to recognize either as literal meanings or as conversational implicatures. From the fact that someone is talking to me on the telephone at 7:00 P.M., I might infer that she is working late, missed her bus and needs a ride home, and she might intend me to draw that conclusion and bear responsibility for my drawing that conclusion (if she knew very well that I would draw that conclusion), but that she needs a ride home is neither a literal meaning nor a conversational implicature of her act. So even if what a speaker intends forms the core of what he or she is responsible for, we could not maintain that there is any special role for the concept of conversational implicature to play in defining this core.

To this it might be said that the core of the contents for which the speaker bears a special responsibility are those that the speaker intends the hearer to draw on the basis of *what the speaker says*, as opposed to the fact of his or her saying it. Even then it is not evident that the concept of conversational implicature will have any role to play in identifying that core. Instead, we might identify those contents simply as conclusions that the speaker intends the hearer to draw on the basis of what the speaker literally says (as opposed to the fact of his or her saying it) and the other features of the situation that the speaker expects the hearer to be aware of.

From the point of view of my alternative theory of linguistic communication, there is just no place for and no need for Grice's theory of conversational implicature. Speakers may indeed expect hearers to draw further conclusions from what they literally say. But speakers need not suppose that these further recognitions on the part of hearers will result from the hearers' contemplating what the speaker had in mind in speaking. Rather, hearers may simply make an inference, taking the speaker's own sentence as premise and relying on other features of the external circumstances in which the conversation takes place, to arrive at the conclusion that the speaker intends the hearer to draw.

In the present framework, to accept what someone literally says is to *take* the context to be one in which the speaker's utterance is indeed assertible. (I have not tried to define *literal meaning* or *understanding literal meaning*.) One's take on the context extends beyond the assertibility of what is actually asserted. Given such a take on the context, the hearer may draw further inferences from what the speaker asserts. These inferences may be merely further articulations of the context governing the conversation. Or in addition, the hearer may have goals that he or she does not share with the speaker, goals that define a context for a conversation that the hearer conducts with himself or herself or with others as well. The hearer's "inference" in such a case may consist in merging two contexts, the one pertinent to his or her conversation with the speaker, identified in part by what the speaker has asserted, and any others governing other conversations that he or she is keeping up with himself or herself or with others.

Semantics

7   Quantification

With this chapter I begin a series of three case studies in semantics, by which I mean simply an account of the logical properties of words, in terms of which we identify logically valid arguments. I want to show that we can give a better account of the logical relations between sentences if we think of logical validity as preservation of assertibility in a context rather than as a relation between propositions. But first, I have to explain what this subject has to do with the received view of linguistic communication.

As I explained in chapter 1, logical implication might be conceived as first of all a relation between propositions. If propositions are modelled as sets of possible worlds, then we might say that one proposition logically implies another if the first is a subset of the second, and we might say that a *set* of propositions logically implies a certain proposition if the intersection of the members of the set is a subset of that proposition. We saw that given such a definition of logical implication as a relation between propositions, logical validity for arguments, considered as consisting of sentences, might be defined thus: An argument is valid if and only if for any context, the set of propositions expressed by the premises in that context logically implies the proposition expressed by the conclusion in that context. Call this the *propositional approach* to logical validity. My alternative to this definition, which I introduced in chapter 3, is to say that an argument is logically valid if and only if for every context in which the premises are assertible, the conclusion is assertible too. Call this the *context-logical approach* to logical validity.

For a proponent of the received view, the propositional approach to logical validity will be almost inevitable, for if we think of linguistic communication as a matter of the speaker's revealing the propositional content of a thought, then it is almost inevitable that one will define logical implication as first of all a relation between propositions. Sentences are conceived as only the vestments in which propositions reveal themselves to the world. Insofar as the quality of our thought is concerned, it is the propositions we think that matter. Insofar as our reasoning is to be criticized, the question is whether the propositions we cite in support of the propositions in question do indeed support them. So insofar as our utterances are expected to be logically consistent and our inferences logically valid, the question concerns first of all a relation between propositions. Normative questions pertaining to speech as such concern only its fidelity to the propositions that we intend to express. In any case, the propositional approach to logical validity is certainly characteristic of the received view, even if not absolutely essential, and is, accordingly, an appropriate target for my critique of the received view.

Further, so long as one accepts the received view of linguistic communication, one will not be able to accept the definition of logical validity as preservation of assertibility in a context. Assertibility in a context is a standard of evaluation governing conversation. Conversation, as here conceived, aims at giving interlocutors a common take on the context objectively pertinent to their conversation in light of the goals. Accordingly, assertibility in a context is a dimension of evaluation for discourse *between* persons. Thinking too may be goal-directed and is in many ways situation-dependent. And thinking of one kind may consist in literally talking with oneself as a way of deciding an issue. But if thinking is conceived, as on the received view, as a kind of processing of propositions that underlies language use, then thinking is not a conversation aimed at giving interlocutors a common take on the context pertinent to the conversation. So while thinking, so conceived, would require a standard of logical validity too, that standard would not be preservation of assertibility in a context.

The topic of this first chapter on semantics is the logical device of *quantification*. I want to show that the context-logical approach yields a more adequate account of the logic of quantification than the propositional approach. By a *quantified* sentence I mean a sentence such as "Everything is new", or "Some people came early", containing *quantifiers* such as "Everything" or "Some people". These are sentences that "talk" about all things or some things without necessarily referring to any particular thing. Quantified sentences contrast with singular sentences such as "This chair is new" or "Paul came early" containing singular terms such as the demonstrative noun phrase "this chair" and the proper name "Paul". These are sentences that, as we say, refer to some particular thing. Since my conception of quantification goes hand-in-hand with a conception of singular terms, I will have to say something about singular terms as well.

The devices of quantification in natural language are many. To simplify my discussion I will pretend that we are dealing with a language in which quantifiers can always be written in the form "For all"ˆv or "For some"ˆv, where v is some object language variable. (Recall that we think of the symbol "ˆ" as denoting a function which forms a single expression from the expressions that fall on either side of it.) The phrase "For all"ˆv is what I will call a *universal quantifier*, and sentences in which it is the dominant logical operator (having all others in its scope) are *universal quantifications*. The phrase "For some"ˆv is an *existential quantifier*, and sentences in which it is the dominant logical operator are *existential quantifications*. So I will assume that instead of saying "Everyone is present," we could say, "For all x, if x is a person then x is present," and that instead of saying "Some animal knocked over a garbage pail," we could say, "For some x and for some y, x is an animal and y is a garbage pail and x knocked over y." I will not stop using other forms of quantification, but whenever it is convenient I will freely substitute these forms.

Students who take a course in elementary symbolic logic invariably learn a rule of inference called *universal instantiation*, which says that if one accepts a premise of the form **for all x F**, then, for any proper name **n** in the language, one may infer a sentence of the form **Fn/x**, by which I mean the result of substituting **n** for any occurrence of **x** in **F** (more precisely, the result of substituting **n** for every occurrence of **x** in **F** that is not "bound" by **for all x** or **for some x** in the sense defined in chapter 2). This rule is supposed to be valid in the sense that every inference conforming to it is supposed to be valid. For example, from "All dogs are mammals", that is, "For all x, if x is a dog, then x is a mammal", one is supposed to be able to validly infer "If Fido is a dog, then Fido is a mammal", which is the result of putting "Fido" in place of "x" in the formula "if x is a dog, then x is a mammal". (Again, I am using boldface to represent *forms* of expression, and I am putting quotation marks around particular instances of those forms.)

The problem, which will be the focus of this chapter, is that there are plenty of cases in which such an inference would be just wrong. For example, suppose that someone is showing a visitor a collection of wooden figurines displayed on a table in front of them and says, "Everything is made of wood," or in other words, "For all x, x is made of wood." Under the circumstances, we should accept such a sentence as true. But even though the philosopher Socrates is not at all at issue in this conversation, the name "Socrates" is still a name in the speaker's language and, we may assume, continues to be the name of the philosopher even in this context. And so, according to the rule of universal instantiation, from "Everything is made of wood" we should be able to infer "Socrates is made of wood". But that's absurd!

It is not an answer to this to insist that in context "Everything is made of wood", that is, "For all x, x is made of wood", expresses the proposition that *every figurine on the table in front of the interlocutors is made of wood*, and that in that same context the sentence "Socrates is made of wood" expresses the proposition that *Socrates is made of wood*, and that the former does not imply the latter. That observation is not a way of defending universal instantiation; it is just a way of explaining the counterexample. The rule of universal instantiation is a formal rule of inference pertaining to sentences. If one sentence logically implies another just in case for every context, the proposition expressed by the first in that context implies the proposition expressed by the second in that context, and in some context "Everything is made of wood" expresses the proposition that *every figurine on the table in front of the interlocutors is made of wood*, while in that same context "Socrates is made of wood" expresses the proposition that *Socrates is made of wood*, then since the former proposition does not imply the latter, the formal rule of universal instantiation is just plain wrong.

Shortly, I will consider what might be said in defense of universal instantiation, but first I want to explain why the propositional approach to logical validity cannot account for these apparent counterexamples to universal instantiation. The problem is not that on the propositional approach the evaluation of quantified sentences cannot be relativized to a contextually supplied domain so that universal instantiation might be rendered invalid. A proponent of the propositional approach might indeed maintain that for any given context and sentence of the form **for all x F**, the proposition that that sentence expresses in the context is a proposition that is true at a world w if and only if for every object *in the domain pertinent to that context*, that object at w

has the property that **F** expresses in that context (more precisely: satisfies the propositional function that **F** expresses in that context).

The problem, rather, is that there is another rule, the rule of *existential generalization*, which, on the propositional approach, stands or falls with universal instantiation but which is not subject to the same doubts. Existential generalization says that given any sentence of the form **Fn/x**, in which the name **n** occurs in place of (every nonbound occurrence of) the variable **x** in **F**, one may infer **for some x F**. For example, from "Socrates is wise", one may validly infer "For some x, x is wise", that is, "Something is wise". Such a rule is surely valid (in the sense that any inference conforming to it is logically valid). For instance, if in any situation "Socrates is wise" would be regarded as true, then by the same token, or equally well, one may regard "Something is wise" as true. Of course, the validity of the inference does not depend on the actual truth of the premise. If one imagines a situation in which "Socrates is made of wood" would be accepted as true, then by the same token, or equally well, one imagines a situation in which "Something is made of wood" would be accepted as true.

In the framework of the propositional approach, one cannot very well accept existential generalization while rejecting universal instantiation. Let $[\mathbf{p}]_c$ be the proposition expressed by the sentence **p** in context c. Every proposition is true or false in fact; there is no in-between case. Therefore, $[\mathbf{not\ p}]_c$ is true if and only if $[\mathbf{p}]_c$ is false. And if $[\mathbf{p}]_c$ cannot be true without $[\mathbf{q}]_c$ being true, then $[\mathbf{q}]_c$ cannot be false without $[\mathbf{p}]_c$ being false. So, if $[\mathbf{p}]_c$ implies $[\mathbf{q}]_c$, then $[\mathbf{not\ q}]_c$

must imply [**not p**]$_c$. So suppose that existential generalization is valid, that is, that for any formula **F** and any name **n**
and any context c, [**Fn/x**]$_c$ implies [**for some x F**]$_c$. In particular, for any name **n** and formula **G**, [**not Gn/x**]$_c$ implies
[**for some x not G**]$_c$. Then, by what we have just shown, for
any name **n**, [**not for some x not G**]$_c$ implies [**not not
Gn/x**]$_c$. But we may presume that **not for some x not G** is
logically equivalent to **for all x G**. That is, for all c, [**not for
some x not G**]$_c$ implies and is implied by [**for all x G**]$_c$. Likewise, **not not Gn/x** is logically equivalent to **Gn/x**. So for
any name **n**, [**for all x G**]$_c$ implies [**Gn/x**]$_c$. But that is precisely what the rule of universal instantiation says. So if existential generalization is valid then universal instantiation
must be valid too.

People's first response to this argument against universal
instantiation is often just to point out that in standard model
theory, an interpretation of a language always includes a
component called the *domain* or *universe*. But the presence of
such a domain in a model-theoretic interpretation does not
acknowledge any kind of context-relativity in the meaning
of the quantifiers. In standard model theory, on every interpretation every name of the language denotes some member
of the domain. Precisely for that reason, universal instantiation turns out to be valid. It would be a mistake to think
that what varies from context to context is the interpretation
of the language, in the model-theoretic sense, because it is
certainly not the case that in every context every name of
the language has to denote some object that belongs to that
context. To allow context-relativity, we have to allow that
within a single interpretation of the language the domain

relative to which we evaluate quantified sentences may vary from one context to another.

Another response I have heard is that the rule of universal instantiation says only that one may infer the result of dropping the quantifier and substituting for the variable any name *that denotes an object in the contextually given domain*. But that is certainly not what the rule says, and that is not the strongest rule that must be valid if the rule of existential generalization is valid. Another common reaction is to say that "Everything is made of wood" may be *elliptical* for "Every figurine on the table is made of wood". But if the apparent counterexamples to universal instantiation are due to confusing the real premise ("Every figurine on the table is made of wood") with something elliptical for it ("Everything is made of wood"), then in the same way, we should expect to get apparent counterexamples to existential generalization. For instance, since "Something is made of wood" might be elliptical for "Something in the refrigerator is made of wood", we should expect the inference from "Socrates is made of wood" to "Something is made of wood" to seem invalid. But in fact there are no such apparent counterexamples to existential generalization.

Another common response is to say that the inference from "Everything is made of wood" to "Socrates is made of wood" is not a counterexample to the rule of universal instantiation because a counterexample requires a true premise and a false conclusion and in this case the premise is simply false. (That is what Kent Bach would probably say. See his 2000.) In many cases we will in some sense *accept* a universal generalization that we know is not true *strictly speaking*. For instance, a child complaining to his mother that he needs a Rock 'em Sock 'em Robot might say, "But mom, *everyone* has one!" Mom's response to this might be, "No, not everyone has one," but it might also be "Why do you have to have what everyone has?" In the latter case, she lets pass the contention that everyone has one, even though she knows it is false, and objects to her child's complaint on other grounds. So similarly, one might say, the sentence "Everything is made of wood" is, strictly speaking, false, even if on occasion it might be accepted as true.

It is true that we have to distinguish between universal quantifications that are false but allowed as exaggerations and universal quantifications that are strictly speaking true. But it would be a mistake to conclude that every universally quantified sentence that would be false if evaluated relative to an absolutely universal domain is not strictly speaking true, for in many of those cases an utterance of that sentence could not plausibly be construed as exaggeration. Exaggeration possesses its own positive characteristics. For instance, the speaker typically aims to impress or deceive.

Even if the position cannot be defended by a comparison with exaggerations, someone might maintain that the apparent counterexamples to universal instantiation are not really counterexamples because the premises in those examples are strictly speaking false. Against this, we may observe that if no universal generalization qualified as strictly speaking true unless it were true relative to an absolutely universal domain, then we would hardly ever utter universally quantified sentences that were strictly speaking true, which is not very plausible. Further, this defense of the validity of universal instantiation renders the rule quite useless. Since most of the universal generalizations we utter will be, by this standard, "strictly speaking false," and the counterexamples show that we need not accept the conclusions that we derive by universal instantiation from such "strictly speaking false" universal generalizations, the rule of universal instantiation will seldom have any application. We can take it as a useful guide to discourse only if we take it together with a maxim to the effect that we should try not to utter universal generalizations if they would be false when evaluated relative to a domain containing absolutely everything. But this latter is certainly not a maxim we have any good reason to try to follow, as ordinary practice amply demonstrates.

Even if we accept that universal instantiation is valid in the sense that it preserves truth *strictly speaking*, there is still a problem for the propositional approach. To see this, consider that even if a universal quantification is never strictly true except when true with respect to an absolutely universal domain, still we need to draw a distinction between those universal quantifications that would be *acceptable* in some sense in a given situation, and not only in the manner of exaggerations, and those that would not be, except perhaps as exaggerations. For example, in the scenario in which someone is showing someone a display of figurines, the sentence "Everything is made of wood" is acceptable, while "Everything is made of glass" is not acceptable, even if both are strictly speaking false. In the classroom scenario from chapter 1, "Everyone is present" might be acceptable if all of the students enrolled in the course are present but might not be acceptable if one of the students enrolled in the course is absent. Even if in that case "Everyone is present" might be tolerable as an exaggeration, there is a sense in which it would still not be *acceptable* but would have been acceptable if that student had been present.

So the problem that remains is this: Existential generalization is valid even in the sense that when the premise is *acceptable*, the conclusion is bound to be acceptable too, but universal instantiation is not valid in that sense. In a situation in which "Everything is made of wood" is acceptable, "Socrates is made of wood" need not be acceptable. The problem is to explain this asymmetry in a way that is compatible with the propositional approach to logical validity. Since it does not solve the central problem anyway, let us leave the idea that our apparent counterexamples to universal instantiation are not really counterexamples, and consider whether a proponent of the propositional approach to validity might have some other way out.

Another way out would be to insist that, despite what I have said, existential generalization is invalid too. We cannot require that every name name some object in the context; so though a proper name like "Jonathan" names different people on different occasions, its denotation does not vary with context in the same way as, say, the reference of "this". So a sentence like "Jonathan is brushing his teeth" might have to be counted as true relative to some context even if "Jonathan" is not the name of anyone in that context. In that case, if we evaluate quantified sentences relative to domains consisting of objects that belong to the context, then "Someone is brushing his teeth" might still be false relative to the context.

One answer to this might be that the objection relies on a conception of some sentences as true or false independently of context in a way that may not prove tenable (see chapter 9). But even without reaching so far for an answer, we may reply that the objection leaves untouched the asymmetry between universal instantiation and existential generalization that has to be accounted for. In any context in which "Jonathan is brushing his teeth" is not only true relative to the context but also relevant, the sentence "Someone is brushing his teeth" will be relevant as well, if only as a step toward the fact that Jonathan is brushing his teeth. In contrast, even if "Everything is made of wood" is both true relative to the context and relevant, it does not follow that "Socrates is made of wood" is relevant. Universal instantiation is *risky* in the sense that it can commit us to conclusions that may be irrelevant in our context, while existential generalization is not risky in this sense.

Finally, a proponent of the propositional approach might offer to give a little and to modify his or her conception of propositions and thereby break the link between universal instantiation and existential generalization. Close examination of my argument showing that if existential generalization is valid then universal instantiation must be valid too reveals that it depends on the assumption that every proposition is either true or false. Thus, the entire problematic might be escaped by allowing that a proposition may be neither true nor false. (Propositions might be modeled as pairs of sets, a set of worlds in which the proposition is true and a set of worlds in which the proposition is false; and some worlds might belong to neither set.)

Technically, we might in this way preserve the assumption that logical validity is first of all a relation between propositions while granting that existential generalization is valid and universal instantiation is not. But the question would remain, what does the technical apparatus really mean? We cannot countenance three values for propositions while maintaining that a proposition is a classification of the world, for there is no third alternative to belonging to a set and not belonging to it. There might be some rationale for the introduction of three-valued propositions in explicating vagueness (so that a proposition to the effect that x is F is false only if x is *definitely* not F), but vagueness is not the source of our present quandary. So while I grant that this strategy for answering my challenge remains, I challenge anyone who would adopt it to give a clear account of what it really means as an account of language.

I turn then to showing that the context-logical approach to logical validity can explain the asymmetry. Toward explaining this, I first need to take a detour through the topic of singular terms, which is important in its own right. One important kind of singular term is the proper name. Philosophers have tended to think of names as like labels that objects carry around with them for longer or shorter stretches of time. If an object carries a label, then we can use that label in various ways to act on that object. For example, if Fido is labelled "Fido", then we can shout "Fido!" to make Fido come. And if Fido is labelled "Fido" then we can use the label "Fido" to *say* things about Fido, such as that Fido is hungry. Thinking of singular terms in this way then creates certain classic problems. For example, if an object has two names such as "Twain" and "Clemens", then how can it be informative to say "Twain = Clemens"? (This is known as Frege's problem, since it was posed by Frege in his 1892/1994.) If referring to a thing by name is not yet saying anything about it, then the proposition expressed by such a sentence is just a proposition to the effect that one thing is itself, which hardly seems informative. If on the other hand, referring by name carries information, then it is hard to see how names can be used effectively in communication, since the information that one person attaches to a name may not be the same as that which another person attaches to it.

I do not intend to take up a full-scale critique of this conception of names, but I do want to suggest an alternative, which starts with what in chapter 3 I called *demonstrative pronouns*. A demonstrative pronoun in my sense may be thought of as an *index* that creates a relation between sentences. If the context contains "*This* is long" and "*That* is short", then what you should do when I tell you to hand me something will depend on whether I say "Give me *this*!" or "Give me *that*!" If I say the former, then you should give me the long one. If I say the latter, then you should give me the short one. If in washing a batch of laundry by hand, we are picking up those pieces of clothing that have been scrubbed, and hanging them up to dry, then the context:

{This is on the left. That is on the right. *This* is clean.}

calls for a different response than the context:

{This is on the left. That is on the right. *That* is clean.}

Acting in accordance with the former will call for picking up and hanging the item lying on the left, while acting in accordance with the latter will call for picking up and hanging the item lying on the right. (I have already acknowledged that the term "demonstrative pronoun" is misleading in suggesting that every use of a demonstrative pronoun must be accompanied by an act of demonstration, which is not my intention.)

In the languages that people actually speak, this role of demonstrative pronouns, as devices for linking sentences, is not easily noticed because there are other common means for creating such relations between sentences. Rather than saying, "This is on the left; this is clean," we can simply say, "The one on the left is clean." Instead of saying, "This is a man; then is yesterday; this came then," we can simply say, "The man came yesterday." (In saying this I do not propose any general analysis of definite descriptions; there would be complications I have not touched on.) Thus we create singular terms that combine the work of demonstrative pronouns with the work of predication. Even most ordinary pronouns are not pure demonstratives because they do not merely serve to link sentences in such ways, but also do some of the work of predication. For example, "He is tall" does the work of "This is male; this is tall." Even "this" and "that", which I have been treating as paradigmatic demonstrative pronouns, are not so pure because "this" indicates a thing that is relatively near to some reference point and "that" indicates a thing that is relatively far.

Still, we might maintain that the role of a *pure* demonstrative pronoun is that of a link between sentences such as I have illustrated, and that the content of the primitive context may be specified by means of literals containing such pure demonstrative pronouns in subject and object positions. The idea is that the content of the context may be specified using such pure demonstrative pronouns and that sentences containing other sorts of singular terms will have their assertibility conditions defined relative to such contexts. However, I will not undertake to give a formal semantics for singular terms of other kinds. (Many ideas for relating natural language sentences to contexts in my sense can be obtained from Discourse Representation Theory, as developed by Kamp and Reyle 1993.)

While in the simple story I told in chapter 3, the content of the context is entirely dictated by the goals of the conversation and the external situation, in fact matters are not quite so simple. Sometimes arbitrary decisions have to be made. As I have already noted (in chapter 5), the use of verbs of motion may require a reference point, which allows us to choose between "come" and "go". It may not always matter much which reference point is chosen so long as the several interlocutors all agree on the same one. Likewise, if we want to create a link between sentences by means of demonstrative pronouns then we may have to make an arbitrary choice among possible pronouns. So for example, we might suppose that a context contains **this is F**, **this is G**, and **that is H**, when we could just as well have supposed that it contains **that is F**, **that is G**, and **this is H**. In that case, the content of the context will be determined by the choices that interlocutors make in forming their sentences.

(This is the element of "free choice" that I referred to at the end of chapter 5.)

In addition, I have been supposing that the content of the context pertinent to a conversation is dictated by the goals of the conversation and the external circumstances irrespective of what may be in the heads of the interlocutors; but that is not entirely correct either. Sometimes when a demonstrative pronoun has to be chosen—for purposes of linking sentences—the choice is not entirely arbitrary. Rather, we may find that there is a certain similarity between the present situation and some other situation in the past in which some singular term has been chosen, and for that reason we use the same one. Returning, finally, to the topic of proper names, I suggest that that is what is special about proper names, such as "Esther" and "Las Vegas". They are demonstrative pronouns that we choose by reason of a certain similarity between the present situation and some prior situation in which that demonstrative pronoun was used. In particular, they are demonstrative pronouns that we choose by reason of a similarity between situations with respect to the individuals (persons, cities, and so on) involved.

In this framework, we can understand a question about the reference of a singular term as a question about the content of the context. If one person says, "That one is good", and another person asks, "Which one?", or "Which one is 'that one'?", or "Which one are you referring to as 'that one'?", then what an answer has to do is, in effect, establish the existence of a suitable identity in the context. For example, if the context contains "*This* is on the left" and "*That* is on the right", then an answer to such questions will suffice if it establishes that "That one = *this*" belongs to the context. The speaker might establish just that by answering, "That one is the one on the left".

Let us now add quantifiers to the simple language introduced in chapter 3. So our simple language will now contain sentences of the form **for all x F** and **for some x F**, where **F** is a formula that may contain the unbound variable **x**. As I mentioned in chapter 3, for every additional logical device that we wish to countenance in our language, we will have to add some complication to our account of contexts. In the case of quantifiers, that complication is that every context must be accompanied by a *domain*. Here we will think of a domain as a set of demonstrative pronouns, not a set of objects such as the demonstrative pronouns might, according to the tradition, be said to denote. Since we are thinking of demonstrative pronouns as linking devices, the objects that such demonstrative pronouns might be said to denote just do not enter into the context-logical account of logical validity. Formally, then, we may define a *Q-context* as a pair consisting of a primitive context and a set of demonstrative pronouns including at least every demonstrative pronoun that occurs in any literal in the primitive context. That is, a *Q-context* Γ is a pair $\langle B_\Gamma, N_\Gamma \rangle$. B_Γ, called the *base* of Γ, is a primitive context as defined in chapter 3, that is, a set of literals such that not both **p** and **not p** belong. N_Γ, the *domain* of Γ, is a set of demonstrative pronouns including every demonstrative pronoun that occurs in any member of B_Γ, as well as perhaps others in addition.

Given this formal definition of Q-contexts, we can state the conditions under which sentences, including quantified sentences, are assertible or deniable. An atomic sentence **p** is assertible in a Q-context Γ if **p** is a member of B$_\Gamma$; an atomic sentence **p** is deniable in Γ if **not p** is a member of B$_\Gamma$. A sentence of the form **not p** is assertible in a Q-context Γ if **p** is deniable in Γ; **not p** is deniable in Γ if **p** is assertible in Γ. A sentence of the form **(p or q)** is assertible in a Q-context Γ if either **p** is assertible in Γ or **q** is assertible in Γ; **(p or q)** is deniable in Γ if both **p** and **q** are deniable in Γ. To these conditions we now add: A sentence of the form **for all x F** is assertible in a Q-context Γ if for every **n** in the set N$_\Gamma$, **Fn/x** is assertible in Γ. A sentence of the form **for all x F** is deniable in a Q-context Γ if there is some demonstrative pronoun **n** such that **Fn/x** is deniable in Γ. A sentence of the form **for some x F** is assertible in Γ if for some **n**, **Fn/x** is assertible in Γ; **for some x F** is deniable in Γ if for every **n** in N$_\Gamma$, **Fn/x** is deniable in Γ. Finally, the closure clause: No sentence is assertible or deniable in a Q-context unless its assertibility or deniability is sanctioned by one of these conditions.

For example, suppose the context Γ is as follows:

B$_\Gamma$ = {*a* is red. *b* is red. *a* is not a cube. *b* is a cube. *a* is large.}

N$_\Gamma$ = {*a*, *b*}.

In that case, "*a* is red" and "*b* is red" are both assertible in Γ. So no matter which demonstrative pronoun in N$_\Gamma$ we choose, the result of substituting that demonstrative pronoun for "*x*" in "*x* is red" is assertible in Γ. So "For all *x*, *x* is red" is assertible in Γ. However, since "*a* is a cube" is deniable in Γ, "For all *x*, *x* is a cube" is deniable in Γ. By contrast, "For all *x*, *x* is large" is neither assertible nor deniable in Γ. It is not assertible because "b is large" is not assertible. It is not deniable because neither "a is large" nor "b is large" is deniable and "a" and "b" are the only demonstrative pronouns in the domain.

As I explained in chapter 3, once we have given the formal definition of a type of context, we still have to go on to give the *substantive* theory of contexts of that type, by explaining what it takes for a given context formally so defined to qualify as the context pertinent to a conversation. (In doing this I make good on the promise at the end of chapter 4 to give a context-logical account of the domain of discourse.) The substantive theory of Q-contexts simply extends the substantive theory of primitive contexts, thus: First, if B_Γ is the primitive context for a given conversation, then N_Γ is a set of demonstrative pronouns including every demonstrative pronoun in B_Γ. But this first point is not quite the end of the story, since we also wish to allow that the domain for a context may contain additional demonstrative pronouns that do not occur in any member of the base for the context. The effect of allowing the domain for a context to contain such "extra" demonstrative pronouns is to block the assertibility of every universal quantification in that particular context. So the substantive theory of Q-contexts has to include something about the circumstances under which no universal quantification should qualify as assertible in a context.

There are perhaps various circumstances under which we should expect to find such an extra pronoun in the domain for the context pertinent to a conversation. One such situation might be one in which conversations are ordered in a series and each conversation in the series has its own context which yields to the next in the series as the conversation moves forward. If we think of these conversations as yielding empirical discoveries, then we might expect assertibility to exhibit a kind of monotonicity with respect to the whole sequence of contexts, so that what is assertible in any one member of the series remains assertible in all subsequent contexts. Accordingly, the content of earlier contexts might, so to speak, anticipate the content of subsequent contexts, and so, since universal generalizations at an early stage might be subject to counterexamples later on, the domain for a context early in the sequence might contain extra pronouns that deprive all universal generalizations of assertibility in that context. Such extra pronouns might be said to represent the relevant unknown.

The validity of existential generalization is an immediate consequence of the assertibility conditions for existential quantifications. If **Fn/x** is assertible in a context Γ, then that is enough to satisfy the sufficient condition for the assertibility of **for some x F** in Γ. However, universal instantiation is invalid. It can easily happen that a sentence of the form **for all x F** is assertible in a context Γ, but some instance **Fn/x** is not assertible in Γ. That will be the case when for all **m** in N_Γ, **Fm/x** is assertible in Γ, so that **for all x F** is assertible, but **n** is not a member of N_Γ, so that **Fn/x** is not assertible. In the example, discussed above, "For all x, x is red" is assertible in Γ, but "c is red" is not assertible in Γ.

8   Conditionals

A *conditional* is a sentence of the form "If"ˆpˆ"then"ˆq, such as "If Fido is a dog, then Fido is a mammal". What kind of relation between Fido's being a dog and Fido's being a mammal do we posit if we assert such a sentence? One common idea has been that a conditional sentence expresses the validity of an inference rule. Thus "If Fido is a dog, then Fido is a mammal" expresses the validity of the inference from "Fido is a dog" to "Fido is a mammal" (Brandom 1994). The obvious problem with this theory is that it does not apply to most of the conditionals we assert. For instance, someone might say, "If you turn left at the next corner, you will see a blue house at the end of the street." This obviously does not mean that in any situation whatsoever in which one accepts the premise "You turn left at the next corner" one may draw the conclusion "You will see a blue house at the end of the street". Still, one might maintain that in some sense any conditional offers a rule of inference that is supposed to be valid *in the context in which it is uttered*. That is the theory of conditionals that I will develop in this chapter.

First, a bit of terminology. In a conditional "If"ˆpˆ"then"ˆq, p is the *antecedent*, and q is the *consequent*. (But in qˆ"only if"ˆp, q is the antecedent and p is the consequent.) For the present, my subject is just *indicative* conditionals, such as "If it fell, then it broke". Later in the chapter, I will distinguish between these and *subjunctive* conditionals, such as "If it *had fallen*, then it *would have broken*".

In elementary logic courses, one stipulates that the *material* conditional is a conditional that is true if and only if either the antecedent is false or the consequent is true. Consequently, if **(if p then q)** is a material conditional, then it is true under exactly the same conditions as **(either not p or q)**. Thus one simple theory of the English indicative conditional is that it is the material conditional. One good thing about this theory is that it confirms the fact that sentences of these two forms seem to be *inter-inferable*. That is:

I. **(if p then q)** implies **(either not p or q)**.

II. **(either not p or q)** implies **(if p then q)**.

Proposition I seems fairly indisputable, even though some studied systems of logic do render it false. Proposition II has been disputed on the basis of some indirect arguments, but as far as I know, no one has ever produced any persuasive counterexamples to this form of argument in which **p** and **q** are conditional-free (that is, do not contain "if-then"). For example, "Either he won't find out or he will be insulted" implies "If he finds out, then he will be insulted". If there are just two possibilities, namely, that he won't find out and that he will be insulted, then if he will find out, so that one of those possibilities, namely, that he does not find out, is ruled out, then the only remaining possibility is that he will be insulted. However, if **q** can be a conditional, then we seem to have a counterexample in the inference from "Either *A* will not take half or if *B* takes half then *C* takes half" to "If *A* takes half, then if *B* takes half then *C* takes half".

One good reason to deny that indicative conditionals are material conditionals is that if they are, then certain arguments will turn out valid that surely are not valid. For example:

III. *Negation of a conditional*

Prem: It is not the case that if I am a millionaire then I drive a Honda.

Conc: I am a millionaire and I do not drive a Honda.

Clearly, the conclusion does not follow from the premise. But it would follow if we said that an indicative conditional is true if and only if either the antecedent is false or the consequent is true, for then the premise, which is the negation of an indicative conditional, would be true if and only if "I am a millionaire" were true and "I drive a Honda" were false, which is exactly the condition under which the conclusion would be true. For another example:

IV. *Adams's switch example*

Prem: If you throw both switch A and switch B, then the motor will start.

Conc: Either if you throw switch A then the motor will start, or if you throw switch B then the motor will start.

In this example (from Adams 1965), the premise might easily be true, if throwing both switches is sufficient to start the motor, but the conclusion may well be false if throwing switch A is not sufficient and throwing switch B is not sufficient. So the argument is not valid. But again, if indicative conditionals such as these are material conditionals, then this argument must be valid, as the reader may verify. So indicative conditionals are not material conditionals.

From this refutation of the identification of indicative conditionals with material conditionals, we may draw some general conclusions. In general, any adequate theory of the semantics of indicative conditionals has to meet the following conditions: It must show that I holds and that II holds, at least in the case in which **p** and **q** do not themselves contain conditionals, and it must show that arguments such as III and IV are invalid. I now want to argue that the propositional approach to logical validity cannot meet these conditions.

On the assumption that the propositional approach yields some kind of sentential logic, the propositional approach will have to respect a principle of compositionality, according to which the proposition expressed by a sentence in a context c is a definable function of the propositions expressed by its sentential components. (This is not what is called compositionality in general.) For example, if we think of propositions as sets of possible worlds, we might hold that $[\textbf{not } \textbf{p}]_c$ is the set of worlds w such that w is not a member of $[\textbf{p}]_c$ and that $[(\textbf{p or q})]_c$ is the set of worlds w such that w belongs either to $[\textbf{p}]_c$ or to $[\textbf{q}]_c$ or both. In this way we may obtain such results as that **p** and **not p** are inconsistent and that **p** implies **(p or q)**.

As a consequence of this compositionality, if any two sentences express the same proposition in every context, then we can substitute the one for the other in any sentence in any argument, and if the original argument was logically valid, then the resulting argument will be logically valid as well. For example, if **(p or q)** logically implies **s** in the sense that applies to sentences, then for all contexts c, $[\textbf{(p or q)}]_c$ implies $[\textbf{s}]_c$ in the sense that applies to propositions; so that if for all c, $[\textbf{p}]_c = [\textbf{r}]_c$, then for all c, $[\textbf{(r or q)}]_c$ implies $[\textbf{s}]_c$ in the sense that applies to propositions, in which case, **(r or q)** implies **s** in the sense that applies to sentences.

Now suppose that we identify propositions with sets of possible worlds and define logical implication as a relation of set inclusion, thus: A set of propositions A logically implies a proposition q if the intersection of the propositions in A is set-theoretically included in q. In particular, $[\textbf{p}]_c$ implies $[\textbf{q}]_c$ if and only if $[\textbf{p}]_c \subseteq [\textbf{q}]_c$ (i.e., $[\textbf{p}]_c$ is a subset of $[\textbf{q}]_c$). In that case, for any pair of sentences **p** and **r**, if each logically implies the other (they are *interinferable*), then for every context c, $[\textbf{p}]_c \subseteq [\textbf{q}]_c$ and $[\textbf{q}]_c \subseteq [\textbf{p}]_c$, in which case, $[\textbf{p}]_c = [\textbf{q}]_c$; in other words, **p** and **q** express the same proposition in every context.

Given these results, the following principle immediately follows:

The Equivalence Principle: For any pair of sentences **p** and **q**, if each logically implies the other, then for any argument in which **p** occurs, either standing alone or as a component of some sentence, if that argument is valid, then the argument that results from substituting **q** for **p** will be valid too.

If logical implication is not defined in terms of propositional inclusion, that is, if we do not say that $[\mathbf{p}]_c$ implies $[\mathbf{q}]_c$ if and only if $[\mathbf{p}]_c$ is a subset of $[\mathbf{q}]_c$, then the equivalence principle cannot be proved so handily, for then the interinferability of two sentences does not demonstrate the identity of the propositions they express. For some purposes (such as explicating the semantics of belief-sentences), theorists have wanted to individuate propositions in such a way that two of them could be distinct though each logically implies the other (e.g., Salmon 1986). This can have the result that interinferable sentences are not intersubstitutable everywhere. In particular, they may not be intersubstitutable in "that"-clauses (as in "John believes that Hesperus appears in the evening"). As far as I know, such a conception of propositions has never been put to use in a general theory of logical implication. Even such theorists have supposed that in all "nonintensional" sentential contexts the replacement of any sentence by any interinferable sentence preserves validity. (Thus, Kaplan, while distinguishing between "contents" that are true in exactly the same possible worlds, holds that such contents are "equivalent" [1989, p. 502].) So since only nonintensional contexts will be at issue in this chapter, we can safely take for granted that the propositional conception of logical validity will respect the equivalence principle. In particular, on the leading theory of conditionals, due to Stalnaker (1968) and Lewis (1973), the substitution of an interinferable sentence for the antecedent or consequent of a conditional will always preserve validity.

Given the equivalence principle, we cannot accept principles I and II while denying the validity of arguments III and IV. To see this, consider the following argument, comparable to IV:

V. Prem: Either you do not throw both switch A and switch B or the motor will start.

   Conc: Either you do not throw switch A or the motor will start, or you do not throw switch B or the motor will start.

This argument is surely valid. But by the equivalence principle, if I and II hold and V is valid, then IV should be valid too. But it is not. So we cannot both accept I and II and deny the validity of IV. Similarly, we cannot both accept I and II and deny the validity of III. So since the equivalence principle is part of the propositional conception of logical validity, that conception of logical validity is mistaken. Some theorists assert the validity of III and IV (this is Lewis's position as regards indicative conditionals). Others (such as Stalnaker 1968, 1975) reject proposition II. But both parties are mistaken, as we have seen.

Let us consider, then, whether we can do better if we adopt the context-logical conception of logical validity and treat conditionals as context-relative rules of inference. The first step is to introduce a more elaborate definition of

contexts. So far, I have defined primitive contexts and
Q-contexts. Since I will not get as far as combining conditionals with quantifiers, we can set aside the domains of
discourse that characterize Q-contexts. But now we want
to define a kind of context that may contain other contexts
as members. Formally, a *primitive* context remains what
I said in chapter 3: a set of literals such that not both **p**
and **not p** are members. I will call the necessary innovation
a *multicontext*. We may define the *set* of multicontexts by
the following construction: The first layer of multicontexts
consists of the set of all subsets of the set of primitive contexts. To form the second layer of multicontexts, we take
the union of the first layer of multicontexts and the set of
all subsets of the first layer. To form the third layer of
multicontexts, we take the union of the second layer of
multicontexts and the set of all subsets of the second layer.
And so on. A *multicontext* is then any member of any of these
layers.

In addition to this formal account of multicontexts we
need a substantive account. Here the basic idea will be that
a context may consist of several other contexts because each
of these several contexts is equally relevant to the conversation. There are various reasons why this might be so. One
is that the course of action we will choose through our conversation affects which primitive context holds, and, inasmuch as the purpose of the conversation may be to decide
which course of action to take, it may be the case that none
of these primitive contexts has any privilege over the others.
For example, suppose we are planning a trip and want to
visit friends. Helen will be in Columbus both today and

tomorrow. But Jerry will be in Columbus today and in Indianapolis tomorrow. Then the multicontext pertinent to our conversation might look something like this:

$\Gamma = \{\Delta_1, \Delta_2, \Delta_3\}$

$\Delta_1 = \{$We go to Columbus today. We go to Indianapolis tomorrow. We see Helen today. We do not see Jerry today. We see Jerry tomorrow.$\}$

$\Delta_2 = \{$We go to Indianapolis today. We go to Columbus tomorrow. We do not see Jerry today. We see Helen tomorrow. We do not see Jerry tomorrow.$\}$

$\Delta_3 = \{$We go to Columbus today. We stay in Columbus tomorrow. We see Jerry today. We see Helen tomorrow. We do not see Jerry tomorrow.$\}$

Yet another possibility is that we are concerned with future events which are not affected by our actions, but which are so unpredictable that for our purposes each of several primitive contexts is equally pertinent to our conversation. For example, suppose we are placing bets on the outcome of a tennis tournament. Our conversation takes place after the quarterfinals have been played, but before the semifinals. The four remaining players are Venus Williams (v), her sister, Serena Williams (s), Martina Hingis (m), and Lindsay Davenport (l), with v facing m, and s facing l. In that case, our multicontext, in outline, is:

$\{\{v$ beats $m.$ s beats $l.$ v meets $s. \ldots\}$, $\{v$ beats $m.$ l beats $s.$ v meets $l. \ldots\}$, $\{m$ beats $v,$ s beats $l,$ m meets $s. \ldots\}$, $\{m$ beats $v,$ l beats $s,$ m meets $l. \ldots\}\}$

(Here the ellipses indicate the negations of all other results, such as "*m* does not meet *s*.") Another possibility is that our purposes are didactic, so that while exactly one primitive context would pertain to our conversation if the goal of our conversation were practical, in fact each of several different primitive contexts equally well pertains to our conversation. For example, in a situation in which someone is near a lake, teaching a fledgling hunter how to track antelope, the pertinent multicontext might be something like this:

{{Tracks are in the mud. Antelope are nearby.}, {Tracks are not in the mud. Antelope are not nearby.}}

With these last two cases, the theory of contexts makes a concession to the epistemic capacities of agents. The context comprises several primitive contexts just because, when compared according to epistemic criteria, they are, or might be, equally good candidates for being *the* primitive context pertinent to the conversation. Even so, multicontexts remain objective in that the members of the multicontext must be equal not just from the point of view of this or that actual agent but from the point of view of a hypothetical, reasonable agent conceived of as present on the occasion.

Yet another possibility is that the context must be, so to speak, respectful of each of several points of view. For example, suppose an MD is firmly convinced that her patient does not have a brain tumor, but her patient, thinking of his frequent headaches, still suspects that he may have one. In this case, the pertinent multicontext may contain a primitive context representing the doctor's point of view and another one representing the patient's point of view:

{{You do not have a tumor. Our tests do not show a tumor.},
{You have a tumor. Our tests do not show a tumor.}}

In other words, the MD, in talking to the patient, can rightfully take for granted that her tests do not show a tumor, but may not take for granted that there is no tumor. Yet another possibility is that there may just not be a single smallest set of literals such that every action in accordance with it is a good way of achieving the goal of the conversation. In that case, the multicontext may contain every such smallest set.

As for assertibility conditions, let us first consider the assertibility conditions of nonconditional sentences. As in chapter 3, we will say that an atomic sentence **p** is assertible in a *primitive* context Γ if it is a member of Γ; and an atomic sentence **p** is deniable in a *primitive* context Γ if **not p** is a member of Γ. Further, any sentence **p** (of any form) is assertible in a *multicontext* Γ if for every context Δ in Γ, **p** is assertible in Δ; likewise, **p** is deniable in Γ if for every context Δ in Γ, **p** is deniable in Δ. Further, any sentence of the form **not p** is assertible in a multicontext Γ if **p** is deniable in Γ; **not p** is deniable in Γ if **p** is assertible in Γ. A sentence of the form **(p or q)** is assertible in Γ if either **p** is assertible in Γ or **q** is assertible in Γ; **(p or q)** is deniable in Γ if both **p** and **q** are deniable in Γ. On this account, there may be two ways in which a sentence might qualify as assertible. For instance, **(p or q)** will be assertible in Γ if one of the disjuncts, either **p** or **q**, is assertible in Γ; but in addition **(p or q)** will be assertible in Γ if for every member Δ of Γ, **(p or q)** is assertible in Δ (which might be the case because for every member Δ of Γ, either **p** is assertible in Δ or **q** is assertible in Δ).

The next step, which we can take before we define the assertibility conditions for conditionals, is to see how we can define a kind of context-relative validity in terms of multicontexts. Let S be a set of sentences, the premises, and let **q** be a sentence, the conclusion. Logical validity simpliciter is preservation of assertibility in a multicontext: The inference from S to **q** is logically valid if and only if for every multicontext Γ, if every member of S is assertible in Γ, then **q** is assertible in Γ too. Context-relative logical validity is defined as follows: The inference from S to **q** is logically valid *relative* to a multicontext Γ (that is, S logically implies **q** relative to Γ) if and only if for every context Δ (primitive or multi) in or identical to Γ, if every member of S is assertible in Δ, then **q** is assertible in Δ too.

For example, suppose Γ = {{**p**, **not r**, **s**}, {**q**, **not r**, **s**}, {**p**, **q**}}. Then relative to Γ, {**(p or q)**, **not r**} logically implies **s**. For if we find any context in or identical to Γ in which **(p or q)** and **not r** are both assertible, we find that **s** is assertible in that context too. The premises, **(p or q)** and **not r**, are both assertible in {**p**, **not r**, **s**} and {**q**, **not r**, **s**}, and **s** is assertible in those primitive contexts too. Although the conclusion **s** is not assertible in {**p**, **q**} and is not assertible in Γ itself, so too the premise **not r** is not assertible in those contexts.

Assertibility and deniability conditions for conditionals may now be formulated as follows. A conditional **(if p then q)** is assertible in a multicontext Γ if for every context Δ in or identical to Γ, if **p** is assertible in Δ, then so is **q**; in other words, {**p**} logically implies **q** relative to Γ. And a conditional **(if p then q)** is deniable in a multicontext Γ if there is a context Δ in or identical to Γ such that **p** is assertible in Δ and **q** is deniable in Δ. Conditionals are neither assertible nor deniable in primitive contexts. These are sufficient conditions, not necessary conditions. Necessary conditions on assertibility and deniability are secured by the usual closure clause.

Thus, in the first of our four examples above, the sentence "If we go to Indianapolis today, then we see Helen tomorrow" is assertible in Γ, because the only context in or identical to Γ in which "We go to Indianapolis today" is assertible is Δ_2, and "We see Helen tomorrow" is assertible in Δ_2 too. Likewise, "If we go to Columbus today, then we see Jerry today or we see Jerry tomorrow" is assertible in Γ because there are two members of Γ in which "We go to Columbus today" is assertible, namely, Δ_1 and Δ_3, and in Δ_3 "We see Jerry today" is assertible, and in Δ_1 "We see Jerry tomorrow" is assertible. On the other hand, "If we go to Indianapolis today, then we see Jerry today" is deniable in Γ, because "We go to Indianapolis today" is assertible in Δ_2 and "We see Jerry today" is deniable in Δ_2. But "If we go to Columbus today, then we see Helen tomorrow" is neither assertible nor deniable in Γ. It is not assertible because "We go to Columbus today" is assertible in Δ_1, but "We see Helen tomorrow" is not assertible in Δ_1. But it is also not deniable because there is no context in Γ where "We go to Columbus today" is assertible and "We see Helen tomorrow" is deniable.

On this theory, proposition II, restricted to conditional-free substituends, is confirmed. To show this we must first make two observations. The first is that if a sentence **p** is conditional-free, then it is assertible in a multicontext if and only if it is assertible in every member of that multicontext. This can be proved by induction on the complexity of sentences. The second necessary observation is that if **(not p or q)** and **p** are both assertible in a context Γ and **p** is conditional-free, then **q** is assertible in Γ too. This can be proved by induction on the levels of multicontexts. With these results in hand, we can prove proposition II as follows: Suppose **(not p or q)** is conditional-free and is assertible in arbitrary multicontext Γ. We need to show that **(if p then q)** is assertible in Γ, for which it suffices to show that for all contexts Δ in or identical to Γ, if **p** is assertible in Δ, then **q** is assertible in Δ too. Let Δ be a context in or identical to Γ, and suppose **p** is assertible in Δ. Case 1: Δ = Γ. By our second observation, **q** is assertible in Δ. Case 2: Δ is a member of Γ. By our first observation, **(not p or q)** is assertible in Δ. So by our second observation, **q** is assertible in Δ.

Furthermore, arguments III and IV are invalid, as desired. Consider for example just IV, Adams's switch example. Suppose:

Γ = {Δ₁, Δ₂, Δ₃}

Δ₁ = {You throw switch A. You throw switch B. The motor will start.}

Δ₂ = {You throw switch A. You do not throw switch B. The motor will not start.}

Δ₃ = {You do not throw switch A. You throw switch B. The motor will not start.}

The premise, "If you throw switch A and you throw switch B, then the motor will start" is assertible in Γ, because Δ₁ is the only context in or identical to Γ where the antecedent "You throw switch A and you throw switch B" is assertible, and the consequent "The motor will start" is assertible in Δ_1 too. But "If you throw switch A, then the motor will start" is not assertible in Γ, because there is a member of Γ, namely, Δ_2, where "You throw switch A" is assertible and "The motor will start" is not assertible. Similarly, "If you throw switch B, then the motor will start" is not assertible, in virtue of Δ_3. So the conclusion of IV, "Either if you throw switch A then the motor will start or if you throw switch B then the motor will start" is not assertible in Γ. (In fact, it is deniable.)

I said at the start that proposition I, according to which **(if p then q)** implies **(not p or q)**, is fairly indisputable. But actually, this inference is not a pure expression of the conception of conditionals as context-relative rules of inference and is not valid according to the theory developed so far. The reason is that a conditional might qualify as assertible in a multicontext Γ just by virtue of there not being any context in or identical to Γ in which the antecedent is assertible. Nonetheless, we can define a closely related sense of validity according to which this inference is valid. To this end, let us define a concept of *salient assertibility*. To define the concept of salient assertibility, we rewrite all of the conditions on assertibility and deniability other than those pertaining to conditionals by substituting "saliently assertible" and "saliently deniable" for "assertible" and "deniable", respectively, throughout. As for conditionals, we say that a conditional **(if p then q)** is *saliently assertible* in a multicontext Γ if for every Δ in or identical to Γ, if **p** is saliently assertible in Δ, then **q** is assertible in Δ, *and* for every context

Δ in Γ, **p** is either saliently assertible or saliently deniable in
Δ. A conditional **(if p then q)** is *saliently deniable* in a multicontext Γ if there is a context Δ in or identical to Γ such that
p is saliently assertible in Δ and **q** is deniable in Δ. Next, we
redefine logical validity (simpliciter) thus: An inference
from a setof sentences S to a sentence **q** is logically valid
(simpliciter) if and only if for every multicontext Γ, if every
member of S is *saliently* assertible in Γ, then **q** is *assertible* in
Γ too. Further, we say that an inference from S to **q** is logically valid *relative* to a multicontext Γ if and only if for every
context Δ (primitive or multi) in or identical to Γ, if every
member of S is saliently assertible in Δ, **q** is assertible in Δ
too. With these modifications in place, one can prove (by
induction on the levels of multicontexts) that proposition I
holds as well.

My theory declares certain arguments to be valid that
some other popular theories declare to be invalid. For
instance, while on Stalnaker's theory of conditionals (1968),
all of the following three arguments are invalid, on my
theory they are all valid:

VI.   *Vacuous Antecedent*

    Prem: I will meet you tomorrow.

    Conc: If I die tonight, then I will meet you tomorrow.

VII. *Strengthening of the Antecedent*

    Prem: If this match is struck, then it will light.

    Conc: If this match is wet and is struck, then it will
           light.

VIII. *Hypothetical Syllogism*

> Prem: If the Democrats lose control of the House, then
> the Republicans will be in control.
>
> Prem: If the Socialist Labor Party gains a majority in
> the House, then the Democrats will lose control.
>
> Conc: If the Socialist Labor Party gains a majority in
> the House, then the Republicans will be in
> control.

As for VI, one must bear in mind that when we ask
whether this is valid, we are asking whether we should
accept the conclusion on the assumption that we accept the
premise. So suppose we do accept the premise. Thus we take
for granted that I will meet you tomorrow. If we take that
for granted, and do not abandon that assumption when
we go to evaluate the conclusion, then we will accept the
conclusion as well. On the assumption that I *will* meet you
tomorrow, my dying tonight is not a possibility we even
countenance, so that the conditional is in a way vacuous. In
evaluating this argument, we must avoid the temptation to
alter the context in which we evaluate the conclusion to one
in which my dying tonight is a live possibility. In such a
context we would not accept the premise "I will meet you
tomorrow" in the first place.

Likewise, if we suppose that the premise of VII is acceptable, then we must be ignoring the possibility that the match
is wet. But in that case the conclusion of the inference is
acceptable just because the antecedent describes no possibility that we even countenance. Against this, it might be

said that the conclusion would be misleading if the basis for accepting it were only the acceptability of the premise. If someone asserts, "If this match is wet and struck, then it will light," someone might get the idea that the match in question is a special kind of match that will light even when wet. But that is no reason to doubt the validity of this inference. Likewise, no one should doubt the validity of the inference from "Harry will do it" to "Either Harry will do it or Jane will do it" just because the conclusion might be misleading (suggesting that there is some chance that Harry might not do it and Jane will).

As for VIII, here the problem is not that the conclusion does not follow from the premises but that the premises are unlikely to be acceptable in any single context. The suggestion that this argument is invalid rests on an equivocation, whereby the first premise is evaluated positively with respect to a context in which the Socialist Labor Party is not a contender for majority party, but the second premise is evaluated positively with respect to a context in which the Socialist Labor Party is a contender. We might imagine a strange context in which both premises receive a positive value—one in which the members of the Socialist Labor Party are all Republicans—but in such a context the conclusion will receive a positive evaluation as well.

The illusion of invalidity in these arguments may be enhanced by a tendency to use an indicative conditional where a more discriminating speaker would choose a subjunctive conditional. This tendency may be due in part to the fact that in many cases where we can use a subjunctive conditional, we can use an indicative conditional just as well. Such a confusion of indicative with subjunctive would lead us to deem VI, VII, and VIII invalid, because in fact if we were to rewrite these arguments in the subjunctive they would be invalid. From the assumption that I will meet you tomorrow, it indeed does not follow that if I *were* to die tonight then I *would* meet you tomorrow.

The context-logical theory of subjunctive conditionals begins with another enhancement to the concept of context. The necessary enhancement is that we will now think of the multicontexts relative to which we evaluate sentences as assertible or deniable as themselves belonging to accompanying multicontexts, called *structures*. Strictly speaking, then, we will not evaluate a sentence relative to a multicontext alone but only relative to a pair $\langle \Gamma, \Theta \rangle$, consisting of a multicontext Γ and a structure Θ, itself a multicontext, where Γ is in or identical to Θ.

We will then say that an atomic sentence **p** is assertible in $\langle \Gamma, \Theta \rangle$ if Γ is a primitive context and **p** is a member of Γ; and an atomic sentence **p** is deniable in $\langle \Gamma, \Theta \rangle$ if Γ is a primitive context and **not p** is a member of Γ. Further, if Γ is a multicontext, then any sentence **p** is assertible in $\langle \Gamma, \Theta \rangle$ if for every context Δ in Γ, **p** is assertible in $\langle \Delta, \Gamma \rangle$; likewise, **p** is deniable in $\langle \Gamma, \Theta \rangle$ if for every context Δ in Γ, **p** is deniable in $\langle \Delta, \Gamma \rangle$. The conditions under which negations and disjunctions are assertible or deniable in $\langle \Gamma, \Theta \rangle$ are formulated in the usual way. As for indicative conditionals, we will say that **(if p then q)** is assertible in $\langle \Gamma, \Theta \rangle$ if for every Δ in or identical to Γ, if **p** is assertible in $\langle \Delta, \Gamma \rangle$, then **q** is assertible in $\langle \Delta, \Gamma \rangle$; **(if p then q)** is deniable in $\langle \Gamma, \Theta \rangle$ if there is a Δ in or identical to Γ such that **p** is assertible in $\langle \Delta, \Gamma \rangle$ and **q** is deniable in $\langle \Delta, \Gamma \rangle$.

We will say that an inference from a set of sentences S to a sentence **q** is logically valid relative to Γ if and only if for every Δ in or identical to Γ, if every member of S is assertible in $\langle \Delta, \Gamma \rangle$, then **q** is assertible in $\langle \Delta, \Gamma \rangle$ too. We will say that an inference from a set of sentences S to a sentence **q** is logically valid (simpliciter) if and only if for every multicontext Γ, the inference from S to **q** is valid relative to Γ. (For simplicity, I am ignoring the salience conditions.)

I will represent subjunctive conditionals, awkwardly, as having the form **(if it were the case that p, then it would be the case that q)**. We say that one multicontext is *smaller* than another if the first is a *proper* subset of the second. (Every set is considered to be a subset of itself, but none is a *proper* subset of itself.) The sufficient conditions on the assertibility of a subjunctive conditional relative to a multicontext Γ and a structure Θ can now be explained as follows: Case 1: There is a multicontext Ω in or identical to Θ such that Γ is a subset of Ω (not necessarily a proper subset) and there is a context Δ (primitive or multi) in or identical to Ω such that **p** is assertible in Δ. In that case, **(if it were the case that p, then it would be the case that q)** is assertible in $\langle \Gamma, \Theta \rangle$ if for *every smallest* multicontext Ω meeting this condition, the corresponding indicative conditional **(if p then q)** is assertible in $\langle \Omega, \Theta \rangle$. Case 2: The condition of Case 1 is not satisfied; there is no such multicontext Ω. In that case, **(if it were the case that p, then it would be the case that q)** is assertible in $\langle \Gamma, \Theta \rangle$. In other words, to decide whether a subjunctive conditional is assertible in a given multicontext Γ, we have to reach just high enough up into the containing structure Θ to find a multicontext Ω such that Γ is a subset of Ω and the antecedent is assertible in some context that is either a member of or identical to Ω. If the corresponding indicative conditional is assertible in $\langle \Omega, \Theta \rangle$, then the subjunctive conditional is assertible in $\langle \Gamma, \Theta \rangle$.

Suppose that Γ is the multicontext pertinent to a conversation, Θ is the structure pertinent to the conversation, and Θ contains another multicontext Ω of which Γ is a subset. In whatever way the members of Γ are relevant to the conversation, the members of Ω should satisfy a less stringent standard of relevance to the conversation. So if we are trying to decide which action to take, and each member of Γ represents the context pertinent to some candidate course of action, then the members of Ω might represent the contexts pertinent to a broader range of possible actions. Or if each member of Γ represents a context pertinent to an interlocutor's point of view, then the members of Ω may represent the contexts pertinent to a broader range of points of view.

For example, returning to the trip-planning example above, it might be that there is another person we would not mind visiting, Polly, who will be in Indianapolis both today and tomorrow. In that case, the structure Θ containing Γ (the multicontext for this example specified above) might also contain Ω, where $\Omega = \{\Delta_1, \Delta_2, \Delta_3, \Delta_4\}$, where $\Delta_1, \Delta_2, \Delta_3$ are as before and

$\Delta_4 = \{$We go to Indianapolis today. We stay in Indianapolis tomorrow. We see Polly today. We see Jerry tomorrow. We do not see Jerry today.$\}$

$\Theta = \{\Gamma, \Omega\}$, Γ is a subset of Ω, and "We go to Indianapolis today and stay there tomorrow" is assertible in a member of Ω, namely, Δ_4, although Γ itself does not meet that condition. The indicative conditional, "If we go to Indianapolis today and stay there tomorrow, then we see Polly today" is assertible in Ω. So the subjunctive conditional "If we were to go to Indianapolis today and stay there tomorrow, then we would see Polly today and Jerry tomorrow" is assertible in $\langle \Gamma, \Theta \rangle$.

On this theory, the subjunctive versions of arguments VI, VII, and VIII are all invalid. For example, consider:

IX. *Strengthening of the Antecedent (subjunctive version)*

> Prem: If this match were struck, then it would light.
>
> Conc: If this match were wet and were struck, then it would light.

To see that this is invalid, suppose:

$\Theta = \{\Gamma_1, \Gamma_2\}$.

$\Gamma_1 = \{\Delta_1\}$, and $\Gamma_2 = \{\Delta_1, \Delta_2\}$.

$\Delta_1 = \{$This match is struck. This match is not wet. This match lights.$\}$.

$\Delta_2 = \{$This match is struck. This match is wet. This match does not light.$\}$.

We will see that the premise of IX is assertible in $\langle \Gamma_1, \Theta \rangle$ and the conclusion is not assertible in $\langle \Gamma_1, \Theta \rangle$. The smallest multicontext Ω in or identical to Θ such that Γ_1 is a subset of Ω and "This match is struck" is assertible in some context in or identical to Ω is Γ_1 itself. Relative to $\langle \Gamma_1, \Theta \rangle$, "If this match is struck, then this match lights" (the indicative conditional corresponding to the premise of IX) is assertible, because the contexts Λ in or equal to Γ_1 such that "This match is struck" is assertible in $\langle \Lambda, \Gamma_1 \rangle$ are Δ_1 and Γ_1 itself, and "This match lights" is assertible in both $\langle \Delta_1, \Gamma_1 \rangle$ and $\langle \Gamma_1, \Gamma_1 \rangle$. So the premise of IX, "If this match were struck, then it would light", is assertible in $\langle \Gamma_1, \Theta \rangle$. Γ_2 is the smallest multicontext in or identical to Θ such that Γ_1 is a subset of it and "This match is wet and struck" is assertible in some context in or identical to it. But "If this match is wet and struck, then it lights" (the indicative conditional corresponding to the conclusion of IX) is not assertible in $\langle \Gamma_2, \Omega \rangle$, because "This match is wet and struck" is assertible in $\langle \Delta_2, \Gamma_2 \rangle$, but "This match lights" is not assertible in $\langle \Delta_2, \Gamma_2 \rangle$. So the conclusion of IX is not assertible in $\langle \Gamma_1, \Theta \rangle$.

9   Truth

As we have seen, the theory of meaning underlying the received view of linguistic communication is formulated in terms of *truth*. Ironically, there is no widely accepted account of the meaning of the truth predicate itself. One thing that stands in the way of any simple account of the meaning of "true" is a classic enigma, the paradox of the liar. Such paradoxes are persistent if we take the basic semantic properties to be truth and falsehood. But, as I will argue in this chapter, they can be cleanly avoided if instead we take the basic semantic properties to be assertibility and deniability in a context and explain the semantics of "true" in terms of those.

Suppose we inscribe the following sentence, known as the *liar sentence*, and call it "λ":

(λ) λ is not true.

Given what is written above, it is just a plain fact that λ = "λ is not true". Given only this plain fact, we seem to be able to derive an explicit contradiction by the following *paradoxical reasoning*:

1. λ = "λ is not true". (A plain fact.)

2. Suppose λ is true.

3. Given 2, "λ is not true" is true. (From 1 and 2, by the laws of identity.)

4. Given 2, λ is not true. (From 3 by *semantic descent*.)

5. λ is not true. (From 2–4, by reductio ad absurdum.)

6. Suppose λ is not true.

7. Given 6, "λ is not true" is true. (From 6, by *semantic ascent*.)

8. Given 6, λ is true. (From 1 and 7, by the laws of identity.)

9. λ is true. (From 6–8, by a form of reductio ad absurdum.)

10. λ is true and λ is not true. (From 5 and 9.)

This conclusion is an explicit contradiction. The liar paradox is said to be a *semantic paradox*, since by reasoning about semantic properties such as truth we seem to derive a contradiction from plain facts.

When one first encounters the liar paradox, a natural first response is to think that there is something illegitimate in our "plain fact," in particular, in the assumption that a sentence can refer to itself. But no lasting solution results from simply forbidding this kind of direct self-reference, because other semantic paradoxes can be constructed without it. For example, consider the notecard paradox. On side A of a certain notecard is written just one sentence: "Every sentence on side B of this notecard is true". On side B of the notecard is written just this: "No sentence on side

A of this notecard is true". In this case, the pertinent plain facts are:

The sole sentence on side A = "Every sentence on side B of this notecard is true".

The sole sentence on side B = "No sentence on side A of this notecard is true".

From these two premises we can derive an explicit contradiction in much the same way we derived one from the premise that λ = "λ is not true". But neither the sentence on side A nor the sentence on side B refers directly to itself. Granted, each refers to itself indirectly, in that each refers to a sentence that in turn refers back to it, but that kind of self-reference cannot be forbidden, because it cannot be prevented from arising by accident.

Classically, the solution has been to deny the inferences from 3 to 4 and from 6 to 7. The first of these is an instance of the rule of semantic descent, which says that the inference from $\sigma^{\smallfrown}$"is true" to sentence s is valid if σ is the result of putting the sentence s in quotation marks. The second is an instance of the rule of semantic ascent, which says that the inference from s to $\sigma^{\smallfrown}$"is true" is valid if σ is the result of putting quotation marks around s. In applying semantic descent and semantic ascent to the sentence "λ is not true" (i.e., in letting s = "λ is not true"), we are in effect assuming that our object language (the language of the material in quotation marks) contains its own *nontruth* predicate, that is, a predicate that applies to a sentence, such as λ, if and only if the sentence is not true. So we have supposed that the object language contains some of its own semantic vocabulary.

Thus, the validity of semantic ascent and semantic descent might be denied by denying that a language can contain its own semantic vocabulary. One supposes that there is a hierarchy of languages each of which could be used to talk about the semantic properties of the language below it, but none of which could be used to talk about the semantic properties of itself. But (as Kripke argued in his 1975) this does not seem to be a very reasonable assumption, because in cases such as the notecard paradox, there does not seem to be any nonarbitrary way to decide which language is higher up in the hierarchy. (Which is higher, the language of the sentence on side A or the language of the sentence on side B?) Since semantic descent and semantic ascent are prima facie plausible, and I know no other reason to reject them, I think we have to accept that they are valid.

A nice feature of the propositional approach to logical validity is that it seems to offer at least the beginnings of a solution to the semantic paradoxes. A sentence is true in a context if it expresses a true proposition in that context, and a sentence is false in a context if it expresses a false proposition in that context, but there is no guarantee that a sentence will express a proposition in every context. The liar sentence λ, it may be said, is a sentence that expresses no proposition in any context in which λ = "λ is not true". Further, the sentence on side A of the notecard, namely, "Every sentence on side B is true", is a sentence that expresses no proposition in any context in which the sentence on side B is "No sentence on side A is true", and the sentence on side B of the notecard is a sentence that expresses no proposition in any context in which the sentence on side A is "Every sentence on side B is true".

Given this, we can diagnose the fallacy in our paradoxical reasoning as follows: All of the inferences are valid so long as the sentences at each step express propositions, but some of them are not valid otherwise. In particular, the reductio ad absurdum steps that we employed in our paradoxical reasoning above (steps 5 and 9) do not go through. For instance, the rule of reductio ad absurdum, which we have employed in step 5, tells us that if, from a set of sentences comprising the sentence **p** and the sentences in some set S, we can validly derive the sentence **not p**, then from S alone we can validly derive **not p**. In the present instance, **p** is "λ is true" (line 2) and S contains just "λ = 'λ is not true'" (line 1). But that principle holds only if **p** expresses a proposition in every context in which the members of S (if there are any) all express true propositions. Since, in this instance, **p** does not express a proposition in any context in which line 1 expresses a true proposition, inference by reductio ad absurdum is fallacious. To make good on this diagnosis, we would still have to construct a precise semantics in which we could demonstrate that the liar sentence does not express a proposition in any context (and, following the example of Kripke 1975, modifying his theory to accommodate context-relativity, we could do that).

If we take this approach, however, then sooner or later we will have to face up to a further problem. Quite generally, anyone who wishes to offer a diagnosis of the semantic paradoxes has to make sure that analogous paradoxes do not re-arise at the level of the semantic metalanguage in which the diagnosis is formulated. (This is something that many theorists grappling with the semantic paradoxes, such as Kripke 1975, Barwise and Etchemendy 1987, and Gupta and Belnap 1993, do not attempt to do. Simmons 1993 uses this as a tool against other theories, but it is not clear to me that he applies the same standard to his own theory.) The strategy proposed is to diagnose the semantic paradoxes in a semantic metalanguage that includes the three-place predicate "... expresses proposition ... in context. ..." The new problem is that further semantic paradoxes can be formulated in terms of this new predicate.

Consider the following sentence:

(γ) γ does not express a true proposition in *this* context.

We seem to be able to derive an explicit contradiction by means of the following second run of paradoxical reasoning:

1. γ = "γ does not express a true proposition in *this* context".

2. Suppose γ expresses a true proposition in *this* context.

3. Given 2, "γ does not express a true proposition in *this* context" expresses a true proposition in *this* context. (From 1 and 2.)

4. Given 2, γ does not express a true proposition in *this* context. (From 3, by a kind of semantic descent.)

5. γ does not express a true proposition in *this* context. (From 2–4, by reductio ad absurdum.)

6. Suppose γ does not express a true proposition in *this* context.

7. Given 6, "γ does not express a true proposition in *this* context" expresses a true proposition in *this* context. (From 6, by a kind of semantic ascent.)

8. Given 6, γ expresses a true proposition in *this* context. (From 1 and 7.)

9. γ expresses a true proposition in *this* context. (From 6–8, by a form of reductio ad absurdum.)

10. γ expresses a true proposition in *this* context and γ does not express a true proposition in *this* context. (From 5 and 9.)

This conclusion is an explicit contradiction.

Offhand, one might guess that we could diagnose a fallacy in this second run of paradoxical reasoning in the same way we diagnosed a fallacy in the first run of paradoxical reasoning (concerning λ), namely, by insisting that γ does not express a proposition in *this* context, the context of our own reasoning, so that the application of reductio ad absurdum in this reasoning is fallacious. Unfortunately, that strategy is not available here. (The remainder of this paragraph was inspired by Glanzberg 2001, p. 229.) The proposal is that we should conclude that γ does not express a proposition in *this* context. But that means, it seems, that in *this* context we ourselves should accept "γ does not express a proposition in *this* context". But by ordinary logic, "γ does not express a proposition in *this* context" implies "γ does not express a *true* proposition in *this* context". So if in *this* context we can accept "γ does not express a proposition in *this* context", then surely in *this* context we can also accept "γ does not express a *true* proposition in *this* context". But we can accept a sentence only if it expresses a proposition in the context in which we accept it. So the proposal requires us to conclude that "γ does not express a *true* proposition in *this* context" expresses a proposition in *this* context. But that sentence is itself γ. So the proposal commits us to the conclusion that γ does after all express a proposition in *this* context, contrary to what we ourselves are trying to say. How ironic!

Still, someone might think that there has to be a way to express, without contradicting ourselves, that γ does not express a proposition. Some philosophers have thought they could lay down as a general principle that:

(S) A sentence σ expresses a proposition (in a context) if and only if the sentence "The proposition that"ˆσˆ"is true if and only if"ˆσ does not contradict plain facts (in that context).

(See Schiffer 1996, pp. 163–166.) From (S) it follows that γ does not express a proposition in this context. To see this, suppose, for a reductio, that γ expresses a proposition in this context. But it is a plain fact in this context that γ = "γ does not express a true proposition in this context". So presumably the proposition γ expresses is the proposition that γ does not express a true proposition in this context. So γ does not express a true proposition in this context if and only if the proposition that γ does not express a true proposition in this context is not true. This conclusion and the additional premise, "The proposition that γ does not express a true proposition in this context is true if and only if γ does not express a true proposition in this context", imply an explicit contradiction. But this additional premise is what results from substituting the sentence "γ does not express a true proposition in this context" for σ in the schema "The proposition that"ˆσˆ"is true if and only if"ˆσ. So by (S), the sentence "γ does not express a true proposition in this context", which is γ, does not express a proposition in this context.

The trouble is that (S) is demonstrably not true in many instances, in particular, in the instance that concerns us. As we have just seen, if (S) is true, then γ does not express a proposition in this context. But we can likewise show that if (S) is true, then γ must express a proposition in this context, as follows: Suppose that γ, which is "γ does not express a true proposition in this context", does not express a proposition in this context. Then the sentence "The proposition that γ does not express a true proposition in this context is true if and only if γ does not express a true proposition in this context" does not contradict anything in this context because the sentence on the right-hand side of the "if and only if" in this sentence does not even so much as express a proposition in this context. So, using the same instance of (S) that we used before, we conclude that "γ does not express a true proposition in this context" expresses a proposition in this context. So (S) implies both that γ expresses a proposition and that γ does not express a proposition in this context. So (S) is not true.

More generally, we must not imagine that we can simply deny those applications of our normal rules of inference that lead us into contradiction while retaining all others. Even plainly unobjectionable instances of our inference rules can play a role in deriving a contradiction. For instance, consider a version of the notecard paradox in which on side A we have just the sentence "Every sentence on side B is true", and on side B we have just the two sentences "No sentence on side A is true" and "The moon is the moon". Then from these plain facts together with the plain fact that the moon is the moon we will be able to derive a contradiction. The inference from "The moon is the moon" to " 'The moon is the moon' is true" will play a role in the derivation of this contradiction, but we cannot on that account declare it to be invalid. (For further discussion, see my 1999.)

There is actually another way out of our second run of paradoxical reasoning (concerning γ), but it is questionable whether it is available to a proponent of the propositional approach to logical validity. How exactly do we move from line 3 to line 4? Suppose, as we say at line 3, that "γ does not express a true proposition in *this* context" expresses a true proposition in *this* context. Assuming that the language contains its own nontruth-in-a-context predicate, that will be so if and only if γ does not express a true proposition in the context that "*this* context" denotes in this context. But if we want to infer, as line 4 says, that γ does not express a true proposition in *this* context, then we have to assume in addition that the context that "*this* context" denotes in *this* context *is this context*. The same assumption is at work in the inference from 6 to 7. What 7 says is that "γ does not express a true proposition in *this* context" expresses a true proposition in *this* context. Assuming that the language contains its own nontruth-in-a-context predicate, that will be so if and only if γ does not express a true proposition in the context that "*this* context" denotes in *this* context. That this is so follows from 6 only given the additional assumption that the context that "*this* context" denotes in *this* context is *this* context. So the second paradoxical run of reasoning will be shown fallacious if we can find some rationale for denying that it is ever the case that the context that "*this* context" denotes in this context is identical to *this* context (that is, the context in which we ourselves are speaking). The identity must fail in every context in which premise 1 is true; otherwise there will be some contexts in which the second run of paradoxical reasoning goes through.

So unless some other kind of remedy can be proposed, it seems that the proponent of the propositional approach to logical validity is committed to denying that it is possible for people to refer to the context they are in. There can never be a singular term t such that in some context c, t denotes c. But what kind of thing could a context be such that this is not possible? If, as is commonly supposed (e.g., by Kaplan 1989), a context is just an n-tuple consisting of such things as the speaker, the audience, the time, and place, what could possibly stand in the way of someone's talking about the very context relative to which we should interpret the sentences he or she utters? Even if we add to the list a set of shared background assumptions, or even if we take the context to be *just* the set of shared background assumptions (as Stalnaker 1998 urges), what could prevent us from referring to the context? From the point of view of the propositional approach, I think there is no answer to this. So I think the propositional approach must be mistaken.

Let us consider then how we might resolve the semantic paradoxes from the point of view of the context-logical approach. In a language in which we can speak of the truth and falsehood of sentences, we must be able to refer to sentences by quoting them. So in addition to demonstrative pronouns, our language must contain the *quotation names* of sentences. Where **s** is any sentence, let **s̄** (*s-bar*) be the quotation name of **s**. For example, if **s** is "This is red", then **s̄** is "'This is red'" (notice the double quotation marks). So if **s** is any sentence of our language, then the language contains also **s̄**. I will refer to demonstrative pronouns and quotation names collectively as *singular terms*.

Since the semantic paradoxes turn on matters of identity (such as the fact that λ is a certain sentence), we need to accommodate the logic of identity. Identity sentences in our language may have the form **a = b**, where **a** and **b** are singular terms in our new sense. To accommodate identity, we must refine our chapter 3 definition of a primitive context slightly. Say that two singular terms **a** and **b** are *identity-linked* in a set of sentences S if and only if either **a = b** is a member of S or **b = a** is a member of S or there is some singular term **e** such that **a** and **e** are identity-linked in S and **e** and **b** are identity-linked in S. As a matter of mere notation, let **p[a/n]** be the result of substituting singular term **a** for every occurrence of demonstrative pronoun **n** in sentence **p**. (For example, "This likes this [that/this]" = "That likes that".) Say that Δ is a primitive context if and only if Δ is a set of literals such that not both **p** and **not p** are in Δ *and* if for each i, $1 \leq i \leq m$, $\mathbf{a}_i$ and $\mathbf{b}_i$ are identity-linked in Δ, then not both $\mathbf{p}[\mathbf{a}_1/\mathbf{n}_1][\mathbf{a}_2/\mathbf{n}_2] \ldots [\mathbf{a}_m/\mathbf{n}_m]$ and **not** $\mathbf{p}[\mathbf{b}_1/\mathbf{n}_1][\mathbf{b}_2/\mathbf{n}_2] \ldots [\mathbf{b}_m/\mathbf{n}_m]$ belong to Δ. Identity may now be accommodated in our theory of assertibility and deniability by stipulating that if **p[a/n]** is assertible in a context Γ (of whatever kind) and either **a = b** or **b = a** is assertible in Γ, then **p[b/n]** is assertible in Γ too, and that if **p[a/n]** is deniable in Γ and either **a = b** or **b = a** is assertible in Γ, then **p[b/n]** is deniable in Γ too. These sufficient conditions on assertibility and deniability generate necessary conditions via the usual closure clause.

Toward defining the assertibility and deniability conditions of sentences of the form **s̄ is true** and **s̄ is false**, we first need to modify the definition of context appropriately. Since we will not be concerned with conditionals in this chapter, we will not deal with the multicontexts of the previous chapter. So let us say that an *alethic* context Γ is a triple $\langle B_\Gamma, N_\Gamma, S_\Gamma \rangle$. B_Γ, the base, is a primitive context in our new sense, with two additional qualifications. The first qualification is that literals in B_Γ may contain any quotation name of any sentence in the language, including quotation names of sentences containing the predicates "is true" and "is false" (as well as other logical vocabulary to be introduced shortly), but the predicates "is true" and "is false" do not occur *as predicates* in sentences in B_Γ. (So "'a is true' = b" might be in B_Γ, but "a is true" will not be in B_Γ.) The second qualification is that if **s** and **r** are distinct sentences, then **s̄** and **r̄** must not be identity-linked in B_Γ (because two different sentences are never the same sentence). N_Γ, the domain, is a set of demonstrative pronouns (not quotation names) including at least all of those demonstrative pronouns that occur in any member of B_Γ. Finally, S_Γ, called the *sentence domain*, is a set of quotation names that includes at least every quotation name that occurs in any member of B_Γ.

An atomic sentence will be assertible in an alethic context if it is actually a member of the base of the alethic context; an atomic sentence will be deniable if its negation is a member of the base. The conditions under which negations (in general) and disjunctions are assertible or deniable in an alethic context will be formulated in the usual way (see chapters 3, 7, or 8). We will say that a sentence of the form **s̄ is true** is assertible in an alethic context Γ if **s** is assertible in Γ; that **s̄ is true** is deniable in an alethic context Γ if **s** is deniable in Γ; that **s̄ is false** is assertible in an alethic context Γ if **s** is deniable in Γ; and that **s̄ is false** is deniable in an alethic context Γ if **s** is assertible in Γ. Further, we can introduce a new quantifier, "for some sentences"$\hat{\ }u$, that binds variables that hold the places where sentence names can go. (Extending the convention of chapter 7, **Fs̄/u** will be the result of substituting **s̄** for every unbound occurrence of **u** in the formula **F**.) Sentences of the form **for some sentences u F** will be assertible in an alethic context Γ if for some sentence **s**, **Fs̄/u** is assertible in Γ; sentences of the form **for some sentences u F** will be deniable in Γ if for every sentence **s** such that either **s̄** is in S_Γ or **s** is assertible or deniable in Γ, **Fs̄/u** is deniable in Γ.

Nothing prevents it from being the case that a sentence of the form "λ = 'λ is not true'" is assertible in some alethic context Γ, for such a sentence might be a member of B_Γ. However, in any such context, "λ is not true" will be neither assertible nor deniable. In order for that sentence to be assertible in Γ, it is necessary that there be some quotation name η such that "λ ="^η is assertible in Γ and η^"is not true" is assertible in Γ. But since "λ = 'λ is not true'" is assertible in Γ, the only such η is "'λ is not true'". So "'λ is not true' is not true" has to be assertible in Γ. But that is assertible in Γ only if "λ is not true" is deniable in Γ. So "λ is not true" is assertible in Γ only if "λ is not true" is deniable in Γ. So "λ is not true" is not assertible in Γ. Similarly, we can show that "λ is not true" is not deniable in Γ. Similarly, in any context in which it is assertible that the sentence on side A = "Every sentence on side B of this notecard is true" and assertible that the sentence on side B = "No sentence on side A of this notecard is true", neither the sentence on side A nor the sentence on side B will be assertible. The reason why our first line of paradoxical reasoning does not go through is that we cannot rely on the rule of reductio ad absurdum. The set {"λ = 'λ is not true'", "λ is true"} implies "λ is not true" (because there is no context in which both premises are assertible) and yet, as we have just seen, {"λ = 'λ is not true'"} does not imply "λ is not true".

That is a nice result, but as we have seen in connection with the propositional approach, the real challenge is to show that no paradoxes arise for our own semantic metalanguage. In the context-logical approach, our semantic metalanguage does not contain the predicate "... expresses proposition ... in context ...?"; so we do not have to worry about that. However, on the context-logical approach, our semantic metalanguage does contain other semantic predicates, such as "... is assertible in ...", and so we have to consider whether we can formulate other semantic paradoxes involving this other vocabulary. To show that that is not so, we need to construct a context-logical account of the assertibility conditions for sentences containing that semantic vocabulary. That is, we have to specify the semantics for our own semantic metalanguage. We will then want to assure ourselves that we cannot derive a contradiction from premises such as that κ = "κ is not assertible in any context".

As is always the case when we introduce some new logical vocabulary into our language, we first need to present a suitable account of the formal structure of contexts. I will call the necessary sort of contexts *metacontexts*. We may define the set of metacontexts as the product of a certain construction. Every metacontext Γ is a quintuple $\langle B_\Gamma, N_\Gamma, S_\Gamma, C_\Gamma, f_\Gamma \rangle$. B_Γ, N_Γ, and S_Γ will be as already described in the definition of alethic contexts, except that the quotation names, which may occur in sentences in B_Γ and S_Γ, will include quotation names of the new sentences in our language containing the predicates "is assertible in", and "is deniable in", and other vocabulary to be introduced shortly. However, these new predicates will also not occur as predicates in sentences in B_Γ. C_Γ, called the *context domain*, will be a set of *context constants* disjoint from both N_Γ and S_Γ. f_Γ, called the *context assignment function*, is a function whose domain is C_Γ, and whose range I will describe presently.

For every such quintuple Γ in the first layer of meta-contexts, f_Γ simply assigns the empty set to every member of C_Γ. Given a first layer of metacontexts, so constructed, we can form a second layer of metacontexts by allowing, for any metacontext Λ in this second layer, that f_Λ may assign to each member of C_Λ either the empty set or one of the metacontexts in the first layer. A third layer of metacontexts may be constructed by allowing, for any metacontext Λ in this third layer, that f_Λ may assign to each member of C_Λ either the empty set or one of the metacontexts in any of the previous layers. And so on. A *metacontext* will then be any member of any of these layers. (We might like to place additional constraints on the construction of metacontexts. For example, we might like to add constraints that would ensure that the inference from " ' "It is raining" is assertible in Γ' is assertible in Γ'' to " 'It is raining' is assertible in Γ'' is valid. That could easily be done by constraining the relation between $f_\Lambda(\mathbf{c})$ and $f_\Gamma(\mathbf{c})$ in the case where $f_\Lambda(\mathbf{c}) = \Gamma$, but I will not take up such details here.)

Now we can define the conditions under which a sentence of the form **s̄ is assertible in c** is assertible or deniable in a metacontext Γ. **s̄ is assertible in c** is assertible in a metacontext Γ if **c** is in the context domain C_Γ for Γ, $f_\Gamma(\mathbf{c})$ is a metacontext (not the empty set), and **s** is assertible in $f_\Gamma(\mathbf{c})$. **s̄ is assertible in c** is deniable in a metacontext Γ if **c** is in C_Γ, $f_\Gamma(\mathbf{c})$ is a metacontext (not the empty set), and **s** is *not* assertible in $f_\Gamma(\mathbf{c})$. **s̄ is deniable in c** is assertible in a metacontext Γ if **c** is in the context domain C_Γ for Γ, $f_\Gamma(\mathbf{c})$ is a metacontext (not the empty set), and **s** is deniable in $f_\Gamma(\mathbf{c})$. **s̄ is deniable in c** is deniable in a metacontext Γ if **c** is in the context domain C_Γ for Γ, $f_\Gamma(\mathbf{c})$ is a metacontext (not the empty set), and **s** is *not* deniable in $f_\Gamma(\mathbf{c})$. Notice that the deniability conditions for **s̄ is assertible in c** are formulated in terms of mere lack of assertibility rather than in terms of deniability; likewise the deniability conditions for **s̄ is deniable in c** are defined in terms of lack of deniability. The rationale for this departure from the usual pattern is that, since the fact that something is not assertible in a context does not mean that it is deniable in that context, we do not want it to turn out that **not s̄ is assertible in c** implies **s̄ is deniable in c**. This does not have the consequence that every sentence of the form **s̄ is assertible in c** is either assertible or deniable in every context, because in some contexts Γ, $f_\Gamma(\mathbf{c})$ will be the empty set.

Further, we can have a quantifier that binds variables that hold the positions that context constants can hold. Thus, **for some contexts g F** is assertible in a metacontext Γ if for some context constant **c**, **Fc/g** is assertible in Γ, and **for some contexts g F** is deniable in a metacontext Γ if for every context constant **c** in C_Γ, **Fc/g** is deniable in Γ. (In view of the new use for quotation names, the deniability conditions for sentences of the form **for some sentences n F** must be revised to read as follows: For every sentence **s** such that either **s̄** is in S_Γ or **s** is assertible or deniable in Γ or for some context constant **c** in C_Γ, **s** is assertible or deniable in $f_\Gamma(\mathbf{c})$, **Fs̄/c** is deniable in Γ.)

Suppose that Γ is the context in which we ourselves are speaking and suppose that "Δ" is a context constant in C_Γ

such that $f_\Gamma(\text{"}\Delta\text{"}) = \Gamma$. We seem to be able to reason para-doxically as follows that if $\alpha = \text{"}\alpha$ is not assertible in $\Delta\text{"}$, then α both is and is not assertible in Γ.

1. $\alpha = \text{"}\alpha$ is not assertible in $\Delta\text{"}$.

2. Suppose α is assertible in Γ.

3. Given 2, "α is not assertible in Δ" is assertible in Γ. (From 1 and 2.)

4. Given 2, "α is assertible in Δ" is deniable in Γ. (From 3.)

5. Given 2, α is not assertible in $f_\Gamma(\text{"}\Delta\text{"}) = \Gamma$. (From 4.)

6. α is not assertible in Γ. (From 2–5.)

7. Suppose α is not assertible in Γ.

8. Given 7, "α is not assertible in Δ" is not assertible in Γ. (From 1 and 7.)

9. Given 7, "α is assertible in Δ" is not deniable in Γ. (From 8.)

10. Given 7, α is assertible in $f_\Gamma(\text{"}\Delta\text{"}) = \Gamma$. (From 9.)

11. α is assertible in Γ. (From 7–9.)

12. α is both assertible in Γ and not assertible in Γ. (From 6 and 11.)

There is no point in questioning the use of reductio ad absurdum at steps 6 and 11, because we could just as well derive a contradiction in the form of a biconditional without using reductio ad absurdum. We may take as our premise that "α is not assertible in Δ" is assertible in Γ if and only if α is not assertible in $f_\Gamma(\text{"}\Delta\text{"}) = \Gamma$ and derive the conclusion that α is assertible in Γ if and only if α is not assertible in Γ.

The answer to this seeming paradox is that we were mistaken to suppose in the first place that it could happen that $f_\Gamma(\text{"}\Delta\text{"}) = \Gamma$. Due to the stagewise manner in which we constructed the set of metacontexts, it can never happen that the context that a context assigns to some context constant in its context domain is that very same context. That is, there cannot be a context Γ and a context constant **c** such that $f_\Gamma(\textbf{c}) = \Gamma$. In other words, no one can talk about the context pertinent to his or her own talk; no one can talk about the context he or she is in.

Another paradox might seem to arise from the assumption that $\kappa = $ "κ is not assertible in any context". From this it might seem that we could infer both that κ is assertible in some context and that κ is not assertible in any context. These inferences might be sound if we could assume that the domain of contexts was constant across all contexts, but that is not the case. On the contrary, due to the stagewise construction of the set of metacontexts, if for some **c**, $f_\Gamma(\textbf{c}) = \Delta$, then the range of the context assignment function f_Γ cannot equal the range of f_Δ (since Δ is in the range of f_Γ but cannot be in the range of f_Δ). In fact, metacontexts can be constructed in which both "$\kappa = $ 'κ is not assertible in any context'" and "κ is not assertible in any context" are assertible. (I have given an example in my forthcoming b.)

We have already observed that in the framework of the propositional approach, it does not make much sense to deny that we can talk about the context we are in. It remains for us to consider whether it makes more sense in the framework of the context-logical approach. An immediate difficulty might seem to be that if we cannot talk about the context we are in, then we cannot even take up the issue of whether we can talk about the context we are in. However, the question that concerns us is really whether participants in a conversation can talk about the context that *they* are in. If we can explain why other people in other contexts cannot talk about the context they are in, then there need not be any further difficulty in understanding why we cannot talk about the context we are in.

Part of the problem is that examples seem to show that one can very well talk about the context one is in. For instance, one might say, "It is assertible in the context of *this* conversation that we cannot make this dish without turmeric", and, in so saying, it may seem to one that the context one is talking about is the very same context as that relative to which one's sentence ought to be evaluated as assertible, deniable, or neither. However, one of the consequences of conceiving of contexts as objective (which is how I have been treating them ever since chapter 3) is that what a speaker takes the context to be is not necessarily what it is. In the example at hand, in particular, it should be plausible that the context relative to which one's assertion is evaluated is not the context one is referring to, because when one makes that assertion, the aim of the conversation shifts, even if only momentarily, from trying to make dinner to settling the conversational score.

Beyond thus accounting for examples, one would like to make intelligible that people cannot talk about the context they are in. What is it about language and the rest of the world that prevents it? My answer to this will rest on the rather vague conception of the context for a conversation as comprising what is objectively relevant to a conversation, which, in chapter 3, I attempted to make more precise (for the simple sort of context presented there) in terms of goals and actions that accord with the contents of the context. Suppose that Γ is the context pertinent to a conversation C, that is, the context relative to which the assertibility of sentences in C ought to be evaluated. Then the content of Γ is a matter of what is relevant to C. In particular, a context Δ is in the range of the context assignment function for Γ only if Δ is relevant to C. Thus, to defend an account of the content of context Γ would be to establish the relevance to C of every context that is taken to belong to the context assignment function for Γ. So if Γ itself were in the range of the context assignment function for Γ, then we would be in the impossible position of having to establish the relevance of Γ to C before we had established the content of Γ. So, assuming that it will be possible to defend an account of the content of Γ, Γ cannot itself be a member of the range of the context assignment function for Γ, as it might be if one could talk about the context one were in. It is fair to assume that it must be possible to defend an account of the content of a context, because, while contexts may be objective, they must also be the sort of thing whose content can in principle be discovered.

Beliefs

10   The Communicative Conception

I believe that today is Friday. You believe that some reptiles can swim. People have a lot of beliefs like that. So why should people not be able to use words to express their beliefs? Why should we not suppose that people choose their words so that, on the basis of their choice of words, hearers can recognize the contents of their beliefs? Why should we not think of language as arising among human beings precisely to enable them to express their beliefs and their other states of mind in this way? I could reply that I have been answering that question throughout this book. But so long as we do not scrutinize the concept of belief, the nagging question will remain: Why should we not think of words as expressing beliefs?

One contemporary conception of the nature of beliefs and desires particularly supports the received view of linguistic communication. Human behavior is a black box; to understand it, we have to guess at what is inside. Supposedly, our hypotheses take the form of attributions of beliefs and desires. Beliefs and desires are the inner mechanisms mediating between sensory inputs and behavioral outputs.

Sensory stimuli set them in motion, they interact with one another, and out come behaviors. Thus, beliefs and desires are supposed to be theoretical entities, postulated for the sake of a certain sort of explanation and prediction of behavior. Ultimately, our postulation of these causes of behavior is supposed to be vindicated by finding that the postulated entities also have a physical identity in the brain. Call this the *postulationist conception* of beliefs and desires.

Perhaps one could accept the received view of linguistic communication without accepting the postulationist conception of beliefs and desires. (After all, the received view of linguistic communication has deeper roots in the history of philosophy.) But the postulationist conception of beliefs and desires supports the received view of linguistic communication rather directly. Not every behavior that is supposed to issue from beliefs and desires will be intended to reveal the content of one's beliefs and desires, of course. Not even every act of speech will have to be conceived as intended to reveal the content of one's beliefs and desires— joking and lying are possible too. But if beliefs and desires guide action, then there would be an obvious utility in being able to reveal the contents of one's beliefs and desires to other people. If we add that the structure within and the relations between sentences are analogous to the structure within and relations between the mental representations bearing the contents of beliefs and desires, then we will have to admit that language would be a very suitable tool for doing just that. So even if we thought that language did not originally develop as a means of communicating the contents of beliefs and desires, we would have to suppose that that soon became its primary function.

Thus it is incumbent upon me to develop an alternative conception of beliefs and desires, one that does not lead to the received view of linguistic communication. One sort of explanation of the nature of beliefs that someone might think to give on my behalf is that beliefs are themselves *in* the languages we speak. The idea would be that if I believe that today is Friday, then that means that somehow the English sentence "Today is Friday" is written in my brain. In general, one might suggest, a person's belief is an inner token of a sentence of a language that the person speaks (see Carruthers 1996). Of course, it has to be written there in such a way that its being written there produces in me whatever behaviors may be expected from me in virtue of my believing that today is Friday. In this case, we would not want to say that speaking is normally a matter of choosing words that enable hearers to recognize the content of the speaker's belief; rather, speaking would be more a matter of letting what is written on the inside show up on the outside.

This is not my explanation in fact. Such a conception of belief would be problematic in a couple of ways. First, it would not make much sense in light of the conception of language that I have been developing. Language, as I have characterized it, has as its function the achievement of goals—paradigmatically, practical goals. It promotes the achievement of goals by creating a common take on the context. On this account, there may still be a role for talking to oneself. One may talk to oneself when one imagines

talking to someone else. One may talk to oneself in deciding a question if one can alternately adopt the different
points of view of different interlocutors. But it is not the case
that whenever it is reasonable to attribute a belief to a person
it is reasonable to suppose that that belief is the product of
some such occasion for talking to oneself.

Even without appealing to my particular conception of
the function of language, it is easy to see that it is not the
case that every time it is reasonable to attribute a belief to
someone, it is also reasonable to think that he or she contains an inner token of a corresponding sentence of natural
language. Perhaps I have plans for Saturday, and I expect to
execute those plans tomorrow, and I know that Saturday
follows Friday; so clearly I believe that today is Friday. Still
I may never have contemplated the question whether today
is Friday, consciously or otherwise. So you might be perfectly well justified in saying that I believe that today is
Friday even though you would have to acknowledge that
the sentence "Today is Friday" may have in no sense passed
through my mind.

Another explanation that one might think to give on my
behalf is that a belief is a *disposition to assert or assent*. If I
believe that today is Friday, it may never have *occurred* to
me that today is Friday, but nonetheless I may be disposed
to assert "Today is Friday" if the question arises, or disposed
to assent if asked "Is today Friday?" But the thesis just does
not seem true. One may be disposed to assert what one does
not believe, and one may have no disposition to assert what
one does believe. If I lived among the Taliban, I might still
believe that there is no God, but I would never *say* that. We

can always imagine circumstances under which one *would* assert those things one believes. Even if I lived among the Taliban, it might still be true that if I did *not* live among the Taliban then I would assert that there is no God. But it is not evident how we can distinguish between those counterfactual circumstances under which one's disposition to assert would reveal the beliefs one actually has and those counterfactual circumstances that would change one's beliefs. So we cannot expect to find a kind of counterfactual circumstance such that what one believes *in fact* is exactly what one is disposed to assert in circumstances of that kind.

Instead, my strategy will be to set aside for the moment the question "What *is* a belief?" and focus on the question "What are we doing when we *attribute* a belief?" Of course, my answer will not be that in attributing a belief we are positing a theoretical entity in the black box of human behavior, so that we might explain and predict that behavior. Having given my account of attribution, I will present, in the next chapter, some independent criticisms of the postulationist conception of beliefs and desires and will explain how the matter of explanation and prediction looks from the point of view of this alternative conception of attribution. Finally, I will argue, in chapter 12, that my theory of belief attribution can qualify as a theory of the *nature* of beliefs as well. Chapter 12 will also extend the context logical approach to semantics to a language in which we can talk about beliefs. (For a different, but possibly compatible, attempt to understand the function of belief and desire attributions as something other than serving to explain and predict behavior, see Morton 1996.)

My account of the attribution of beliefs and desires begins
with an alternative conception of asserting and commanding (which I have not had occasion to develop until now).
To *assert* something is, on my view, to utter a declarative sentence of a language subject to the norms of asserting for that
language, where the declaratives are those that, by their
form, are especially suited for the making of assertions. The
norms of asserting include the sorts of conditions on assertibility that I have been concerned to explicate, but may
include others as well. To *command* something is to utter an
imperative sentence subject to the norms governing commanding (about which I have not said much). A speaker is
subject to the norms of asserting and commanding for a language whenever he or she is *obligated* to conform to those
norms.

The hard part is to explain when a speaker is obligated to
conform to the norms of a language. For this purpose I will
simply help myself to the concept of *being a speaker* of a given
language. I will assume that we know what it is for a person
to be a speaker of English or a speaker of Korean. A speaker
of a language is *always* obligated to conform to the norms of
that language unless . . . , and now we have to list all of the
possible exceptions. I cannot do that, but I can give some
examples: exceptions include speaking on the stage, writing
poetry, telling an obvious joke. Whenever we are doing
those things we are, at least in liberal, democratic societies,
liberated from the usual obligation to speak in conformity
to the norms (or at least the primary norms). In addition, we
should expect there to be the sorts of exceptions to which
obligations in general are subject, for example, cases in

which a higher obligation takes precedence over a lower one. A large body of ethical theory is devoted to this topic, and I do not want to say anything overly simple about it here.

In addition to *asserting* and *commanding*, there is such a thing as asserting and commanding *on someone else's behalf.* Here I mean to speak of doing something on someone's behalf in the sense of doing it *in their stead*, not in the sense of *doing it for their benefit*. For instance, imagine a tribe of hunter-gatherers. They send a scout into distant territories to look for game. Rather than make the scout come all the way back to camp to report his findings, they send out an intermediary who, by prearrangement, meets with the scout halfway out and then reports back to the tribe. The scout tells the intermediary "Herds are in the northern hills." The intermediary returns to the camp and replies "Scout says herds are in the northern hills." This is an example of what I call asserting on someone's behalf. The intermediary does not himself assert that herds are in the northern hills; rather, he asserts this on the scout's behalf. In this example, the intermediary attributes a *saying* to the scout. But likewise, attributions of beliefs in general are assertions on another person's behalf. An attribution of a desire is a command, or request, on someone else's behalf. (In addition, to say that someone *wonders* something is to ask a question on his or her behalf, but I will say no more about wondering.) I call this account of the attribution of beliefs and desires, considered as an account of the very nature of beliefs and desires (as I will argue it is in chapter 12), the *communicative conception* of beliefs and desires.

Suppose, for another example, that a group of builders aims to build a house. One of the builders, Balam, wants some rope, so that he can hoist up the logs for the roof using the scaffold and pulley he has put together. Balam may say to his assistant Namu, "Bring me some rope!" One possibility is that Namu may in turn go to the keeper of supplies and say, "Give me some rope!" But this may not be a very satisfactory solution for a variety of reasons. One reason is that it cannot be allowed that anyone at any time may go to the supply house and take out whatever he or she wants. Someone has to be in charge. So Namu, the assistant, may be allowed to take out some rope if he is merely relaying a command from Balam, but not if the command originates with himself. Another reason is that it may not be very clear to the supply keeper how to comply with Namu's command. How much rope? What thickness? But Namu may be prepared to amplify the command in an appropriate way because he understands Balam's goal. So Namu may say to the supply keeper, "Balam wants at least 50 yards of thick rope." In this way, Namu both establishes his credentials and transmits Balam's command in a form adjusted to the removed circumstances. This is an example of what I will call *commanding on someone's behalf*. In general, I suggest, an attribution of a desire is a command on someone else's behalf.

Consider another example of *asserting* on someone's behalf. The builders need more logs for use in building the house. The loggers have been cutting logs somewhere in the forest, but where? Perhaps Balam's assistant Namu does not know where the logs are, but he knows where the loggers are camped. So Namu can go to the loggers' camp and ask them, "Where are the logs that we are to use to build the chief's house?" Hanul, the leader of the loggers, may tell Namu, "The logs are at the south fork of the river." As a result, Namu knows how to get the logs. But he cannot do it all by himself. He has to go get the others and the wagons and the oxen. So Namu might go back to the other builders and say to them, "The logs are at the south fork." But this may not be a very satisfactory solution for a variety of reasons. For one thing, Namu's assertion may not carry adequate authority. The others will want to know where Namu got this information. Moreover, Namu may not wish to take the blame if it turns out that the logs are not at the south fork. Furthermore, there may be several building projects under way, so that Namu has to specify which logs he is talking about. So Namu says, "Hanul says that the logs for the chief's house are at the south fork." This is an example of what I call *asserting on someone's behalf*. In general, I suggest, an attribution of a belief is an assertion on someone else's behalf.

In this case we are again dealing with an attribution of belief that is also an attribution of *saying*. In other cases, where our assertion on another's behalf is not so directly grounded in the other person's own words, we will speak of belief rather than saying. For instance, suppose that Namu and Bosok together witness Balam stealing grain from the tribal store house. Under these circumstances, Namu may wish to call on Bosok as a corroborating witness. Bosok did not herself assert that Balam stole the grain. Indeed, fearing retaliation, she may be very ill-disposed to do so. Still, Namu, having been at Bosok's side when the event occurred, may make an assertion on Bosok's behalf, thus: "Bosok believes that Balam stole the grain." Namu's assertion on Bosok's behalf will have the same function as Bosok's own assertion that Balam stole the grain would have, although it might be less effective in bringing about the result that Namu desires. One thing that distinguishes attributions of beliefs, as the broader class, from attributions of sayings, is that attributions of beliefs are assertions on someone else's behalf that may not be very directly grounded in anything that the person to whom the belief is attributed actually said.

What we assert on another person's behalf may be very directly grounded in another person's own words if what we say in making our assertion on the other's behalf is basically the speaker's own words, adjusting only for the difference in who is speaking and when. For example, if Namu says, "I will go hunting today," then on the next day, Bosok may say, "Namu *said* that *he would* go hunting *yesterday*." But we may speak of what is *said* even when the grounding is in various ways less direct than this. If Namu says, "That one is good" in a context in which "That one is the one on the left" goes without saying, then Bosok may say, "Namu *says* that the one on the left is good." In such cases, one may optionally speak of belief rather than saying, but in other cases, we will have to speak of belief rather than saying.

Just like unmediated assertions and commands, assertions and commands on another person's behalf are subject to norms. The norms governing assertions include the norms of assertibility such as I have been defining throughout this book. Assertions on another person's behalf are likewise governed by norms of assertibility. What is properly assertible in a conversation is what is assertible relative to the context pertinent to that conversation. Likewise, what is assertible on someone's behalf is what is assertible on that person's behalf relative to the context pertinent to that conversation. But what is assertible on another person's behalf is of course not identical with what is properly assertible. What is assertible on another person's behalf is also not simply what the person is himself or herself willing to assert. It is also a matter of what has really happened in the person's environment, provided that the person was in a position to take it all in. Namu's assertion, "Bosok believes that Balam stole the grain," may be assertible in the context in which he speaks because Bosok was indeed watching as Balam stole the grain and was well positioned to take in what she saw.

Again, something may be assertible on someone's behalf although the person on whose behalf the assertion is made is not at all *disposed* to make that assertion as well. Though Namu may be correct in asserting "Balam stole the grain" on Bosok's behalf, it may not be the case that Bosok is in any sense disposed to assert that herself. Ultimately, as I say, I intend the communicative conception to qualify as a theory of the *nature* of beliefs and desires and not merely as a theory of their attribution. Nonetheless, it is not an account of their nature that works by identifying beliefs and desires with something else. In particular, the idea is not that beliefs and desires may be identified with dispositions to make assertions and commands.

Nor, certainly, does the communicative conception identify beliefs and desires with *inner* assertions and commands. Sometimes when we are warranted in making an assertion or command on someone else's behalf there may be an inner assertion or command in that person corresponding to our assertion or command on his or her behalf. But I know no reason to assume that whenever we are warranted in making an assertion or command on someone else's behalf, that person likewise asserts or commands something, overtly or covertly.

According to the postulationist conception, the *raison d'être* of attributions of beliefs and desires is the explanation and prediction of behavior. As I will explain in the next chapter, the practice of attributing beliefs and desires may indeed yield a certain kind of explanation of behavior, but on the communicative conception that is not at all the primary reason for being of attributions of beliefs and desires. Rather, their reason for being is linguistic communication. If two people are present to one another, then they can converse by making assertions and commands. But even if someone is absent from a conversation, he or she can, to a certain extent, participate in the conversation inasmuch as he or she may be represented by someone present who makes assertions and commands on his or her behalf. The primary function of attributions of beliefs and desires is to extend the range of participation in conversations in just this way.

I acknowledge that the practice of attributing beliefs and desires may be rather fragile in the sense that in some cases no determinate judgment as to whether someone believes something or not may be possible. If someone "saw" something but claims not to have been paying attention or not to remember, there may simply be no right answer to the question whether he believes that it happened or not. If something jars him and suddenly he reports that he remembers, then we may say that he believed it all along or that he did not believe it until he remembered. If someone claims to understand that smoking tobacco is harmful to his health but takes no steps to quit smoking, then we may wonder whether he really believes that tobacco is harmful or is just saying what he has been trained to say. In such cases, further observations and crucial tests might resolve our question; or they might not.

Next, I want to discuss a couple of problems concerning belief and desire to which the communicative conception perhaps contributes a solution. One of the classic problems of epistemology, touched on in the previous paragraph, is: Exactly what attitude toward a proposition is the attitude of believing it? (The same sort of question can be asked about desire, but I will focus on belief.) There are many belief-like attitudes one can take toward a proposition. One may take for granted that p without ever really thinking about it, or one may deliberately conclude that p after carefully considering both sides of the question. One might be willing to agree that p when someone else says it but be unwilling to place any bets on it, or one might be willing to bet one's whole share that p. One may accept that p for the sake of argument, or one may commit one's entire research program to defending the proposition that p. One may regard the proposition that p as the best confirmed of the currently recognized hypotheses, or, while admitting some possibility that one is in error, one may predict that there will never again be any grounds to doubt whether p. One may maintain that p though one has long forgotten the reasons why one ever began asserting that p, or one may be prepared to defend the proposition that p against all objections that anyone has proposed. One may consider one's belief to be fit for disputation, and be prepared to abandon it in the face of stronger reasons, or one may consider one's belief to be not open to dispute for fear of what life would be like without it. There is a continuum of cases along each of the dimensions just described; so it is hard to believe that we will be able to draw a sharp line between those cases that qualify as belief and those that do not.

For those epistemologists who think of knowledge acquisition as primarily a matter of deciding what probabilities we should assign to propositions, it seems reasonable to identify belief with assigning a high probability. The problem is that, while we cannot be said to believe only those propositions we regard as absolutely certain (because there are too few of those), if we say that any probability short of certainty is sufficient for belief, then we will find that we may believe things logically incompatible with other things we believe. Suppose that I may be said to believe any proposition to which I assign a probability of at least 0.9 (where the probability of propositions I regard as certain is 1). Then if there are a dozen lottery tickets and I believe that each one is equally likely to be the winning ticket, then of each one I believe that it will not win (since I assign to each a probability of not winning greater than 0.9). So if I know, and thus believe, that those dozen tickets are all the tickets there are, then what I believe implies that no ticket will win. So if I must not believe anything logically incompatible with my beliefs—at least when I recognize them as such—then I must not believe that some ticket will win. But that is wrong; I may very well believe that some ticket will win. Of course, the same sort of problem will arise no matter how high we set the threshold short of 1. So either nothing short of certainty qualifies as belief, or there is nothing against adopting logically incompatible beliefs.

A virtue of the communicative conception of belief is that it evades such quandaries. On this conception there need not be any special relation between believing something and taking one of these belief-like attitudes. The nature of these attitudes can perhaps not be very adequately explicated in terms of the grounds on which we might attribute them, but the fact that the grounds on which we might attribute these attitudes look very different from the grounds on which we might assert something on someone's behalf indicates that there is a difference between each of these attitudes and the attitude of belief. A willingness to bet on the truth of a proposition may be revealed in the bets a person actually takes. But a person might be willing to bet on something that cannot be asserted on his or her behalf. The fact that someone has deliberately concluded that p may be evident in the fact that she emerges from the library declaring, "Now at last I can at least be sure that"$^\frown p$. But even after she says that, p may not be assertible on her behalf. Conversely, in some contexts p may be assertible on someone's behalf, although that person has never seriously considered his grounds for claiming that p and would probably stop claiming that p, given the slightest reason to do so. Accordingly, there need not be any very tight relation between these various attitudes and the attitude of belief.

As for the lottery paradox, the solution lies in the facts of co-assertibility in a context. The following fourteen sentences are not all assertible in any one context:

Ticket #1 will not win.

Ticket #2 will not win.

    .

    .

    .

Ticket #12 will not win.

Every ticket is either #1, or #2, or . . . #12.

Some ticket will win.

Accordingly, those fourteen sentences are not assertible together on anyone's behalf. And so, it will not be assertible in any one context that someone believes that ticket #1 will not win, that ticket #2 will not win, . . . , that every ticket is either #1, or #2, or . . . #12, and that some ticket will win. Still, there may be contexts in which all three of the following sentences are assertible but not the rest:

Ticket #5 will not win.

Every ticket is either #1, or #2, or . . . #12.

Some ticket will win.

For instance, this might be a context in which ticket #5 in particular is being offered for sale. Accordingly, all three of these sentences might be assertible on someone's behalf, and it might be assertible that someone believes that ticket #5 will not win, that every ticket is either #1, or #2, or . . . #12, and that some ticket will win. The trick is just to see that from the fact that any of the twelve tickets could just as well stand in place of ticket #5 in such a context, it does not follow that there is some context in which all fourteen of the sentences in question are assertible together.

Finally, I want to say something about "privileged access." Typically we are authoritative over the contents of our own beliefs. That is, if someone asserts, "I believe that"$^\frown p$, and the assertion is deemed sincere, then usually the rest of us just have to accept that; doubts about whether the person really does believe that p are deemed inappropriate. This is not always true, of course. We may set aside lies as cases of insincerity. We may set aside also utterances that are not really assertions (such as quotations of someone else's words). Still, people may be mistaken in what they say about their own beliefs, for they may be self-deceived, or just eager to please. But not every sort of challenge that in other cases would be appropriate to a claim of the form, $S^\frown$"believes that"$^\frown p$, would be appropriate to a claim of the form "I believe that"$^\frown p$. For example, we might doubt that Joe believes that the office will be closed on Monday on the grounds that Joe did not receive the memo that would have informed him of that fact. But if someone sincerely asserts "I believe that the office will be closed on Monday," then we cannot doubt on such grounds that he or she believes the office will be closed on Monday. The problem of privileged access is to explain this difference between first-person and third-person attributions of beliefs.

The problem of privileged access can be framed as a problem concerning the difference between the following two arguments:

The argument from self-ascription

Prem: A believes that A believes that p

Conc: A believes that p.

The argument from other-ascription

Prem: B believes that A believes that p

Conc: A believes that p.

The problem is to explain in what way the argument from self-ascription is more persuasive than the argument from other-ascription (although even the argument from self-ascription is not strictly speaking valid). According to the communicative conception, the premise of the argument from other-ascription is assertible (in a given context) only if "A believes that"^p is assertible on B's behalf (in that context). That in turn means that p itself is assertible on A's behalf (in that context) *from the point of view of things that are assertible on B's behalf* (in that context). But there is no special reason to expect that things that are assertible on A's behalf from the point of view of things that are assertible on B's behalf will in fact be assertible on A's behalf. So the conclusion of the argument from other-ascription may not be assertible even if the premise is. Similarly, the premise of the argument from self-ascription is assertible (in a given context) only if "A believes that"$\hat{}p$ is assertible on A's own behalf (in that context). That in turn means that p itself is assertible on A's behalf *from the point of view of things that are assertible on A's behalf*. But as I will explain presently, what is assertible on A's behalf from the point of view of things that are assertible on A's behalf is likely to be assertible on A's behalf as well. In that case, if the premise of the argument from self-ascription is assertible, then the conclusion is likely to be assertible as well.

So the problem of explaining privileged access comes down to this: To explain why it is that what is assertible on A's behalf (in a given context) from the point of view of things that are assertible on A's behalf (in that context) will likewise be assertible on A's behalf (in that context). That may be explained as follows: (i) What a person asserts, or would be willing to assert in a given context, is a fairly good guide to what is in fact assertible on his or her behalf in that context. By the same token, A's willingness to assert "I believe that"$\hat{}p$ is a fairly good guide to whether "A believes that"$\hat{}p$ is assertible on A's behalf. In other words, (ii) what a person asserts on his or her own behalf, or would be willing to assert on his or her own behalf, is a fairly good guide to what is assertible on his or her behalf from the point of view of things assertible on his or her behalf. But asserting something on one's own behalf is tantamount to just asserting it (while asserting something on someone else's behalf is not at all tantamount to asserting it). So (iii) one would be willing to assert anything that one would be willing to assert on one's own behalf. So, by (i), (ii), and (iii), chances are that anything assertible on A's behalf from the point of view of things that are assertible on A's behalf will likewise be assertible on A's behalf. That is my explanation of privileged access. The explanation does not demonstrate that a person's access to his or her own beliefs is perfect, because what a person would be willing to assert is only a good guide and is not a perfect guide to what is assertible on that person's behalf.

This explanation of privileged access raises the question, if attributing a belief to oneself is just asserting something on one's own behalf, why would anyone ever attribute beliefs to himself or herself rather than just making assertions? In fact, self-attributions of beliefs are often nothing more than politeness hedges. The real point is to make an assertion, but one does not wish to seem too assertive, and so one merely makes the assertion on one's own behalf, as if offering to treat any challenge to one's assertion with the same detachment with which one might treat a challenge to someone else's beliefs. (See Sbisà 2001.) Thus, if one asks people whether they believe, say, that their salary is too low, then they will answer not by thinking about their own states of mind, but by thinking about their salary.

However, there are some other cases as well. Sometimes a first-person attribution of a belief serves as a declaration of allegiance to a cause or an idea. For example, someone who declares that he believes that "all men are created equal" is probably not putting forward a proposition that he is prepared to defend with arguments but is instead declaring his allegiance to an ideal of justice. The reason to do this by means of an assertion on one's own behalf rather than by a plain assertion may be just that, since the question at issue is really his allegiances, the answer requires some kind of reference to himself. In still other cases, which I estimate are quite rare, one might offer to explain one's behavior as another might explain it, and for that reason make assertions on one's own behalf. This takes us to the next chapter, which concerns the nature of explanation in terms of beliefs and desires.

11   Explanation and Prediction

Many contemporary philosophers seriously exaggerate the extent to which we explain one another's behavior in terms of beliefs and desires. No doubt we sometimes do it. If someone is late for class on the first day, we might explain that he had *thought* that the class would meet in another room. But I do not think we do this so often that the practice ought to encourage the notion that beliefs and desires are theoretical entities postulated for the sake of explanation and prediction.

Certainly there are occasions on which we attribute a belief or a desire to a person although our intention is not at all to explain or predict. Often our objective is to persuade. For example, if I wonder whether I should believe that it is safe to drink the water from this stream, someone might try to persuade me that it is by telling me that that is what the trail guide believes. Or if I am trying to decide whether to cut down a tree, someone might try to persuade me to do so by telling me that my neighbor wants me to cut it down. One could maintain that the best test of the truth of such attributions of beliefs and desires is whether they serve to explain the subject's behavior. But if there is reason to doubt the postulationist conception, then we might appeal to such attributions, as I have done in the previous chapter, to motivate a different conception of what we are doing in attributing beliefs and desires.

A postulationist conception of beliefs and desires cannot rest solely on the observation that we sometimes explain behavior in terms of beliefs and desires, for this does not all by itself entail that beliefs and desires are theoretical entities postulated precisely for the sake of explanation and prediction. The usual addition (see Loar 1981) is a conception of beliefs and desires as conforming to constitutive folk psychological laws. These laws are supposed to tell us what we can expect a person to believe and desire, given that he or she has had a certain course of training and then is exposed to certain stimuli, and these laws are supposed to tell us what actions we can expect a person to take given that he or she has certain beliefs and desires. If we find that for some person the sensory inputs and the behavioral outputs are such as we should expect, according to the theory, on the assumption that certain beliefs and desires have intervened between the inputs and the outputs, then we may infer that those beliefs and desires are indeed present.

Thus postulationism, in its usual formulation, acquiesces in the widespread notion that theoretical explanation rests on laws describing the behavior of theoretical entities. I myself am not so sure that that is the best way to understand the nature of theoretical explanation. Perhaps it would be better to think of theories as descriptions of significant structures—be it the structure of cells, the structure of the economy, or the structure of space-time. But this conception of the aims of science might not diminish the postulationist's commitment to the existence of folk psychological laws governing the behavior of beliefs and desires. Beliefs and desires are not mechanisms whose interactions we can observe under a microscope or record with electrodes or track with radioactive tracer molecules or chemically dissect. If we are able to detect the presence of certain beliefs and desires by inference to the best explanation of behavior, then that will be so only because we have a general theory telling us where beliefs and desires come from and what they will do.

So one major problem for the postulationist conception of beliefs and desires is that no one has ever given any plausible examples of the tenets of the folk psychological theory. To be sure, even if it is true that all of us who attribute beliefs and desires to one another are in possession of such a folk psychological theory, it need not be very easy for us to figure out exactly what it is we know. What we ourselves know could be, as they say, an empirical question; empirical research might be necessary for us to make explicit to ourselves what we already tacitly know. But if we really do employ such a theory, then it should at least be possible to come up with some plausible hypotheses concerning the content of our commonsense knowledge, between which empirical research could then decide. That is what no one has ever been able to do.

Sometimes it is said that we know something like this: *People do what they believe will satisfy their desires.* (See Loar 1981, p. 90, or, for another example, Horgan and Woodward

1985.) But that is not right, and what is wrong with it is not corrected by adding a few provisos or a ceteris paribus clause. A person always has many desires, and which one he or she tries to fulfill at a given moment is in part a matter of what he or she takes to be most feasible under the circumstances. We might say that the reason why someone stooped over and took a drink from the drinking fountain was that he desired to quench his thirst and believed that by drinking from the fountain he would quench his thirst, but then the reason why that is a good explanation, if it is one, is not that this belief and this desire are lawfully sufficient. He might have had that belief and that desire and might nonetheless have kept on walking in order to get where he was going sooner. Or he might have waited for a tastier beverage. Or he might have stopped to talk to a friend who was passing by at just that moment. If we wish to have a general principle, then at the very least we will have to suppose that beliefs and desires come in degrees and that what people do depends on the strengths of their beliefs and the strengths of their desires. In that way we might at least acknowledge that a person might try to obtain his second choice rather than his first choice if his belief that he can obtain his second choice is stronger than his belief that he can obtain his first choice.

Accepting that our choice depends on degrees of belief and degrees of desire, some philosophers have thought that we could look to decision theory for a general principle relating a person's mental state to his or her actions (e.g., Rey 1997, pp. 216–220.) That too is an error. The only kind of general, all-purpose advice that decision theory offers about how to make a decision is that we should maximize expected utility. But degrees of utility cannot be measured with a stick. To define a utility scale we first of all need a ranking of all lotteries over all of the basic outcomes pertinent to the decision problem (see Resnik 1987 for an elementary exposition). But if we already have a ranking of all such lotteries, then there is nothing left to decide. We just choose the top-ranked lottery of those that are available. Decision theory merely offers some very rudimentary (but nevertheless controversial) constraints on how the lotteries may be ranked. Indeed, the principle that one should maximize expected utility really means no more than that one's rankings of lotteries over basic outcomes should satisfy these constraints. (For further discussion, see my 1994, chapter 5.)

The dearth of folk psychological principles is only more obvious when we turn from decision-making to theory confirmation. There is simply no general theory whatsoever that tells us what theories people will accept on the basis of their evidence. Furthermore, we can expect no help from the normative theory of inference. Statisticians have methods for selecting among statistical hypotheses. Philosophers of science can perhaps identify in a vague way some of the virtues that a theory ought to have. Ideally, we would have a true, all-purpose principle that, given a range of hypotheses and given a body of evidence, would tell us which of those hypotheses we should believe or should regard as most probable. Certainly no one knows any such principle. Before we even get to the point of selecting among hypotheses, we first of all have to think some hypotheses up, and there is even less to say about how a person does or ought to do that.

A basic question for anyone who imagines that our attributions of beliefs and desires are guided by folk psychological laws is whether (a) we should think of those laws as describing the way people actually do think, or (b) we should think of those laws as rules of rational thought. The problem with option (a) is that there are at least as many styles of thinking as there are personality types, and there is no fixed number of the latter. We should not expect the determining differences between thinkers of different types to be characterizable in folk psychological terms. Folk psychology certainly has nothing useful to say about why one person jumps to conclusions while another ponders the evidence, or why one person accepts short-term gratification while another patiently waits for the larger prize, or why one person draws analogies while another writes equations instead. Perhaps there is just a small number of parameters of variation and all of the differences in styles of thought result from different combinations of the values of these parameters. But folk psychology says nothing about these parameters, and even if it does, it does not tell us how to calculate their values in particular cases on the basis of a person's overt behavior. So we should not expect there to be general folk psychological principles that subsume all the various styles of thought. (For an exposition of the concepts of folk psychology that brings out their *Mannigfaltigkeit* and defies any attempt to subsume them under universal principles, see Morton 1980.)

Option (b) is to think of the principles of folk psychology as a general theory of rationality. If we take this option, then we might say that what the different styles of thinking have in common is only that they approximate to the same ideal. We can learn to understand people by learning in what ways their thinking diverges from this ideal. The problem with this option is that in fact the theory of rationality is an invention, not a discovery. It is not something hidden deep within our souls that can be teased out into the open through clever thought experiments. The theory of rational thought is a collection of tools, each limited in its sphere of application, invented by people who study scientific, economic, and rhetorical practice and try to improve performance where they can. In teaching logic and probability theory to my students, I am not merely making explicit for them what they have long taken for granted without ever really thinking about it. I am forcing them to do something new. Their present patterns of thought provide only hand-holds by which I can try to drag them into the light.

If it is not by applying a folk psychological theory of beliefs and desires that we explain and predict human behavior, then how do we do it? In order to show that we are not bound to understand the attribution of beliefs and desires as descriptions of the gears in the machine that produce behavior, it is not enough just to present an alternative account of the point of such attributions, as I have done in the previous chapter, or to question the viability of folk psychological theory as a source of explanations and predictions, as I have just done. It is necessary also to show that there might be some other means by which we anticipate other people's behavior and coordinate ourselves with others. It is necessary beyond that to acknowledge and accommodate the fact that in some manner we can sometimes explain people's behavior in terms of beliefs and desires.

One of the main ways to predict people's behavior is just by generalizing from the past, that is, by straight induction. For instance, we might predict that a person crossing a street will look both ways before crossing. We can think of good reasons to do this, but we can expect that people will do it just because we know that they tend to do it. We may predict that a panting, sweating jogger will stop at the drinking fountain and take a drink, not because we think that he desires to drink water and believes that he can drink water from the fountain, but just because we know that panting, sweating people tend to drink water when presented with it. We could be wrong of course—he might not see the fountain, or he might be testing his stamina—but we could be wrong no matter how we do it. I predict that most of my students will show up for class, not because I know that they desire to do well and believe that in order to do well they must attend class, but just because every day I come to class and there they are!

The reference class for such generalizations may be the actions of people in general, or just the actions of the particular person in question, or just the actions of the person in question in circumstances like the present. Naturally, we will have reason to define the reference class narrowly. In that way we take account of what distinguishes the person and circumstances in question from other things. And we will have reason to define the reference class broadly. In that case our prediction is supported by a larger body of data. Our skill at prediction will depend on how well we balance these conflicting desiderata.

To say that we can predict what a person will do by straight induction is not to say that what he or she does is thoughtless, the product of sheer conditioning. The behavior may be the product of a complicated mental process and still be predictable through straight induction. Indeed, the conditions in terms of which we define the reference class may be conditions that a creature's behavior would not be sensitive to unless that creature were capable of thinking in some way. For instance, we might predict that a baboon who is being groomed by another baboon will allow himself to be displaced by another baboon higher up in the social hierarchy, because that is what baboons tend to do. We would not expect baboons to behave in this way unless they were in some way sensitive to one another's position in a social hierarchy, and we would not expect that they could be sensitive to this unless they were capable of some kind of mental process characterizable as *thought*. But to make the prediction, it is not necessary to make any assumptions at all about the nature of the thinking that goes on in them beyond the fact that it somehow allows them to be sensitive to hierarchy.

Certainly straight induction is not the only method by which we might predict a person's behavior. Another important method is to find that a person has a certain skill or competence and to extrapolate from that. If on the basis of past experience I know that my opponent is a competent chess player, and if on the basis of the arrangement of chess pieces on the board I can see that the best thing for her to do would be to take my rook, then I may predict that she will take my rook. This method can work as well if my opponent is not a person but a chess-playing computer. My prediction in this case is not just a generalization from the past, because I may make the prediction even if I have never observed a chess game in which the pieces were arranged on the board in any way quite like this. Generalizations may be involved, of course, such as the generalization that this computer tends to keep on playing and does not tend just to quit due to no apparent cause. But it is also necessary to apply a conception of what the rules of chess allow and what good strategy dictates, and applying such a conception is not the same as generalizing from the past.

If the question arises what my opponent, or the computer, believes and desires, there may be definite answers: She may believe that my rook is vulnerable. She may desire to win the game. And if the circumstances were such that I could not attribute these beliefs and desires to her then I might not predict that she would take my rook. But the inference to the conclusion that she will take my rook need not be mediated by any premises about her beliefs and desires (contrary to the philosophy of the "intentional stance" popularized by Daniel Dennett 1971). Rather, I simply make an inference from the assumption that in playing chess she tends to do whatever is most likely to promote her winning, which in this case means that she will take my rook.

A particularly important kind of prediction based on an attribution of competence is prediction based on the supposition that a person is competent in the use of a language. If I ask a student to meet me at my office at 10 o'clock and he agrees, then I expect to find him there at roughly 10 o'clock. To normally do what one says one will do is part of one's competence in language. To normally expect people to do what they say they will do is another part of that competence. So as a consequence of my own competence I expect that the student will show up. Of course, various things may prevent him from showing up, and I know that. Or I may know from past experience that this particular student is especially unreliable. Or I may have reason to doubt that he knows where my office is. But if I do not have any such specific grounds to doubt that the student will do what he agreed to do, then, as a consequence of our both being competent speakers of English, I am justified in assuming that he will show up.

One of the main reasons why philosophers are so readily persuaded that the reason for being of attributions of beliefs and desires is explanation and prediction may be that human beings do coordinate their behavior and therefore must have some means of doing so. But it is not necessary to think of this coordination as a matter of predicting on the basis of attributions of beliefs and desires. The better way to think of it is as a matter of making agreements. The linguistic means for making agreements range from explicit promises to simply taking part in a conversation that has a goal. Our expectation that a person will do as he or she agrees to do, whether that is a matter of keeping a promise or merely remaining party to the conversation, is a consequence of our presumption of people's linguistic competence.

How, one might ask, do we know what a person's competence in language entails? A rather superficial answer is that that knowledge is itself an aspect of one's competence. A person's competence as a speaker of a language entails not only an ability to speak appropriately for himself or herself and to respond appropriately to words, but also an ability to recognize what it would be appropriate for someone else to say or to do in response to words. If one is competent, then by virtue of that competence one will know what would be appropriate, and one will be able to predict that another will say one of those things that would be appropriate in light of the other things he has said and the circumstances in which he finds himself, and one will be able to predict that another will respond to what is said in one of those ways that would be appropriate. However, to presume that someone is a competent speaker of a language and to behave toward that person accordingly need not amount to *ascribing* competence. In a context where everyone we meet is a competent speaker of the language, there is no need to specifically ascribe competence.

The deeper question, then, is, what does this competence consist in? One kind of answer to this would be a characterization of the norms of discourse, conformity to which defines competence. I certainly have not provided a complete answer of that kind, but I hope that part of the answer is everything that I have said in this book about assertibility in a context. But another kind of answer is also required, namely, a description of the mental processes underlying language use. I have acknowledged (in chapter 3) an obligation to provide an alternative account of this, which does not treat language as the expression of beliefs and desires, but I have declined to take up that subject in this book. Certainly, I am not suggesting that straight induction and inference from competence are alternatives to scientific psychology. On the contrary, I expect that the deep explanations of human behavior will be ones with which we have no ordinary acquaintance.

Someone might think that prediction on the basis of a presumption of a competence in some skill might be described as *simulation*, but that would be a mistake. (So what I am proposing is not a version of the so-called simulation theory, as developed by Gordon 1986, 1995, and Goldman 1989.) Simulation of another person's thought or behavior requires imagining oneself in the other's shoes, looking out at the world from his or her point of view, with his or her motives and conceptions of things. Having done this, one is supposed to think in the manner of someone so situated. On one version, one is supposed to identify the products of this thinking introspectively and then infer that they must be present in the other as well. On another version, there need be no such introspection or inference; rather one speaks or acts *for* the other in the way this thinking motivates. My own proposal involves none of this. In drawing conclusions from the presumption that someone possesses some competence, one has no need to imagine oneself in his or her place or in any other way to use one's own mental machinery as a model for the other's. A person's knowledge of what it is appropriate for another person to say in a given situation is an exercise of his or her competence with language that is no less fundamental than his or her knowledge of what it is appropriate for himself or herself to say; the former sort of knowledge needs no grounding in the latter.

Whenever we could have *predicted*, we will be able to produce at least one kind of *explanation* in the same way. If we might have predicted by straight induction, then we can explain what we observe as having been predictable in just that way. (I do not say that this is a very deep kind of explanation, but there is a commonplace practice of explaining things in this way all the same.) If we might have predicted on the presumption of a skill, then what we observe will be explicable as what might have been expected on just that basis. In other cases, we may be able to explain post hoc what we could not have predicted. One such case is that in which we explain by representing the behavior in question as integral to a conversation, either overt or covert, on the presumption that the agent is a competent speaker of the language. For instance, if we explain why *A* gave *B* a pencil, the answer may be that *B* asked *A* whether he could borrow a pencil.

In such cases, the connection between the thing explained and the explanation is not a general law relating effects of that kind to causes of that kind. Nor does the connection consist in the fact that we see that such a response is one that we ourselves might make if such a thing were said to us. As competent speakers of a language, if we are acquainted with the context pertaining to a conversation, then we understand what it would be appropriate to say at a given juncture in the conversation, and we understand what it would be appropriate to say if the context were in specific ways different from what it is in fact. This understanding allows us both to participate in conversations ourselves and to explain a contribution to a conversation or a response to words by citing the prior stages of the conversation. It also allows us to recognize as explanatory such explanations that are given to us by others. But again, such explanations are no substitute for scientific psychology; at best they contribute to our ability to conduct ourselves in society.

In some of these cases in which we explain by representing the behavior in question as integral to a conversation, it makes sense to treat the explanation as an explanation in terms of beliefs and desires. Among the assertions and commands that we make, there will be assertions and commands that we issue to *ourselves*. I command myself: "Eat lunch now," and consequently I go to the kitchen. I assert to myself: "The bread is in the refrigerator," and consequently I open the refrigerator when I start to prepare lunch. Further, just as we may make assertions and commands directed to ourselves, we may make assertions and commands on another person's behalf directed at that person. For instance, I might be able to command you, on your behalf, to prepare lunch now, and assert, on your behalf, that the bread is in the refrigerator. These commands and assertions on your behalf may take the form of attributions of desires and beliefs. In this way, it may be possible to explain your behavior by citing your desire to prepare lunch and your belief that the bread is in the refrigerator. Generalizing, when we explain a person's behavior by citing beliefs and desires, we represent that behavior as integral to a conversation that that person has with himself or herself. Such explanations in terms of beliefs and desires are explanatory to us because we ourselves know how to carry on a conversation such as that which is reconstructed when we make them on another's behalf.

While little can be explained in terms of beliefs and desires, much less can be predicted in that way. Nonetheless, attributions of beliefs and desires may occasionally play a role even in prediction. As noted, one of our ways of explaining a person's behavior may be to issue assertions and commands on that person's behalf directed to that same person. On some occasions, it might even be possible to make these assertions and commands on a person's behalf directed at him or her in advance of the behavior that we think of as the person's response to those assertions and commands and, in that way, predict in terms of beliefs and desires. As a competent speaker of the language, one may be able to reconstruct on another person's behalf brief conversations between that person and himself or herself, which one may expect to have a certain behavioral outcome. However, the implications of a person's linguistic competence are not very often definite enough to allow us to predict his or her behavior in this manner.

Sometimes behavior that is predictable only by straight induction is nonetheless explicable in terms of beliefs and desires. I may predict that you will take measures to stop the leak in the roof of your house just because I know that people take measures to avoid getting wet, and in this case that would mean plugging up the holes in your roof. Having predicted this merely by generalizing from what people tend to do, I might also explain it in terms of what you must have been thinking. You said to yourself something like this: "I don't want to get wet. I'll get wet if I don't plug those holes. So get yourself up there and plug those holes!" I could make these assertions and commands on your behalf just as well using the idioms of "belief" and "desire."

This fact, that behavior predictable only by straight induction is sometimes explicable in terms of beliefs and desires, even before the predicted action occurs, may be one source of the tendency to exaggerate the extent to which we can predict people's behavior in terms of beliefs and desires. We can sometimes predict what people will do, although seldom on the basis of their beliefs and desires. But even where we could not have *predicted* on the basis of the agent's beliefs and desires, we can sometimes *explain* in advance the agent's behavior on the basis of beliefs and desires. So it is easy to get confused and think that the basis for our prediction is the beliefs and desires cited in explanation.

A natural reaction to my thesis on the part of analytically trained philosophers will be to try to think of counterexamples. A counterexample would be a case in which we explain what another person has done, or predict what another person will do, on the basis of attributions of beliefs and desires but in which our attributions cannot be construed as assertions and commands on the other's behalf. Such counterexamples will probably be hard to find, because it is actually rather easy to reconstruct ordinary claims about beliefs and desires as assertions and commands on another's behalf and then to characterize whatever predictive power we may derive from these attributions as a consequence of our competence in the language. By the same token, finding examples that pass this test does little to confirm the communicative conception.

Consider, for example, the following case (suggested to me by John Perry):

The Helpful Onlooker

1. A lecture is taking place in the evening in Cordura Hall. Shortly before the lecture is to start, Alfred sees somebody, Barbara, pulling on the locked door of Ventura Hall, which is just across the patio from Cordura Hall.

2. Alfred asks Barbara, "Are you looking for the lecture?"

3. Barbara says, "Yes, I am."

4. Alfred says, "It's in the other building." Alfred and Barbara walk over to Cordura together.

5. Chen, who has observed the above sequence of events, asks Alfred, "Why did you ask her that question?"

6. Alfred says, "I thought she might be looking for the lecture and wanted to help."

7. Chen asks Alfred, "Why did you think she might be looking for the lecture?"

8. Alfred replies, "I didn't recognize her as someone who might have a reason to get into Ventura at this hour, and I knew that a lot of people would be coming over here tonight to hear the lecture."

This example is confusing because four explanations are involved, namely, Barbara's explanation of her own behavior at line 3, Alfred's explanation of Barbara's behavior at line 6, Alfred's explanation of his own behavior at line 6, and Alfred's explanation of his own thought at line 8.

Barbara's explanation of her own behavior at line 3 answers Alfred's question at line 2. Her answer at line 3 is elliptical for "Yes, I am looking for the lecture." Toward understanding this answer, compare a simple conversation in which someone says, "Go into the other room," and this command is followed by somebody's going into the other room, or a conversation in which someone says, "Find the lecture," and this command is followed by somebody's finding the lecture. Some of these conversations will be conversations that people have with themselves. For instance, someone might tell himself, "Find the lecture," and this might be followed by his finding the lecture. We may view Barbara's answer at line 3, "I am looking for the lecture," as a reconstruction of just such an internal conversation that she has with herself. (But to take it as such is not to say that any such conversation actually took place.) In saying this to Alfred, Barbara is carrying on, on behalf of her former self, a simple conversation in which Barbara says to herself, "Find the lecture," and responds by pulling on the front door of Ventura Hall. She carries on this conversation on behalf of her former self, rather than just carrying it on, because at this point she is not trying to find the lecture but is explaining her behavior to Alfred, or, more precisely, affirming the explanation that he had entertained. The reason why Alfred asks whether she was *looking* for the lecture, using that particular expression of desire, is that such a formulation acknowledges that what she had commanded herself to do was specifically to *find* something, namely, the location of the lecture. In acquiescing in this formulation, Barbara acknowledges that the command she had given herself was of this kind.

We may now take up Alfred's explanation of his own behavior at line 6. Here Alfred cites his own thought about a thought, namely, Alfred's thought about Barbara's looking. We may understand Alfred's ascription of a thought to himself here as an assertion on his own past self's behalf. What Alfred asserts on his own past self's behalf is that this person (Barbara) had possibly commanded herself to find the lecture. In response to Chen's question at 5, this explains Alfred's question to Barbara at line 2 in that Chen will understand that Alfred might have wished to confirm that Barbara had commanded herself to find the lecture by, in effect, asking her whether she had done so. In the second half of line 6, Alfred says "and I wanted to help." This we may understand as a command that Alfred issues to his former self on behalf of his former self, commanding himself to help Barbara find the lecture.

Line 8 can be reconstructed as a matter of Alfred's making or disavowing assertions on his own behalf. When Alfred says, "I didn't recognize her as someone who might have a reason to get into Ventura at this hour," he denies that he asserts on his own behalf, "She has a reason to get into Ventura at this hour." By denying this, he explains why it occurred to him to wonder why this person (Barbara) was pulling on the door of Ventura Hall. When Alfred says, "I knew that a lot of people would be coming over here tonight to hear the lecture," he asserts on his own behalf that a lot of people would be going to Cordura to hear the lecture. By doing this, he provides an explanation for his own speculation that Barbara was looking for the lecture. (I do not attempt to explain what is achieved by means of the verbs "recognize" and "know" over and above what might be achieved by means of the word "believe.")

A common ploy of charlatans is to take some commonsensical account of things and translate it into some arcane lingo. So anyone not persuaded on other grounds by my account of belief and desire attribution will not be persuaded by this construal of the case of the helpful onlooker. It is indeed just too easy to take any ordinary explanation in terms of states such as belief and desire and reformulate it in the lingo of assertions and commands on another person's behalf. My only purpose has been to demonstrate to anyone who might have doubted whether it can be done that it can be. The real test of my theory is not whether we can reformulate attributions of beliefs and desires in this manner, but whether we can go on to give satisfactory theoretical explanations of the terms of the reformulation. That is what I hope to have made a start at in everything else I have said in this book. I will answer some important further questions in the next chapter.

12 Semantics and Ontology

In two respects my account of the communicative conception of beliefs and desires is incomplete. First, I need to show that the theory of belief attribution that I have been developing in the previous two chapters can be extended to provide a comprehensive semantics for sentences of the form S^"believes that"^p. Second, I need to show that this account of belief *attribution* can qualify as a theory of the very *nature* of beliefs as well. In completing my account in these ways I will at the same time be addressing two remaining motives for employing some kind of concept of meaning, or proposition, in our theory of language.

From the received point of view, what semantics requires is an account of the truth conditions of sentences of the form S^"believes that"^p. This account must extend as well to more complex sentences in which sentences of that form are embedded. In the tradition stemming from Frege (and carried on by, for example, Stalnaker 1987), the solution to this semantic problem has been to say that a sentence of the form S^"believes that"^p is true if and only if the thinker that S refers to stands in the belief-relation to the proposition that "that"^p refers to. Thus, in a sentence such as "Janice believes that dinosaurs are extinct", the "that"-clause refers to the proposition that dinosaurs are extinct. Even among proponents of the received view it is well recognized that the semantics of "that"-clauses is not at all that simple, but it is nonetheless widely assumed that propositions will play a role here somehow.

The theory of belief attribution that I have developed in the previous two chapters does not immediately provide an alternative to this semantics since it does not immediately tell us anything about the use of "believes" in complex sentences. If what I am doing when I say "Harry believes the cookie jar is empty" is asserting on Harry's behalf that the cookie jar is empty, what am I doing if I assert, "*If* Harry believes that the cookie jar is empty, *then* he will not open it"? If what I am doing when I say that "Janice believes that dinosaurs are extinct" is asserting on Janice's behalf that dinosaurs are extinct, what am I doing if I say, "Everything that Janice believes about dinosaurs is true"?

However, the communicative conception of beliefs can be extended to include a theory of such embedded occurrences of "believes" by means of a context-logical semantics for languages containing sentences of the form, S^"believes that"^p. The relation of the theory of belief presented in the previous chapters to this semantics is that it will play a role in the substantive account of the pertinent notion of context. I will assume that a similar semantics for "desire" could be given, but I will not go so far as to actually give one. I should acknowledge my debt here to the work of Walter Edelberg (1995). Although Edelberg works within a model-theoretic, possible worlds framework, his paper helped me to see what my semantics had to achieve and gave me some ideas about how to achieve it.

Let us consider a language that permits negation, disjunction, and ordinary quantification, and which contains the identity sign "=", but, for simplicity, let us ignore the complications brought on by conditionals, truth predicates, and assertibility predicates. To this language, we want to add a predicate "believes that", which we use to form sentences of the form **n believes that p**, and which we want to understand as a predicate by means of which we make assertions on other people's behalf. We now want to define the pertinent sort of context for such a language and define assertibility and deniability conditions for the sentences of such a language relative to such contexts, including assertibility and deniability conditions for sentences of the form **n believes that p**.

As usual, the first thing to do is to explain the formal structure of contexts for such a language. Here, the basic idea is that we want contexts to include assignments of other contexts to agents. Let us say that, formally, a *perspectival context* Γ is a quadruple $\langle B_\Gamma, N_\Gamma, A_\Gamma, h_\Gamma \rangle$. B_Γ, the *base* of the context, is a primitive context in the sense of chapter 9 (which, recall, differs from the definition in chapter 3 in that it accommodates identity). Sentences in B_Γ do not contain "believes that". N_Γ, the domain of the context, is a set of demonstrative pronouns containing every demonstrative pronoun that occurs in any member of B_Γ and possibly others as well. A_Γ is a set of names, or demonstrative pronouns, which we may think of as denoting agents pertinent to the conversation. There may be some overlap between N_Γ and A_Γ. h_Γ is a function that assigns to every member of A_Γ a perspectival context of the same kind as I am here describing. In the first layer of perspectival contexts, A_Γ is empty. In the second layer, A_Γ is nonempty and h_Γ assigns to every member of A_Γ a perspectival context in the first layer. In the third layer, A_Γ is again nonempty and h_Γ assigns to every member of A_Γ a perspectival context from any of the previous layers. And so on. A *perspectival context* is any such quadruple in any of these layers.

In terms of perspectival contexts, we can now define the assertibility and deniability conditions for sentences of the form **n believes that p**. For other sorts of sentences, conditions on assertibility and deniability will be formulated in the usual way (see chapters 3 and 7, and for the theory of identity, see chapter 9). We then add: **n believes that p** is assertible in a perspectival context Γ if **p** is assertible in $h_\Gamma(\mathbf{n})$, and **n believes that p** is deniable in a perspectival context Γ if **p** is deniable in $h_\Gamma(\mathbf{n})$. In this way a belief-predicate can be incorporated into a language so as to allow sentences such as "Either John does not believe that it is raining or John believes that it is precipitating".

It remains to explain in a substantive way what a perspectival context is supposed to be. The substantive definition will tell us the conditions under which a perspectival context, formally so defined, pertains to a given conversation. This is where the theory of belief developed in chapter 10 makes its showing in the semantics of belief-predicates. As always, B_Γ, N_Γ, and A_Γ are identified in terms of relevance to the goals of the conversation. As for h_Γ, if **n** is the name of agent S and $h_\Gamma(\mathbf{n}) = \Delta$, then the sentences assertible in Δ should be just those that are assertible on S's behalf in the conversation in question. In particular, the literals in the base of $h_\Gamma(\mathbf{n}) = \Delta$ should be the literals that are assertible on S's behalf. In effect, the present semantics for belief-predicates extends the communicative conception of belief attribution to belief attributions occurring as components of compound sentences.

We can take this style of semantics a step further and allow quantifications into "that"-clauses as follows: Let $\Sigma(\Gamma)$ be the set of contexts in the range of h_Γ plus Γ itself. Let $N_{\Sigma(\Gamma)}$ be the union of all of the domains of the contexts in $\Sigma(\Gamma)$. Call this the *outer domain* for Γ, and to emphasize the distinction, call N_Γ the *inner domain*. Overlooking the equation of things with their names, one could say that $N_{\Sigma(\Gamma)}$, the outer domain, is the set of all things that anyone in Γ believes to exist (as well as the things that exist according to Γ). Just as we defined assertibility and deniability conditions for ordinary quantifications with reference to N_Γ, we can define assertibility and deniability conditions for "intensional" quantifications with reference to $N_{\Sigma(\Gamma)}$. Suppose, then, that we add to our language a quantifier "for some*" (read "for some-star"). Then we can formulate assertibility and deniability conditions for sentences of the form **for some* x F** as follows: **for some* x F** is assertible in a perspectival context Γ if for some singular term $\mathbf{n}$ in $N_{\Sigma(\Gamma)}$, **Fn/x** is assertible in Γ; and **for some* x F** is deniable in a perspectival context Γ if for every $\mathbf{n}$ in $N_{\Sigma(\Gamma)}$, **Fn/x** is deniable in Γ. Since we will now have two kinds of quantifiers in play, it is also necessary to make the reference to the domain explicit in the assertibility conditions for ordinary existential quantifications (which we did not need to do in chapter 7), thus: **for some x F** is assertible in Γ if for some **n** in N_Γ, **Fn/x** is assertible in Γ. (It's the "in N_Γ" that is new here; it has been explicit all along in our statement of the deniability conditions for existential quantifications.)

Someone murdered Jones. No one murdered Smith; he drowned by accident. Detectives Arsky and Barsky both believe that someone murdered Jones. Arsky and Barsky also both believe that someone murdered Smith, but while Arsky believes that Jones's murderer and Smith's murderer are one and the same, Barsky believes that different people murdered Jones and Smith. However, Arsky thinks that the person who Barsky believes murdered Smith is the person who murdered both Jones and Smith. This is a tricky situation in that, while in some sense Arsky believes something of something real (Jones's murderer) and Barsky believes something of something unreal (Smith's murderer), nonetheless the object of Arsky's belief is in some sense the same as the object of Barsky's belief. How can something real be the same as something unreal?

The perspectival context Γ pertinent to our story may be represented thus:

B_Γ = {This murdered Jones. This did not murder Smith. Jones did not murder Smith. Smith did not murder Smith.}.

N_Γ = {Jones, Smith, This}.

A_Γ = {Arsky, Barsky}.

h_Γ(Arsky) = Δ.

h_Γ(Barsky) = Ω.

B_Δ = {This murdered Jones. This murdered Smith. This = that.}.

N_Δ = {Jones, Smith, This, That}.

A_Δ = {Barsky}.

h_Δ(Barsky) = Ω.

B_Ω = {This murdered Jones. That murdered Smith. This ≠ that.}.

N_Ω = {Jones, Smith, This, That}.

(To avoid clutter I have omitted quotation marks. The items in these sets are all linguistic items. For instance, A_Γ contains the name "Arsky", not Arsky himself, and h_Γ assigns Δ to "Arsky", not to Arsky.) Relative to this context, the story of Arsky and Barsky comes out just as we should expect. For example:

• "For some x, Arsky believes that x murdered Jones and Barsky believes that x murdered Jones" is assertible in Γ, because "This" belongs to N_Γ and "This murdered Jones" is assertible in both h_Γ(Arsky) = Δ and h_Γ(Barsky) = Ω.

• "For some x, x murdered Jones and Arsky believes that x murdered Jones" is assertible in Γ, because "This" belongs to N_Γ and "This murdered Jones" is assertible both in Γ and in h_Γ(Arsky) = Δ. Likewise, "For some x, x murdered Jones and Arsky believes that x murdered Smith" is assertible in Γ.

• "Arsky believes that for some x, x murdered Smith" is assertible in Γ because "For some x, x murdered Smith" is assertible in $h_\Gamma(\text{Arsky}) = \Delta$.

• "For some x, x murdered Smith and Arsky believes that x murdered Smith" is *not* assertible in Γ, since there is no n in N_Γ such that $n^\wedge$"murdered Smith" is assertible in Γ.

• "For some x, Barsky believes that x murdered Smith" is not assertible in Γ because there is no n in N_Γ such that $n^\wedge$"murdered Smith" is assertible in $h_\Gamma(\text{Barsky}) = \Omega$. Consequently, "For some x, x murdered Jones and Barsky believes x murdered Smith" is not assertible in Γ, and "For some x, Barsky believes that x murdered Smith and Arsky believes that x murdered Jones" is not assertible in Γ.

• However, "For some* x, Barsky believes that x murdered Smith" is assertible in Γ, because "That" is in $N_{\Sigma(\Gamma)}$ and "That murdered Smith" is assertible in $h_\Gamma(\text{Barsky}) = \Omega$.

• Likewise, "For some* x, Barsky believes that x murdered Smith and Arsky believes x murdered Jones" is assertible in Γ, because "That" is in $N_{\Sigma(\Gamma)}$ and "That murdered Smith" is assertible in $h_\Gamma(\text{Barsky}) = \Omega$ and "That murdered Jones" is assertible in $h_\Gamma(\text{Arsky}) = \Delta$. The reason why "That murdered Jones" is assertible in $h_\Gamma(\text{Arsky}) = \Delta$ is that both "This = that" and "This murdered Jones" are assertible in Δ. (See the treatment of identity in chapter 9.)

• "Arsky believes that for some x, x murdered Jones and Barsky believes that x murdered Smith" (with "for some x" having "Barsky believes" in its scope) is assertible in Γ, because "For some x, x murdered Jones and Barsky believes that x murdered Smith" is assertible in $h_\Gamma(\text{Arsky}) = \Delta$. The reason for that, in turn, is that "That" is in N_Δ and "That murdered Jones" is assertible in Δ, as I have already explained, and "That murdered Smith" is assertible in $h_\Delta(\text{Barsky}) = \Omega$.

• But, "For some* x, x murdered Jones and Barsky believes he murdered Smith" is not assertible in Γ, for there is no n in $N_{\Sigma(\Gamma)}$ such that both $n\hat{}$"murdered Jones" is assertible in Γ and $n\hat{}$"murdered Smith" is assertible in $h_\Gamma(\text{Barsky}) = \Omega$.

(What I am proposing to explain here is only the assertibility conditions for sentences of a certain regimented syntax. To convert ordinary English sentences into sentences of this more regimented syntax we need a theory of a kind I have not attempted to develop here.)

I do not wish to suggest that the languages we actually speak contain two different kinds of quantifiers, normal quantifiers and intensional quantifiers. But I do think that our ordinary quantifiers can be understood in two different ways, so that sometimes they work like our "for some x" and sometimes like our "for some* x". In the story of Arsky and Barsky, we can say, without being misleading, "Someone murdered Jones and Arsky believes he murdered Jones." Here we understand the quantification as normal. Likewise, we can say, treating the quantifier as having wide scope, "Barsky believes that someone murdered Smith and Arsky believes he murdered Jones." Here we understand the quantification as intensional. (Read it as "For some* x, Barsky believes that x murdered Smith and Arsky believes x murdered Jones.") Giving the quantifier wide scope and understanding the quantification as intensional, we can even say, "Arsky believes that someone murdered Jones and Barsky believes he murdered Smith." (I take it that this does not imply that Barsky thinks that Jones's murderer and Smith's murderer are identical.) What shows that we are really dealing with two kinds of quantification is that we cannot, without being misleading, say, "Someone murdered Jones, Arsky believes he murdered Jones, and Barsky believes he murdered Smith." That would imply that the person who murdered Jones is the one of whom Barsky believes that he murdered Smith; but since we cannot say, "Someone murdered Jones and Barsky believes he murdered Smith," regardless of how we understand the quantifier, that is not right.

To accommodate the validity of the inference from **n believes that p** to **n believes something** and the assertibility of sentences such as **There is something that n and m both believe**, we would need to introduce yet another kind of quantifier, one that binds the position held by "that"-clauses. That would be easy to do, but I will not take the space to do it here. Perhaps we do not have to say that natural language contains an additional kind of quantifier—propositional in addition to objectual, but I think we do have to recognize at least an additional "understanding" of quantifiers in our formal semantics. If we suppose that there is only one sort of quantifier and only one sort of domain, then we might have to countenance the validity of an inference from "Peter believes that the movers have finished" and "Everything is in the truck" to the conclusion "That the movers have finished is in the truck".

Nothing in this account corresponds to the distinction sometimes drawn between *de re* and *de dicto* belief-sentences. It is sometimes thought that a sentence such as "Ralph believes that the shortest spy is a spy" can be taken in two ways. On the *de re* reading, "the shortest spy" refers to the shortest spy, and on the *de dicto* reading, those words refer, rather, to some other kind of thing, such as Ralph's concept, *the shortest spy*. Philosophers have even gone so far as to claim that this sentence is true on the *de re* reading only if Ralph is in some special sense *en rapport* with the shortest spy. (A primary source is Kaplan 1968–1969, although Kaplan does not use the *de re/de dicto* terminology. Kaplan, in turn, relies heavily on the work of Quine.) I myself do not see any reason to countenance such a distinction. What I do acknowledge is a distinction between two domains of discourse, the outer domain and the inner domain, and that of course makes a difference to the kinds of existential quantification that will be assertible in a context.

Some people have persuaded themselves that the *de re* reading can be equivalently expressed with the sentence "Ralph believes *of* the shortest spy that he is a spy" (with stress on "*of*"). But as far as I can see, ordinary linguistic practice does not in any way encourage this idea. Though someone might say, "Andy believes of Santa Claus that he drives a flying sleigh," the speaker would not thereby commit himself or herself to the existence of Santa Claus. English grammar provides this form of sentence as a way of letting the speaker put the emphasis, or focus, on "Santa Claus" or whatever other noun phrase occupies that position; but the use of the "of"-locution does not carry any special commitment on the part of the speaker to the existence of something denoted by the phrase that follows "of".

Nothing in the present account of the semantics of belief-sentences entails that a sentence of the form Sˆ"believes that"ˆp is assertible only if p is a sentence that the person we are talking about might actually speak. For instance, while p will be a sentence of English (since Sˆ"believes that"ˆp is English), the person we are talking about might speak no English, for we might still speak in English on that person's behalf. Moreover, the sentence we use in the "that"-clause need not be any very direct translation of any sentence that the person we are talking about would actually use to express his or her belief. If a person were speaking for himself, he might say, "*I* need to go now"; whereas if we spoke on his behalf, we would say, "He thinks *he* needs to go now." Or while someone might express her thought saying, "The first man to walk on the moon was born in Ohio," we might speak on her behalf saying, "Neil Armstrong was born in Ohio."

So we might ask, what relation must obtain between the sentences that appear in the "that"-clause of a sentence by which we attribute a belief to someone and the sentences by which the person would, as we say, express his or her belief? An answer might take the form of a theory of the conditions under which two sentences "say the same" in context. Here I will not attempt any general theory of samesaying but will merely comment that the context-logical account might be liberating in that it might allow an account of samesaying more nuanced than the usual; we will not be confined to the relations of *expressing the same proposition*, or *having the same meaning.* (For an approach to this matter that is not bound to the usual categories, see Sbisà, forthcoming.)

Perhaps I need to add that it would be a basic misunderstanding to characterize my theory as holding that belief is a relation between a believer and a sentence. That would be a fair characterization only if I had interpreted "believes" as denoting, or expressing, a relation—one that holds between believers and sentences. But in fact the devices of context logic manage to define assertibility conditions for sentences and validity for arguments without ever interpreting expressions as denoting or expressing things at all. Nor am I saying that a belief is a relation between a believer and a context. A perspectival context Γ includes a function h_Γ that assigns a context to each member of A_Γ, but h_Γ is clearly not the belief-relation either since h_Γ assigns a whole context, not the thing that a believer is said to believe. We may retain the slogan "A belief is a relation to a proposition," but we should understand it as merely a characterization of the grammatical form of "belief"-sentences. In just the same sense we might say that a conjunction is a relation between propositions as a way of characterizing the syntax of "and"-sentences. In saying that conjunction is a relation between propositions, we distinguish the syntax of "and" from the syntax of "next to", which we may characterize by saying that contiguity is a relation between objects.

So much for the semantics of Sˆ"believes that"ˆp. I now turn to the other question that I raised at the beginning of this chapter, concerning the *nature* of beliefs and desires. What I want to say about this is that my account of the attribution of beliefs and desires is already an account of the nature of beliefs and desires. At first, this might look like a perverse inversion of the proper order of explanation. The proper order of explanation, one might presume, would be to first explain what beliefs *are* and then to explain the attribution of beliefs by explaining how we recognize the presence of such things. If we want to say what beliefs *are*, then what we have to do is characterize at some level the distinctive physical structure of things that have beliefs and explain how having that physical structure puts a thing that has it into the belief-relation to propositions. This does not in itself entail "internalism" regarding the nature of beliefs. We do not have to say that it is only the intrinsic structure of the belief or the belief-having organism that determines the propositional content of the belief; the relations between that structure and the rest of the world may matter as well.

In order not to be fooled by this objection, it is helpful to bear in mind the variety of ways in which we may explain the nature of a thing. Sometimes it is possible to say a lot about the nature of a thing by describing its internal structure and the manner of its interaction with other things. In this way, we could explain what a proton is. In other cases, the appropriate sort of explanation is an identification of function. There are many kinds of faucet; what they have in common is only a function; so there is no point in trying to describe in a general way the physical structure of a faucet. In other cases, the appropriate explanation locates the entity in question in a system of human conventions. For example, that is how we will explain what a Wednesday is. In still other cases, the key point will be a function within a system of human conventions. That is how we will explain what an apology is.

It is too narrow to think that an explanation of the nature of a thing must always amount to identifying its relation to the things in a privileged ontology, such as the basic elements of matter. What we can say in general about explanations of the natures of things is only that they must facilitate the hearer's entry into a form of discourse. In formulating our explanation, we have to imagine that we are explaining things to a student who is largely party to a form of discourse, but who for some reason does not know what to do with, say, the word "proton", or "faucet", or "Wednesday", or "apology". Our explanation of the kind of thing in question, be it protons, faucets, Wednesdays, or apologies, ought to provide a bridge from the forms of discourse in which the student is competent to the form of discourse that we imagine him or her to be lacking.

If we thus bear in mind the variety among explanations of the natures of things and the general purpose of such explanations, we should not be shocked by the claim that the communicative conception's account of the attribution of beliefs and desires is itself a theory of the *nature* of beliefs and desires. When we set out to explain the nature of beliefs and desires, we have to imagine a student who has somehow learned to talk about many things, to make assertions and issue commands, and in general to participate in linguistic interaction, but who has not latched on to the specific practice of attributing beliefs and desires. Our question concerns what we can say to such a person that would facilitate his or her entry into this further aspect of discourse. One thing that distinguishes this case from many others is that we would have to say something explicitly about language, namely, that in attributing a belief or a desire to a person, the student should think of himself or herself as making an assertion or command, respectively, on behalf of the person in question.

A further aspect of the doubt about the legitimacy of explaining the nature of a thing in terms of the way people talk about it stems from the sense that if a thing really exists then it must have a nature that can be investigated quite apart from the way people talk about it. For example, we would not want to have to countenance the existence of *fate* just because we find that there exists in our culture a certain practice of attributing events to fate. If fate really exists, then it must be something whose nature we can investigate quite apart from what people say about it. If electrons really exist, then they must have a nature that we can cite in explanation of observable phenomena, and this nature is not determined by how we talk about electrons. Similarly, if beliefs and desires really exist, it might be said, then they must have a nature that we can investigate quite apart from what people say about them, contrary to what the communicative conception claims.

This objection appears to stem from a postulationist prejudice, namely, the assumption that if anything can be said to exist, then our claim that it exists must be vindicated in light of our success in explaining and predicting in terms of it. It is certainly true that in some cases an existence claim can be justified in only this way, and in those cases the nature of the thing said to exist cannot be determined through an examination of the way people talk about it. Fate, if it existed, would have a nature apart from what people say about it, because we can have no reason to think that it exists apart from the success of explanations in terms of it. Fate has no nature apart from what people say about it, and does not exist, because there are no good explanations in terms of it. Electrons really do exist, and our reason for thinking so is that in positing the existence of electrons, we can explain observable phenomena, such as the illumination of a cathode ray tube.

The case of beliefs and desires is different, however, for in this case, we are not talking about a kind of thing the existence of which is demonstrated only through the success of explanations and predictions in terms of it. Explanation and prediction are not the main reasons for attributing beliefs and desires. Accordingly, we need not assume that if beliefs and desires really exist, then they must have a nature that can be investigated quite apart from the way people talk about them. This is not to say that the hypothesis that beliefs and desires exist cannot be criticized. It can be, but only by showing that the practice of making assertions and commands on behalf of others is defective in some way.

Yet another reason not to ground our theory of the nature of beliefs in our theory of their attribution is the intuition that a person may have beliefs even when there is no reason to attribute them. At any given time, I have all kinds of beliefs—for instance, that Timisoara is in Romania—that no one has any reason to attribute to me at that time. In general, people have many beliefs the attribution of which would have no special relevance to our current goals. My answer to this is that such suppositions belong to a derivative, exclusively philosophical practice. I can imagine someone before me, asking me all sorts of questions, such as "Where is Timisoara?" or "Would you describe your relationship with the accused as a friendly one?" and I can imagine myself answering them. I call the answers I might give, or that might be given on my behalf, *beliefs*. But what I might say will depend on who I imagine is asking and the reasons for asking I imagine him or her to have. (What I say to my wife might differ from what I would say to a prosecuting attorney. What I say to a student might differ from what I would publish in a book.) Since in this way we fall back on a context, even if it is only an imaginary context, in the evaluation of such "contextless" attributions of belief, such contextless attributions give us no reason to think that beliefs must have a nature that can be understood apart from the practice of attributing beliefs in a context.

Over and above these general objections against putting attribution before nature, a doubt might be raised against the particular theory of attribution developed here on the grounds that it seems to rule out the attribution of beliefs and desires to nonlinguistic animals or even to people with whom we have no linguistic interaction. What is right about this is that since the practice of attributing beliefs and desires does not primarily serve explanation and prediction, the practice of attributing beliefs and desires would not arise apart from a need to make assertions and commands on behalf of members of our own linguistic community. But the objection is mistaken about the commitments of the present theory of beliefs because not every correct exercise of a practice that has a certain function need directly serve that function. The practice of stopping at red lights serves the function of preventing collisions, but stopping at a red light at 2 a.m. when there are no other cars around is also a correct exercise of that practice. Similarly, making assertions and commands on behalf of people with whom we cannot interact, and who cannot even make assertions and commands of their own, may be a correct exercise of the practice of making assertions and commands on behalf of others if the way we do it is relevantly similar to the way we do it in interaction with members of our own linguistic community.

As for the attribution of beliefs and desires to nonlinguistic animals, the usual rationale for these is that such attributions yield good explanations of their behavior. But I have questioned the utility of attributions of beliefs and desires even in the explanation of human behavior, and I have suggested that such explanation succeeds only insofar as it reconstructs a hypothetical conversation. If we cannot explain even human behavior very well in terms of beliefs and desires, then surely we will not do very well in explaining the behavior of nonlinguistic creatures in terms of beliefs and desires. Consequently, I think we should not be impressed by this rationale. A practice of making assertions and commands on behalf of nonlinguistic animals might be useful in some ways. For instance, if there is something we can learn from their way of negotiating their environment, a good way for us to learn it and communicate it to others might be to make assertions on their behalf. For instance, we might say of some polar bears, "They believe they will actually be warmer if they dig a hole in the snow and climb in." In saying this, we may incidentally offer some analogical explanation of the polar bears' behavior; for they behave as though they had said to themselves "We will be warmer in the snow" (and then understood what they said). But the main point is that in doing so we bring the polar bears into the conversation, and let them teach us something that may be useful to us all.

In other cases, though, animals may have nothing to contribute to our conversation, and attributions of belief to them will serve us only as a convenient way of describing behavior. Thus we might say of a dog that he "believes that his master will be home soon." Or we might say of a chimp that he "thinks he can mislead you by heading toward the barrel on the left; but then at the last moment, he'll dart over to the one on the right." So long as we do not misunderstand these attributions as serious explanations of behavior, which they are not, they might help us imagine what happened. The way they do that, however, is not by allowing us to infer the effects of such beliefs. I doubt that the claim that the dog thinks his master will be home soon would be of much use to anyone who was not already familiar with dog behavior. What does a dog do when he is waiting for his master? Does he go out and shoot some hoops? Does he cook the master's dinner? Such an attribution serves merely to pick out one of a limited variety of already familiar dog behaviors.

At this point, it should be clear that the conception of beliefs that I have developed in this and the previous two chapters is entirely incompatible with the received view of linguistic communication. The incompatibility is not due to a disagreement over the priority of thought over language with respect to genesis, for a proponent of the received view does not have to say that language arises from the need to express prior beliefs. A proponent of the received view may acknowledge that language and contentful thought arise in the world together. He or she might acknowledge that we form many of our concepts in an effort to grasp the concepts that underlie other people's use of words, or, more generally, in learning what they tell us.

The reason for the incompatibility is also not that according to the communicative conception, it never makes sense to describe a person's words as an expression of his or her belief; we can grant that that does sometimes make sense. If someone says something and the question arises whether she was speaking sincerely, or perhaps dissembling, or merely quoting or parodying someone else, then we may reply that, no, she really believed what she said. Her words, we might say, expressed what she truly believes. Thus, our ordinary, nontheoretical talk of expressing belief can play a useful role in discourse. Similarly, asking someone what he "meant," or undertaking to clarify someone's "meaning," may play a distinctive role in conversation. We might even attempt to develop a normative theory pertaining to these forms of discourse, although I have not attempted that in this book.

However, if we wish to adhere to the received view of linguistic communication, then we must at least maintain that beliefs have a nature independent of language so that we might explain people's acts of speech as expressions of their beliefs. That independent nature is what I have here denied. We understand the nature of beliefs only insofar as we can explain it in terms of the practice of attributing beliefs. We understand that practice only insofar as we independently grasp the nature of assertion. Thus we cannot, in a fundamental formulation of the norms of discourse, or in a fundamental psychological theory of language, treat words as the expression of beliefs.

Afterword

Above all, this essay has been a critique of the received view of linguistic communication. I have disputed the conception of linguistic communication according to which a speaker's aim in speaking is to enable a hearer to grasp the propositional content of a thought underlying the speaker's act of speech. This doctrine does not seem to be labelled with any special *ism* in the contemporary literature. Probably that is because hardly anyone in recent times has imagined that anyone would disagree. So perhaps, in closing, I ought to accentuate the relevance of my point of view to current debates by comparing it with a number of other contemporary *isms*.

One of these is *representationalism*. This is the doctrine that the processes of cognition may be thought of as the manipulation of sentence-like representations bearing propositional content. I have acknowledged that to a certain extent we can explain people's behavior in terms of intentional states such as beliefs and desires. But I have denied representationalism in that I have denied that the explanation of behavior is the *raison d'être* for attributions of intentional states, and I have denied that there would be any basis for the interpretation of such mental representations. In this work, I have not advanced any other conception of the processes of cognition, but I have suggested that the alternative will be a theory that at some level characterizes events in the brain. This theory might even posit states that qualify as some kind of representations. In any case, it should be perfectly clear that my rejection of representationalism in no way signifies a return to behaviorism.

No one should want to be caught denying *realism*—until one discovers what the term is supposed to mean. I have certainly not endorsed *relativism*, the doctrine that two people may really disagree and still both be right. Contexts in my sense are objective. The context defines that which interlocutors ought to agree in asserting, whether they are so disposed or not, and the content of the context depends on how the world really is. But in rejecting all attempts to explain how mental representations acquire meaning, I have rejected as well the explication of truth in terms of real reference relations, and in that way I have rejected what is very prejudicially called realism.

My position on truth could be described as a kind of *deflationism*—if this is understood broadly as just the rejection of the explication of truth in terms of real reference relations. Deflationism is often defined more narrowly as the claim that the following schema somehow expresses the whole truth about truth: *the proposition that p is true if and only if p.* (The key text is Horwich 1998.) However, that narrower thesis is more or less demonstrably mistaken (see my 1999 and 2001a.). The lesson of that failure should be that we need real semantics; that is, we need to find a semantic property of sentences that we can define recursively for all sentences of a language, and we need to define logical validity in terms of that property in such a way that we can precisely demonstrate the *in*validity of invalid arguments. According to me, that property is assertibility in a context.

Elsewhere, I have written extensively about the *internalism/externalism* debate in the philosophy of mind. (For a recent statement, see my forthcoming a.) For a long time, I would have described myself as an externalist. I accepted that a person's thought content was essentially relative to the character of the environment in which he or she was embedded, and, in particular, to the way words are used in his or her linguistic community (Burge 1979). I still think that externalism provides a good point of entry into my present perspective. But I have now come to think that it is better to simply deny that there is any such thing as propositional, or conceptual, content. The idea that there is such a thing as content begins with the idea that content is what a hearer recognizes in a speaker when linguistic communication is successful. In denying this conception of linguistic communication, we should abandon all theoretical use of the concept of content.

However, this kind of dispensing with propositional, or conceptual, content must be contrasted with what is usually called *eliminativism*. Starting with his 1979 book, Paul Churchland launched an attack on the idea that there is a folk psychological theory of belief and desire that forms a credible theory of mind. (This had an important precedent in Rorty 1965.) Churchland understood this critique of folk psychology as casting doubt on the very existence of beliefs and desires. Despite this, in subsequent work Churchland developed a conception of concepts according to which they really do exist in brains as regions of "hidden unit activation spaces" (1989). Thus Churchland's point of view is approximately just the inverse of mine. I agree that there is no credible belief-desire theory (see chapter 11 above); but, according to me, the practice of attributing beliefs and desires never rested on the existence of such a theory in the first place. I agree that scientific psychology leads to the structure of the brain, but I deny that we should expect to find conceptual representations in there.

Robert Brandom's *inferentialism* (1994, 2000) bears a kinship with my theory, in that he and I are opposed to many of the same dogmas. (As one of my teachers in graduate school, he is no doubt a source of some of my present inclinations.) However, Brandom represents himself as explicating the nature of *content*, and I do not see what theoretical role he thinks the concept of content ought to have. Moreover, a lot seems to be missing from his conception of linguistic practice. In particular, he does not provide any semantic theory in terms of which we can precisely demonstrate the invalidity of invalid arguments. It is hard to be sure that in Brandom's theory the world beyond society plays any role at all in determining what people *ought* to say.

If I had to choose an *ism* by which I would like my conception of language to be known, perhaps it would be *contextualism*, for the primary positive thesis of this book has been that assertibility in a context, not proposition expressed, is the semantic property in terms of which we

should formulate the norms of discourse. The larger, metaphysical lesson of this book is that we thoroughly misunderstand the relation of minds to the world if we think of
ourselves as grasping propositions and thereby classifying
the world in its entirety. There is objective right and wrong,
but that is not a matter of whether the world as a whole
really is as we take it to be; rather, it is a matter of whether
our assertions accurately reflect the context objectively
relevant to our conversation.

References

Adams, Ernest. 1965. "On the Logic of Conditionals," *Inquiry* 8: 166–197.

Bach, Kent. 1994. "Conversational Impliciture," *Mind and Language* 9: 124–162.

Bach, Kent. 2000. "Quantification, Qualification and Context: A Reply to Stanley and Szabó," *Mind and Language* 15: 262–283.

Bach, Kent. 2001. "You Don't Say?," *Synthese* 128: 15–44.

Barwise, Jon and John Etchemendy. 1987. *The Liar: An Essay on Truth and Circularity*, Oxford University Press.

Bickle, John. forthcoming. "Empirical Evidence for a Narrative Concept of Self," in G. Greman, T. McVay, and O. Flanagan, eds., *Narrative and Consciousness: Literature, Psychology, and the Brain*, Oxford University Press.

Brandom, Robert. 1994. *Making It Explicit: Reasoning, Representing and Discursive Commitment*, Harvard University Press.

Brandom, Robert. 2000. *Articulating Reasons*. Harvard University Press.

Burge, Tyler. 1979. "Individualism and the Mental," in *Midwest Studies in Philosophy*, vol. 4, *Studies in Metaphysics*, ed. Peter A. French, Theodore E. Uehling, Jr., and Howard K. Wettstein, University of Minnesota Press: 73–121.

Carruthers, Peter. 1996. *Language, Thought and Consciousness: An Essay in Philosophical Psychology*. Cambridge University Press.

Churchland, Paul. 1979. *Scientific Realism and the Plasticity of Mind*. Cambridge University Press.

Churchland, Paul. 1989. *A Neurocomputational Perspective: The Nature of Mind and the Structure of Science*. MIT Press.

Clark, H. H. 1992. *Arenas of Language Use*. University of Chicago Press.

Cowie, Fiona. 1999. *What's Within? Nativism Reconsidered*. Oxford University Press.

Cummins, Robert. 1996. *Representations, Targets and Attitudes*, MIT Press.

Davidson, Donald. 1967. "Truth and Meaning," *Synthese* 17: 304–323.

Davis, Wayne A. 1998. *Implicature, Intention, Convention and the Principle of the Failure of the Gricean Theory*. Cambridge University Press.

Dennett, Daniel. 1971. "Intentional Systems," *Journal of Philosophy* 87: 279–328.

Dretske, Fred. 1988. *Explaining Behavior*. MIT Press.

Edelberg, Walter. 1995. "A Perspectivalist Semantics for the Attitudes," *Noûs* 29: 316–342.

Fodor, Jerry. 1987. *Psychosemantics: The Problem of Meaning in the Philosophy of Mind.* MIT Press.

Frege, Gottlob. 1994. "Über Sinn und Bedeutung" in Günther Patzig, ed., *Funktion, Begriff, Bedeutung,* Vandenhoeck & Ruprecht, pp. 40–66. Originally published in 1892.

Gärdenfors, Peter. 2000. *Conceptual Spaces: The Geometry of Thought.* MIT Press.

Gauker, Christopher. 1994. *Thinking Out Loud: An Essay on the Relation between Thought and Language.* Princeton University Press.

Gauker, Christopher. 1995. "Review of Ruth Garrett Millikan, *White Queen Psychology and Other Essays for Alice,*" *Philosophical Psychology* 8: 305–309.

Gauker, Christopher. 1997a. "Domain of Discourse," *Mind,* 106, 1–32.

Gauker, Christopher. 1997b. "Universal Instantiation: A Study of the Role of Context in Logic," *Erkenntnis,* 46, 185–214.

Gauker, Christopher. 1998. "What is a Context of Utterance?," *Philosophical Studies,* 91, 149–172.

Gauker, Christopher. 1999. "Deflationism and Logic," *Facta Philosophica* 1: 167–195.

Gauker, Christopher. 2001a. "T-Schema Deflationism and Gödel's First Incompleteness Theorem," *Analysis* 61: 129–136.

Gauker, Christopher. 2001b. "Situated Inference Versus Conversational Implicature," *Noûs* 35: 163–189.

Gauker, Christopher. forthcoming a. "Social Externalism and Linguistic Communication," forthcoming in María-José Frápolli and Esther Romero, eds., *Meaning, Basic Self-Knowledge and Mind: Essays on Tyler Burge*, CSLI Publications.

Gauker, Christopher. forthcoming b. "Semantics for Deflationists," in JC Beall and Bradley Armour-Garb, eds., *Deflationism and Paradox*, Oxford University Press.

Gauker, Christopher. forthcoming c. "Attitudes without Psychology," *Facta Philosophica*.

Glanzberg, Michael. 2001. "The Liar in Context," *Philosophical Studies* 103: 217–251.

Grice, Paul. 1989. *Studies in the Way of Words*, Harvard University Press.

Goldman, Alvin. 1989. "Interpretation Psychologized," *Mind and Language* 4: 161–185.

Gordon, Robert M. 1986. "Folk Psychology as Simulation," *Mind and Language* 1: 158–171.

Gordon, Robert M. 1995. "Simulation without Introspection or Inference from Me to You," in Martin Davies and Tony Stone, eds., *Mental Simulation*, Blackwell, pp. 53–67.

Gupta, Anil and Nuel Belnap. 1993. *The Revision Theory of Truth*. MIT Press.

Haugeland, John. 1985. *Artificial Intelligence: The Very Idea*. MIT Press.

Horgan, Terence and James Woodward. 1985. "Folk Psychology is Here to Stay," *Philosophical Review* 94: 197–226.

Horwich, Paul. 1998. *Truth*, 2nd edition. Oxford University Press.

Kamp, Hans and Uwe Reyle. 1993. *From Discourse to Logic*. Kluwer.

Kaplan, David. 1968–1969. "On Quantifying In," *Synthese* 19: 178–214.

Kaplan, David. 1989. "Demonstratives: An Essay on the Semantics, Logic, Metaphysics, and Epistemology of Demonstratives and Other Indexicals," in Joseph Almog, John Perry, and Howard Wettstein, eds., *Themes from Kaplan*, Oxford University, pp. 481–564.

Karttunen, Lauri. 1974. "Presupposition and Linguistic Contexts," *Theoretical Linguistics* 1: 181–194.

Keenan, Edward L. 1973. "Presupposition in Natural Logic," *The Monist* 57, 344–370.

King, Jeffrey C. 1999. "Are Complex 'That' Phrases Devices of Direct Reference?" *Noûs* 33: 155–182.

Kripke, Saul. 1975. "Outline of a Theory of Truth," *Journal of Philosophy* 72: 690–716.

Kripke, Saul. 1982. *Wittgenstein on Rules and Private Language: An Elementary Exposition*. Harvard University Press.

Levinson, Stephen C. 2000. *Presumptive Meanings: The Theory of Generalized Conversational Implicature*. MIT Press.

Lewis, David. 1969. *Convention*. Harvard University Press.

Lewis, David. 1973. *Counterfactuals*. Harvard University Press.

Lewis, David. 1975. "Languages and Language," in Keith Gunderson, ed., *Language, Mind and Knowledge*, University of Minnesota Press, pp. 3–35.

Lewis, David. 1979. "Scorekeeping in a Language Game," *Journal of Philosophical Logic* 8: 339–359.

Loar, Brian. 1981. *Mind and Meaning*. Cambridge University Press.

Martin, John N. 1975. "Some Misconceptions in the Critique of Semantic Presupposition," *Theoretical Linguistics* 6: 235–282.

Millikan, Ruth. 1993. *White Queen Psychology and Other Essays for Alice*. MIT Press.

Morton, Adam. 1980. *Frames of Mind*. Oxford University Press.

Morton, Adam. 1996. "Folk Psychology is not a Predictive Device," *Mind* 105: 119–137.

Pelczar, Michael. 2000. "Wittgensteinian Semantics," *Nôus* 34: 483–516.

Perry, John. 1993. "Thought without Representation," in his *The Problem of the Essential Indexical and Other Essays*, Oxford University Press, pp. 205–225. (Originally published 1986.)

Pickering, Martin and Nick Chater. 1995. "Why Cognitive Science is Not Formalized Folk Psychology," *Minds and Machines* 5: 309–337.

Putnam, Hilary. 1981. *Reason, Truth, and History*. Cambridge University Press.

Quine, W. v. O. 1960. *Word and Object*. MIT Press.

Recanati, François. 2001. "What is Said," *Synthese* 128: 75–91.

Resnik, Michael. 1987. *Choices: An Introduction to Decision Theory*. University of Minnesota Press.

Rey, George. 1997. *Contemporary Philosophy of Mind*. Blackwell.

Rorty, Richard. 1965. "Mind-Body Identity, Privacy and the Categories," *The Review of Metaphysics* 19: 24–54.

Salmon, Nathan. 1986. *Frege's Puzzle*. MIT Press.

Sbisà, Marina. 2001. "Illocutionary Force and Degrees of Strength in Language Use," *Journal of Pragmatics* 33: 1791–1814.

Sbisà, Marina. forthcoming. "Belief Reports: What Role for Contexts?," *Facta Philosophica*.

Schiffer, Stephen. 1987. *Remnants of Meaning*. MIT Press.

Schiffer, Stephen. 1996. "Language-Created Language-Independent Entities," *Philosophical Topics* 24: 149–167.

Simmons, Keith. 1993. *Universality and the Liar: An Essay on Truth and the Diagonal Argument*. Cambridge University Press.

Simons, Mandy. 2001. "Contexts for Presupposition," presented at the Context-Relativity in Semantics Conference, University of Cincinnati, November 16, 2001.

Soames, Scott. 1982. "How Presuppositions are Inherited: A Solution to the Projection Problem," *Linguistic Inquiry* 13: 483–545.

Sperber, Dan and Deirdre Wilson. 1995. *Relevance: Communication and Cognition*, 2nd edition. Blackwell.

Stalnaker, Robert. 1968. "A Theory of Conditionals," in N. Rescher, ed., *Studies in Logical Theory*, American Philosophical Quarterly Monograph Series, no. 2, Basil Blackwell, pp. 98–112.

Stalnaker, Robert. 1972. "Pragmatics," in Donald Davidson and Gilbert Harman, eds., *Semantics of Natural Language*, Reidel Publishers, pp. 380–397.

Stalnaker, Robert. 1973. "Presuppositions," *Journal of Philosophical Logic* 2, 447–457.

Stalnaker, Robert. 1974. "Pragmatic Presuppositions," in Milton K. Munitz and Peter K. Unger, eds., *Semantics and Philosophy*, New York University Press, pp. 197–213.

Stalnaker, Robert. 1975. "Indicative Conditionals," *Philosophia* 5: 269–286.

Stalnaker, Robert. 1987. "Semantics for Belief," *Philosophical Topics* 15: 177–190.

Stalnaker, Robert. 1998. "On the Representation of Context," *Journal of Language, Logic and Information* 7: 3–19.

Stanley, Jason. 2000. "Context and Logical Form," *Linguistics and Philosophy* 23, 391–434.

Stanley, Jason and Zoltán Gendler Szabó. 2000. "On Quantifier Domain Restriction," *Mind and Language* 15, 219–261.

Thomason, Richmond. 1990. "Accommodation, Meaning, and Implicature: Interdisciplinary Foundations for Pragmatics," in Philip R. Cohen, Jerry Morgan, and Martha E. Pollack, *Intentions in Communication*, MIT Press: 325–363.

van Deemter, Kees. 1998. "Domains of Discourse and the Semantics of Ambiguous Utterances: A Reply to Gauker," *Mind* 107: 433–445.

Wilson, Deirdre. 1975. *Presuppositions and Non-Truth-Conditional Semantics*. Academic Press.

Wittgenstein, Ludwig. 1953. *Philosophical Investigations*, trans. G. E. M. Anscombe. Macmillan.

Index